Moses, Paul, and Swedenborg

Stages of Growth in Rational Spirituality

Leon James, Ph.D.

Volume 2

Theistic Psychology Series

© 2018 Leon James and Diane Nahl Kailua

Moses, Paul, and Swedenborg

Contents

Volume 2

Preface
17. Recapitulation and Study Questions and Exercises
   17.2 True Science and Theistic Psychology
   17.3 Why do scientists oppose scientific revelations in the Word of God?
   17.4 Why do religious people oppose the idea that the Word of God is a scientific revelation?
   17.5 What is the relation between the mind and the spiritual world?
   17.6 What is heaven and hell?
   17.7 Why do some people oppose the idea that hell is forever?
   17.7 If God is omnipotent and pure love, why does he allow evil?
   17.8 What are the three phases of consciousness?
   17.9 What is the ennead matrix or the nine zones of spiritual development?
   17.10a What are the laws of space and time in the spiritual world?
   17.10b Are there devils and angels there?
   17.11a What's the difference between sensuous and rational consciousness? 17.11b Is spirituality closer to mysticism or to rationality?
   17.12 How does True Science view religious rituals and faith?
   17.13 What is the Science of Correspondences?
   17.14 Can it be shown that genuine spirituality is rational and scientific?
18. Discovering the Writings of Swedenborg
   18.1 The Holy Spirit -- Rational Consciousness of God's Co-Presence
   18.2 Dual Citizenship -- Horizontal and Vertical Community
   18.3 As-of Self – First Fruits of Rational Consciousness
   18.4 Self-Witnessing – The Psychology of Cooperation
   18.5 What is God Talking About?
   18.6 Christianity Demystified
   18.7 Forming the New Church Mind in Ourselves
   18.8 On Discrete Degrees and Correspondences
   18.9 On Personality, Sacred Scripture, And the Afterlife
19. Further Exercises
   19.1 Characterize the thinking and feeling levels of every day activities
   19.2 Explain the level of thinking in each religious tradition sampled below
   19.2.a Charity and Buddhism
   19.2.b Charity and Christianity

19.2.c Charity and Judaism
19.2.d Charity and Islam
19.2.e Charity and Hinduism
19.2.f Charity and Secular Humanism
19.2.g Charity and New Church or New Christianity
Answer to 19.2.a Charity for Buddhism
Answer to 19.2.b Charity for Christianity
Answer to 19.2.c Charity for Judaism
Answer to 19.2.e Charity for Hinduism
Answer to 19.2.f Charity for Secular Humanism
Answer to 19.2.g Charity for New Christianity

Exercise 19.3 Use the ennead matrix to characterize Judaism, Christianity, New Church

Appendix: Diagnostic Test of Rational Spirituality 100 Items
   ANSWER SHEET
   ANSWER KEY
   How to Interpret Your Score
   Summary List of Characteristics for the Three Phases
   Phase 1 Thinking
   Phase 2 Thinking
   Phase 3 Thinking
   A Listing of the 100 Items Test Without the Alternatives
Other Recent Books by Leon James
About the Author
Contents of Volume 1
END

Preface

I wrote this book in 1999 and posted it on the Web where it has been since and still appears on the theisticpsychology.org Web site maintained by Dr. Ian Thompson. I revised it slightly in 2003 and again slightly in 2008. The text therefore antedates by about two decades my recent books in the Theistic Psychology Series. Today I would use the expression "theistic psychology" instead of "rational spirituality" but the two expressions are equivalent except for style and context.

Moses, Paul, and Swedenborg

This book is based on the Swedenborg Reports and presents a point of view on religion and theistic science that may be found in the Writings of Swedenborg. The perspective of theistic psychology is that God instructs us through two levels of meaning of *Sacred Scripture*. The literal and historical meaning of the verses of *Sacred Scripture* is addressed to our natural mind and involves materialistic ideas about God, creation, punishment, and life after death. God instructs our natural mind through this natural phase of thinking about religion and worship. This religion is called *"blind faith"*.

At the same time, God instructs our rational mind through the psychological meaning that is hidden by correspondence within each verse, each expression, every word, name, and number. This "spiritual meaning" of *Sacred Scripture* is the basis for theistic psychology.

This text describes three historical phases of Divine Revelations that are embodied, first, in the Books of Moses and the *Old Testament* Prophets, second, in the Gospels and Epistles of the *New Testament*, and third, in the *Writings of Swedenborg*. These three sets of Divine Revelations have also been called the *Old Testament*, The *New Testament*, and the *Third Testament*. Together they form one rational unit called the *Threefold Word*.

I constructed a Diagnostic Test of Rational Spirituality with 100 objective multiple-choice items and a scoring sheet to record your answers along with an Answer Key from the perspective of Phase . This test helps readers to pinpoint the specific differences in their own thinking in relation to the three phases of rationality regarding their ideas about God, religion, and theistic psychology.

Leon James
Kailua, Hawaii
November 2018

Moses, Paul, and Swedenborg

Note: For your convenience the Table of Contents for Volume 1 is reproduced at the end of this Volume.

17. Recapitulation and Study Questions and Exercises

Take each question in turn, and follow these steps:

1) Formulate an answer to the question. Write it out.

2) Find passages in the book that address that subject. You can use the Table of Contents and you can also use the Find Command repeatedly until you locate all the relevant passages. Read them. Go back to your answer and expand it as necessary.

3) Read the answer I formulated for the question (see below). Notice the sequence of logical steps in my answer. The topic has to be built up appropriately and logically.

4) Look at your answer now. Examine its sequence – does it follow a logical pattern? Are all terms defined before using them? Are there important elements or concepts left out? Edit your answer accordingly.

5) Make up several sub-questions to reflect your final answer.

The questions are:

17.1 What does the title mean -- Moses, Paul, and Swedenborg: -- The Three Phases of Spiritual Consciousness

17.2 What is True Science and what is dualism?

17.3 Why do scientists oppose dualism and scientific revelations in the Word of God?

17.4 Why do religious people oppose the idea that the Word of God is a scientific revelation?

17.5 What is the relation between the mind and the spiritual world?

Moses, Paul, and Swedenborg

17.6 What is heaven and hell?

17.7a Why do some people oppose the idea that hell is forever?

17.7b If God is omnipotent and pure love, why does he allow evil?

17.8a What are the three phases of consciousness?

17.8b What is the ennead matrix or the nine zones of spiritual development?

17.9a What is spiritual enlightenment?

17.9b What is spiritual regeneration?

17.10a What are the laws of space and time in the spiritual world?

17.10b Are there devils and angels there?

17.11c How does True Science view religious rituals and faith?

17.11d How does thinking and willing change across the three phases?

Here are my answers:

17.1 What does the title mean -- Moses, Paul, and Swedenborg: -- -- The Three Phases of Spiritual Consciousness

This book is written from the perspective of the Writings of Swedenborg. From this perspective, God communicates with the human race on earth by means of scientific revelations given in inspired writings called "the Word of the Lord." Each civilization on this earth has received a version of the Word that is suited for its understanding and designed to elevate the consciousness of its generations. Consciousness is the capacity of human beings to perceive reality rationally by thinking and feeling at the required level of operation.

Human beings are so created as to be able to receive Divine Truth in their understanding, and thereby to receive a spiritual level of consciousness. By reading the Word of God and understanding it, people were able to have their consciousness raised to the spiritual level. This level is necessary for a heavenly life after death in the spiritual world. Without developing a spiritual consciousness in this life, we are condemning ourselves to a life in

Moses, Paul, and Swedenborg

hell to eternity, for without this consciousness, we are unwilling to believe that there is God and a heaven.

What we refuse to believe, remains unattainable to us. Thus people in hell keep themselves there by refusing to believe that heaven exists. Is that not such a horrible irony for the fate of those people! This book shows how you can avoid such a sad fate and how you can form for yourself a mind and consciousness that can live in heaven to eternity.

The Word of God that we know today is referred to here as the Threefold Word because it has taken three civilizations or eras in human history, to deliver the entire Word. The first portion is known as the Word of the *Old Testament* (the Hebrew Word), and was written by God through the willing mind of Moses and the Prophets of the Hebrew and Israelite nations between the 11th and 8th century B.C., approximately. The second portion is known as the Word of the *New Testament* (the Greek Word), and was written by God through the willing mind of the Gospel Writers at the time of the Lord's First Coming.

The third portion is known as the *Word of the Second Coming* (the Latin Word), and was written by God through the willing mind of a scientist in the 18th century A.D., also known as the *Writings of Swedenborg*. The *Threefold Word* is now complete and the human race can enter a new civilization that will bring about the spiritual consciousness of heaven, the highest human beings are capable of perceiving.

The title of this book refers to the three historical architects for God who wrote the Threefold Word under His immediate supervision and determination. Moses represents the level of thinking and consciousness that characterizes the human race on earth in the centuries preceding the Incarnation. A rise in spiritual consciousness was experienced by the human race when the New Testament came into being and began to spread in many parts of the world, but especially the Western world.

Paul represents this second civilization forged by the New Testament. He was the intellectual architect for the Christian religion that allowed it to become a variety of Churches all based on the theological doctrines Paul constructed as a human edifice for the New Testament. Swedenborg represents that last phase of the race's spiritual development. The Writings that God authored through Swedenborg completes the *Threefold Word*.

17.2 True Science and Theistic Psychology

True Science is dualist and theistic while the science we know today is atheistic and materialistic or monistic. Monism is the philosophy of nonduality, which means that there is only world, one substance, one reality, and this is it – what your senses see around you and what your brain figures out about how it works. All things are material. God is not part of reality that science recognizes because God is not material. What is not material is not real.

This monistic premise of science today does not allow the inclusion of the scientific revelations in the Threefold Word. Science denies that scientific revelations exist, along with any revelation that has to do with reality. Reality has to be discovered by materialistic research and abstract thinking.

However, there is an alternative to this negative bias of scientists today, an alternative that is shown in this book to be rational and practical. This alternative is the positive bias which I, as a scientist, have adopted. The positive bias assumes as a departing premise, that dualism is the reality. This means that one accepts the idea that God exists and that the universe, in whole and in every detailed part, is created and managed by God moment by moment. This is called dualism because God is not of the same substance as His creation. Creation furthermore is a dual reality because two interacting worlds were created simultaneously, one spiritual and the other natural.

True Science refers to the scientific revelations given in the *Threefold Word of God*.

17.3 Why do scientists oppose scientific revelations in the Word of God?

Scientists are trained to follow the scientific method and protect the premises upon which the method rests. The premises of science today includes atheism and materialism. There is therefore a prohibition against using explanatory concepts that have no definition within the materialist and atheistic premises. In other words, God cannot be used as a concept for explaining the source, direction, or power of any phenomenon. Neither can angels be used as a concept. Neither can resuscitation of the dead, a phenomenon witnessed by Swedenborg thousands of times. Neither can you relate in your theory to heaven or hell, yet Swedenborg has seen numberless inhabitants of these two spiritual states and their related phenomena. Neither can you talk about dualism or correspondences as an explanatory concept for natural phenomena.

Neither can you talk about revelation or the Word of God by which He communicates with the human race. Neither can you talk about the Laws of Divine Providence and how God directs the outcome of events, physical and historical. Neither can you talk about the vertical community we participate in, that is, spiritual influx from the world of spirits into our mind, without which we could neither think nor sense anything. In fact, as scientists today, we cannot talk about the numerous facts the Word of the Writings reveal regarding life after death, regarding the human mind, society, animals, and much more. Such is the negative bias of materialistic and monist science today. It keeps all scientific revelations out, preventing them from entering.

17.4 Why do religious people oppose the idea that the Word of God is a scientific revelation?

Most people are socialized into a culture that is characterized by phase 1 and phase 2 level consciousness, as explained in the book. In other words, they see science and religion as separate. For example, scientists practice their theories and explanations during the week, but evenings or weekends, they are among family, Bible study classes, and Church services. They do not feel a tension because they segregate science and religion in their mind. Society does this, so individuals do it as can be expected.

Therefore people tend to oppose new ideas that eliminate the segregation between science and religion. To stop segregating them in the mind would pose as serious problems as it would in society. The bloodiest wars in history are said to have been fought when religion got in the way of politics, industry, and science. For the individual, removing the segregation in the mind would cause intellectual havoc and emotional conflict and stress.

The negative consequences of not segregating religion and science in the mind come from phase 1 and phase 2 levels of thinking. In phase 3 thinking no such conflict is produced because one sees the thinking level we do in religion does not allow us to raise our consciousness to the highest level possible. This is because religion is not just about God, but about our relation to God, and this varies from culture to culture, and even among different social groups. But when we see that the Word of God is a scientific revelation, then

Moses, Paul, and Swedenborg

we move up to phase 3 thinking where we are freed from the filters imposed on us by staying in the framework of our culture and religion.

There is opposition to the idea that science is above religion. This opposition is based on valid grounds because science is materialistic and atheistic. This puts science below religion intellectually and rationally. Religion is much closer to truth and reality than science because religion has the Word of God to rely on for knowledge while science sees nothing whatsoever about God, heaven, and hell.

But it's all together different with True Science, which refers to the scientific revelations in the Threefold Word. Since True Science is based directly on the Threefold Word of God, it can be higher than religion since True Science uses systematic methods of discovery employing the procedures taught by the Word.

17.5 What is the relation between the mind and the spiritual world?

The mind is an organ housed in the spirit-body. The spirit-body is "within" the physical body which houses the physical brain. The meaning of "within" is with reference to discrete degrees. In other words, the physical body in the natural world acts synchronously with the spirit-body in the world of spirits. The two are created together at birth and are tied together by correspondent actions. Every detail in the physical body and brain must be accompanied at the same time by correspondent details in the spirit-body and mind.

Our consciousness, or conscious awareness, is produced by the action or operation of the spirit-body and the mental organs it houses. The mind has two types of organs – affective and cognitive, also called "the will" and "the understanding." These two types of organs correspond to the two types of operation in the physical body – circulatory and respiratory.

The two types of mental organs operate at three different levels of consciousness. The highest level of consciousness in the mind is called heaven. At this level, our thinking and feeling is celestial and gives us the power to experience happiness, love, and wisdom to eternity. The middle level of consciousness in the mind is called the spiritual mind. At this level, our thinking and feeling is spiritual and gives us the power to experience happiness, love, and wisdom to similar to the celestial mind, but not as sublime, rich, and complex. The lowest level of consciousness in the mind is called hell. At this level, our thinking and feeling

Moses, Paul, and Swedenborg

is infernal and gives us the power to experience misery, hatred, and stupidity to eternity.

It's easy to accept the idea that the mind is not material, and therefore it has no size, distance, or location. It's more difficult to see that because it has no size, weight, or location, therefore all minds overlap and are not separated from each other by place or distance, like physical bodies are. Once you can accept this rational conception of a non-material mind, you can begin to understand that the spiritual world doesn't have place and distance because it too is non-material. What is non-material is called spiritual.

Therefore the spiritual world and the mind must logically be the same overlapping phenomenon or creation. The mind of every human being past and present, which must be a big number, was born as a spiritual entity, and therefore is (a) immortal, and (b) overlaps with all other minds. This follows from the fact that there is no physical space or time in the spiritual world or mind.

As a result of this overlap anyone who is awake in the spiritual world has access to anyone else there. While we are tied to the physical body, we are not consciously awake in the spiritual mind, only in the natural mind. But when we resuscitate a few hours after the death of the physical body, we then have conscious awareness in the spirit-body, and thereafter we have access to all other minds who are awake in the spiritual world, that is heaven, hell, and the world of spirits which is in between. Access to others in the spiritual world is by altering our mental state.

For example, when we are in a similar mood with others, and think similar thoughts, we see them and we can talk to them or touch them. As soon as our thoughts or feelings clash or differ, we are no longer with them but with others who now match our new mood and thoughts.

The spiritual geography of the world of spirits, of heaven, and of hell, is the map of mental states in which minds can be. The chart below gives the relation between consciousness and the spiritual world. Read chart from bottom up.

CONSCIOUSNESS	SPIRITUAL WORLD
celestial-rational mind	celestial heavens or Third Heaven of angels
spiritual-rational mind	spiritual heavens or Second Heaven of angelic spirits
spiritual-natural or	natural heavens or First Heaven of good spirits

interior natural mind		
SPIRIT-BODY IN THE WORLD OF SPIRITS		
natural-rational mind	mild hells	
sensuous mind	severe hells	
corporeal mind	worst hells	

The chart above shows the relation between the degree of development of our rational spirituality and our fate in the afterlife. Those end up in the hells who remain natural in their thinking and feeling, and the severity of the hells varies with one's moral feelings and thoughts. Those who are more rational and moral – but not yet spiritual or dualist – are in the mild hells compared to the others. A moral person who is not also dualist and spiritual does not regenerate the inner character of inherited evils. As a result, their moral behavior is external and covers up the raging and insane internal loves. In the afterlife, covering up the internal loves is no longer possible in the spirit-body.

Those have a heavenly life who have regenerated their inherited character by means of a life of religion (phase 2) and a life guided by True Science (phase 3). A life of religion, unlike natural morality, confronts the inner loves that are evil and condemned by the doctrine of one's religion. There are three heavens and everyone enters the heaven that is suitable to the understanding of spiritual truths acquired by the regenerated mind. This varies according to the level of temptations one was willing to undergo –interior-natural, spiritual, or celestial.

17.6 What is heaven and hell?

The *New Testament* makes the awesome scientific revelation that heaven and hell are inside the mind of every person. They are not places in the spiritual world where people are kept in gardens or caverns. Hell is not a prison for the damned as punishment of sins. Heaven is not a place of reward where people are admitted for their good deeds. The Writings give a lot more detail about heaven and hell. Hell is the bottom of every human mind, and heaven is the topmost region of the mind called the celestial mind. In between is the natural mind and the spiritual mind.

Moses, Paul, and Swedenborg

The *Threefold Word* has been given to the race so that we might study the facts and principles given there and live accordingly. This means to use the facts and principles from scientific revelations to apply to oneself, especially one's struggle against evil loves and habits with which we acquire in daily life through the choices we make. Our inherited tendencies incline us to bad choices, selfish perspectives, and irrational ways of thinking, including rejecting the Lord's close partnership in our every thought and feeling.

We are exposed to scientific revelations from many sources as we grow up, including secondary sources from books, movies, lectures, and what others say about God, religion, conscience, morality, heaven and hell. Those who have a tradition of reading and worshipping Sacred Scripture, can use those ideas, truths, principles, doctrines, and spiritual facts, to evaluate the rightness or wrongness of their decisions and feelings. Some go still further and try to modify their thinking and willing so that they can gradually change their character and their nefarious hereditary influences.

This slow process of character change through self-modification using truths from revelation, is called in the Threefold Word "regeneration." The Writings reveal that everyone is born with ties to the hells, and these ties lead us to developing a character that is made mostly of evil loves and false ideas. We are not necessarily aware of this connection, especially if we do not acknowledge the Word of God or Divine Truth by which we are to modify ourselves.

We are therefore born in a state called "unregenerate." The Writings say that this state automatically leads to an evil character whose consciousness can live only in the bottom of the mind. Hence when we pass on, our spirit-body automatically sinks to the lower regions of the spiritual world called the hells where are also all the other people who keep their consciousness in the bottom of their mind. They are unwilling to remove themselves from the bottom because when they try, and are given the opportunity to explore the higher regions of their mind, they feel like they are losing their life. Therefore they throw themselves back into the bottom of their mind called the hells where they are in company with many others.

But those who persist in their self-modification have the opportunity to be reborn, that is, start a new character that is filled with truths and loves from the Word. This is possible only under the condition where we look to God for help, that He may give power to overcome our inherited and acquired loves, lusts, cupidities, insanities. God always gives this power as He works closely with every person, participating in every thought sequence and every emotion or fantasy. God must continually supply the power for the mind to operate, moment by moment, second by second, or else it would shut down instantly and disintegrate, just like the physical body shuts down and disintegrates when God removes from it the endeavor of life.

Those who undergo rebirth, reformation, and regeneration, arrive in the world of spirits prepared and capable of ascending to the top region of their mind, where they find a heaven in company of many others. Heaven is not a reward because no one deserves good since everyone is evil. Only God is God and deserves merit and righteousness. It is impossible for human beings to acquire or be given God's merit and righteousness. Instead, we need to think of heaven medically or scientifically. It's the ability to remain in the highest consciousness of the mind and to exist there. This ability comes from God as He prepared every person for it. But only some cooperate, and therefore they make it to heaven, while the others make it to hell. No other alternative exists.

Clearly therefore, nothing can be more important in this life than to work as hard as we can for our regeneration. When we do this, we are also most useful to others and to society, since we are being regenerated by God and God's will is that we have mutual love for one another. God cannot regenerate us except by means of our voluntary cooperation, which means reading the Word, understanding it, applying its principles to our willing and thinking all day long. This will get us to shun our evils as sins against the Lord against our ability to live

in heaven. After we shun an evil, the Lord gives power to detest it, and we can then live in good. This must be done over and over again, every day with our numberless evils. When we are done with this process, the Lord detaches the physical body and we undergo resuscitation, awakening in our spirit-body. Our fate to eternity then depends on what we came with in terms loves and cognitions.

17.7 Why do some people oppose the idea that hell is forever?
17.7 If God is omnipotent and pure love, why does he allow evil?

One line of objection is that there is something inhuman about the idea of hell forever. Hell implies people suffering miserably and the idea that suffering can go on forever seems too much for humans to live through. It's just too horrible an idea to be true. Then there is another line of objection, namely that God couldn't damn some people to eternal suffering no mater how heinous their deeds were on this earth. Then there is the objection that the punishment of hell forever would not be just or fair no matter what the crime or sin was. The human mind needs to think that every crime has its punishment, and every punishment has its limit, after which the person has "served time" or "taken it" and is now over it, and continues to have rights that must be respected.

And finally, there is the objection that a person who is repentant and has been punished enough, can be rehabilitated and turned into a useful productive citizen deserving of rights and opportunities. These various objections all assume that hell is a place of punishment, like a prison on earth, and that eventually they have a right to another chance. Some sentences judges hand down carry a term of three lifetimes without the possibility of parole.

I've heard of some really bad guy who was handed ten life sentences without the possibility of parole. These are ways in which society tries to keep an individual segregated to prevent more harm being done to others and to society. No one has yet returned from the dead to serve their second life sentence after they completed their first!

But True Science has a different answer, one that rationally explains why hell is forever, despite a loving omnipotent God. The Writings reveal that God forgives every evil deed before it's even completed in the act. God is pure Divine Love and Good in His essence and it would be impossible for God to act or feel against His Own Character of Pure Love and Good. God loves every angel in heaven, every earthling on the planets, every devil in hell.

Furthermore, the Writings reveal that no event, no matter how small, could occur without God's active participation. A murderer could not point the gun unless God gave the power to the finger on the trigger. And God must also guide the bullet to its target. And God must bring about the anatomical destruction by the bullet, and God must participate in the sensation of pain, for without God there is no sensation. And on and on to every single detail there exists. This participation and determination by God of every detail of a phenomenon is called "omnipotence."

A logical issue must therefore be brought up and must be answered rationally, and understood. Let's phrase the issue as two propositions: (a) God is pure love; (b) God is

Moses, Paul, and Swedenborg

omnipotent. How do we logically reconcile these two propositions? Why would God participate giving power to the bandit's trigger hand, or intelligence to a terrorist plotting to kill innocents? Why doesn't God withdraw His power to freeze up the trigger-finger, or confusion to foil the terrorist's plot that kills children and innocent bystanders? And what about the child abuser – Why does God give him the slyness and the cleverness by which he entraps and rapes young children? True Science gives the rational answer without which we fall into error about God, or into suppressed doubts, or even open resentment against God. And the answer is this:

God had a choice to make when creating human beings. The explanation in phase 1 thinking, which I received as a boy in *Cheder* (Orthodox Jewish school) is that God created human beings on earth and angels in heaven. The angels in heaven were sexless human robots that automatically obeyed God's will. One of the main things God wanted them to do is to stand around God's Divine Court and to sing "Glory to God the Most High" in variations and multiplications.

God also created a devil and "fallen angels" and gave them the power to bring misery upon earthlings. Sometimes God would feel sorry for the human race being tortured by the devil, and at other times He would bring on hellish plagues and misfortunes to punish people for offending Him or to test their loyalty to Him by making terrible things to happen to them. This level of thinking about God is natural, not yet spiritual, not yet rational.

Phase 2 thinking gives a more humane interpretation of God as a Divine Person who loves everyone and hates no one. This loving God would never damn anyone to hell, even less to eternal hell. But, God has two natures according to this level of thinking, one nature that is good and loving, and the other nature that is without love and pity. The good side of God is called Mercy, and the punishing side is called Justice. Mercy is motivated by love and forgiveness of all sins and deeds by anyone no matter who they are. Justice is motivated by truth and the laws of punishment of evil that are built into creation. Every crime has its built in punishment, for evil returns to the source, which hell.

Those have turned away from God, lead themselves into evil, and when they pass on, their evil takes them to hell, and since the evil clings to them, they remain in hell. Some phase 2 thinking allows the idea of "hell forever" while others do not. Those who are opposed to the idea of hell forever point back to God's other side, which is Mercy, and they have the certitude that Mercy eventually wins over Justice, and that those in hell can repent and give up their contact with evil, leave it behind, and ascend to heaven where they can worship

Moses, Paul, and Swedenborg

God.

Note that much is left out in the phase 2 explanation that one needs to have in order to gain a full logical understanding. Unless we gain a full rational understanding of the idea of "hell forever", we will either doubt its reality, or we will experience some conflict regarding God's character (Is He really all good?) or God's Omnipotence (Is He really in total charge?). I've heard people say that God is not fully totally omnipotent because the created world cannot be perfect as God would want it to be. Others speculate that the devil was given certain powers at creation, and God cannot undo this, and therefore God has no power over certain situations (e.g., in the *Book of Job* in the *Old Testament*).

But phase 3 thinking from True Science (or theistic psychology) gives a fully rational answer to all these puzzles. The short answer is this – *those who are in hell are unwilling to leave.*

Would you have thought of it? It's hard to believe because we put ourselves in that frightening unbearable place and the feeling we have is, "Help, quick, how do I get out of here. God, are you there?" And if God were to remain silent, as if nonexistent, we would indeed have rational grounds for impeachment. But this is just a fantasy. The people in hell are reacting in the same way as we do when we imagine ourselves to be there. The people are in hell only because their consciousness or level of thinking, is at the sub-human level. This is the bottom of the natural mind and is called the corporeal and sensuous mind. Animals on earth are at this level of thinking.

And what keeps them at this sub-human level of thinking filled with insanity, unreality, fantasy and instantly translating all true statements they hear into their opposites? The answer is that it is their loves that keep them at the sub-human level of thinking. The Writings go into the many details of why it is that every love has its own companion of thought. This is a necessity by creation, for reasons are fully explained.

And therefore infernal loves must have their own insane thoughts, and when we are in a state of evil lust or cupidity, our mental apparatus becomes a opposite machine, taking every incoming truth and turning into its opposite. Swedenborg reports experiments he performed with inhabitants of hell who were allowed to go up into the world of spirits (but not heaven, which they could not stand). Swedenborg made precise observations of when and how they turned true statements he gave them to explain, into their opposites. As long as they are unwilling to give up their infernal loves they cannot rise in consciousness above the bottom of the human mind.

Moses, Paul, and Swedenborg

This unwillingness is what keeps them there, unable to receive truth, without which they cannot ascend to a higher consciousness. God works through angel volunteers in hell who constantly try to therapize or instruct them, but it has never yet happened that one would be willing to give up their infernal lusts. They say that when they try, they feel like all life departs from them. In other words, they are unwilling to live the life of rational loves and goodness.

One final puzzle needs to be answered. Why did God not prevent them from getting attached to their evil loves while they were still on earth? After all, God must have participated in their experiences, decisions, acts, and God must have provided for them a physical environment in which they could live and become attached to their infernal loves. Why did God allow this to happen in the first place?

The answer is that God created two worlds, one natural the other spiritual. When we are born we receive a physical body in the natural world and a spirit-body in the spiritual world, the two being tied by the laws of synchronous correspondences. God did not create a heaven and have people born in it, or even create people as adults in heaven. Why not? We must understand this in order not to threaten our complete love and confidence in God's omnipotence and goodness. Neither does God want us to have blind faith and accept this as a mystery for limited capacity humans, since mystery and blind faith does not provide us with full spiritual comprehension, and therefore, we are barred from God's full love for us, barred from progressing in our spiritual development which goes on to eternity.

God could not create something like that. He could not create full blown adults, or children, in heaven. He created a natural world for the natural mind and a spiritual world for this natural within which is a celestial mind. In other words it's a question of anatomy. The human mind is made of a natural portion and a spiritual portion.

The natural mind must contain the order and experience of the natural world. Without the natural mind there cannot be a spiritual mind for heaven. We must grow up on some planet, develop our natural mind, become rational, and then we can understand and accept spiritual things from rationality, not blind faith or mystery. Swedenborg reports that those who arrive in the world of spirits with blind faith and mystery, are instructed by the angels in truths and rationality, but they are unwilling to accept anything. Therefore they sink down to their corporeal mind.

Only rationality by means of revealed truths can raise our consciousness to higher levels.

Moses, Paul, and Swedenborg

Refusing to receive rationality is therefore a stumbling block to heavenly life. This is why the Lord has now given the Writings to the modern mind so that all the endless future generations to come will be able to understand Him and His reality in a rational way through education in True Science.

So now you can see the entire picture a little better. God allows evil on the planets and gives power to its consequences and details, out of love and goodness in order to protect and maintain the individual's capacity to acquire truths and think rationally. The finger on the trigger, the terrorist's plotting, the injury from carelessness, the rapist's violence, etc., are the things God enforces and empowers to save the ability of the planet, and society, to remain a place of nursery for the human mind so that we can ascend to the top of our mind, where we can receive the love and truth God intends for us from His creation.

The top of our mind, called celestial mind or heaven, is attainable in our consciousness through Divine Truth given in revelations. Receiving these truths must involve our rationality and understanding, or else we do not receive them permanently. At the same time, God must maintain our feeling or sense that we are free to choose either to act from this truth or to act from the opposite of this truth. Rationality allows us to choose one way or the other, to chose as-of self, seemingly independently from God.

If we lose this sense of freedom to do as we please according to our own mind, then we lose the capacity to be rational, lose the capacity to be celestial, lose the capacity to operationalize the top of our mind, thus condemning every human being to sub-human level. By not allowing evil when we insist on it, God would eliminate the possibility of anyone going to heaven, or reaching his or her highest consciousness. Yet it is only in this highest consciousness that we begin to be truly human. Below that, we are not yet genuinely human.

From the Writings of Swedenborg:

> *At this point I shall add the following account of an experience.*
>
> *After completing my reflections on conjugial love and beginning to think about scortatory love, two angels suddenly came to me and said, 'We perceived and understood your previous reflections, but the things you are now thinking about pass us by, and we do not perceive them. Abandon them, because they are of no value.'*
>
> *'The love which is the subject of my present reflection,' I replied, 'is not nothing, since*

it certainly exists.'

'How,' they said, 'can any love exist which is not from creation? Surely conjugial love is from creation, and this is a love between two people who are able to become one. How can there be a love which divides and separates people? Can any young man love a girl unless she loves him in return? Does not the love of the one know and recognize that of the other, and so when these loves meet they join of their own accord? Can anyone love something which is not love? Is not conjugial love the only one which is mutual and reciprocal? If it is not reciprocated, does it not rebound and become nothing?'

[2] On hearing this I asked the two angels what community of heaven they came from. 'We are,' they said, 'from the heaven of innocence. We came as children into this heavenly world and were brought up under the Lord's

guidance. When I grew up and my wife, who is with me here, became old enough to get married, we were engaged and betrothed, and joined for the first time** in marriage. Since we know of no other love than the true love of marriage, conjugial love, when the ideas you thought about came across to us about a different kind of love, the exact opposite of ours, we could understand nothing. So we have come down to ask why you are reflecting on things we cannot perceive. Tell us then how a love can exist which is not only not from creation, but is opposed to creation. We regard what is opposed to creation as subjects of no validity.'

[3] When he said this, I was heartily glad to talk with angels so innocent that they were totally ignorant of sexual impropriety. So I opened my mouth to tell them. 'Are you not aware,' I said, 'that good and evil exist, and good is from creation, but evil is not? Yet evil regarded in essence is not nothing, even though it is nothing from the point of view of good. Good exists from creation, and it varies in degree from the highest to the lowest. When its lowest degree reaches zero, evil arises on the other side. So there is no relationship or progress of good to evil, but it relates and progresses to what is more or less good. Evil relates and progresses to what is more or is less evil, because these are opposites in every single detail. Since evil and good are opposites, there must be a mean point distinguished by equilibrium, where evil acts against good; but because it is not stronger, it cannot advance beyond making the effort.

Moses, Paul, and Swedenborg

'Everyone is brought up in this state of equilibrium; and since this is between good and evil, or what is the same thing, between heaven and hell, it is a spiritual equilibrium, and this confers freedom on those who enjoy it. As the result of this equilibrium the Lord draws all to Himself; and if a person freely follows Him, He leads him out of evil into good, and so to heaven. It is much the same with love, especially conjugial love and scortatory love. The latter is an evil, the former a good. Everyone who hears the Lord's voice and freely follows is brought by the Lord into conjugial love and into all its joys and happiness. But someone who does not hear and follow brings himself into scortatory love and first into its joys, and then into its unpleasantnesses, and finally into unhappiness.'

[4] When I said this, the two angels asked, 'How could evil come into being, when nothing but good had come into being from creation? For anything to come into being it must have a source; good could not be the source of evil, because evil is a negation of good, since it takes away and destroys good. Still, because evil exists and is felt, it is not nothing, but it is something. Tell us then from what source this comes from nothing into being something.'

I replied to them, 'This secret cannot be revealed without knowing that none is good save God alone, and that there is nothing good that is inherently good unless it comes from God. Anyone therefore who looks to the Lord and wants to be guided by Him is in a state of good. But anyone who turns away from God and wants to be guided by himself is not in a state of good; for the good he does is done either for his own sake or for worldly reasons, so that it is either intended to acquire merit, or pretended, or hypocritical. This makes it plain that man himself is the source of evil, not because man had that fate assigned to him from creation, but because he assigned it to himself by turning away from God. That source of evil was not in Adam and his wife; but when the serpent said:

> *On the day when you eat of the tree of the knowledge of good and evil, you will be like God. Gen. 3:5.*

And then they turned away from God, and turned towards themselves as if they were gods, they produced the source of evil in themselves. "Eating of that tree" means believing that one knows good and evil and is wise of oneself, and not from God.'

[5] But then the two angels asked, 'How could man turn away from God and towards

himself, when it is still true that man can will nothing, think nothing and so do nothing except from God? Why did God allow this?'

'Man was created,' I replied, 'so that everything he wills, thinks and does appears to be inside him and so to come from him. Without this appearance he would not be a man, for he could not receive, retain or make as it were his own any trace of good and truth, or of love and wisdom. It follows from this that unless this were exactly the appearance, man could not be linked with God, and so he could not have everlasting life.

However, if this appearance induces him to believe that he himself, and not the Lord, is the source of what he wills, thinks and does, however much it looks as if he were the source, he turns good in himself into evil and so produces a source of evil in himself. This was Adam's sin.

[6] 'But I can cast a little more light on this subject. The Lord looks on every person in the forehead, and His gaze passes through to the back of the head. Behind the forehead is the cerebrum, and beneath the rear of the head is the cerebellum. This is devoted to love and the various kinds of good it produces; the cerebrum is devoted to wisdom and the truths which compose it. Anyone therefore who looks face first towards the Lord receives wisdom from Him, and by this means he receives love.

But anyone who turns his back and looks away from the Lord receives love but not wisdom, and love without wisdom is the love that comes from man and not from the Lord. Since this love links itself with false beliefs, it does not acknowledge God, but puts itself in God's place, finding silent confirmation of this through the ability to understand and to be wise with which he is endowed from creation, as if it came from himself. This love is

therefore the source of evil. I can give you a visual demonstration that this is so, by calling here a wicked spirit who has turned away from God; I shall speak to his back, that is, to the back of his head, and you will see that what he is told turns into its opposite.'

[7] So I called such a spirit, and when he came, spoke to him from behind. 'Do you know,' I said, anything about hell, damnation and the torments of hell?' At once he turned towards me, and I asked him, 'What did you hear me say?'

'This,' he answered, 'is what I heard: "Do you know anything about heaven, salvation and the happiness of heaven?"' Then when he was asked this question behind his back, he said that what he heard was the first question.

Afterwards the following question was put from behind his back. 'Are you not aware that those in hell are made mad by false ideas?' When I asked him what he had heard, he said, 'Are you not aware that those in heaven are made wise by truths?' When this question was repeated to him behind his back, he said that what he heard was, 'Are you not aware that those in hell are made mad by false ideas?' and so on.

These facts made it obvious that when a mind turns away from the Lord, it turns towards itself and so perceives the reverse of everything. This is the reason why, as you know, in the spiritual world no one is allowed to stand behind another's back and talk to him. For by doing so love is breathed into him, and because it is pleasant the intelligence approves and obeys it. But since it comes from man and not from God, it is a love of evil or of falsity. (CL 444)

17.8 What are the three phases of consciousness?

Phase 1 thinking is the level of operation that is built up by abstraction from the natural world and the way our senses inform us of this order. Science at this level of operation is materialistic and atheistic, attributing nothing to anything that cannot be based on the physical senses or something abstracted derived from their order. At this level of thinking, all causes of physical phenomena are physical, even those explanations that involve "emergent phenomena" like mind and consciousness. In other words, consciousness and spiritual truth do not have an existence other than what they have drawn or abstracted from the natural world. This level of thinking does not see any contradiction in the idea that something physical can produce itself.

And so we have the theory that life was produced by physical elements coming together in the just the right way to produce life. And it sees no contradiction in the theory that the universe produced itself somehow, say a Big Bang from a large mass of matter compressed together. As to where that mass came from, one thinks that it's always been there. As to how this mass could develop in an organized orderly way, one thinks that it's just happened by chance, and then it evolved by trying to survive.

Moses, Paul, and Swedenborg

Phase 2 thinking is the level of operation that is built from revelation. Phase 1 thinking can progress and improve endlessly, yet it can never turn into phase 2 thinking. The Writings declare that truth cannot be discovered or invented, only received from God as revelation. Phase 2 thinking begins when one receives the truth of revelation in one's understanding. This truth comes from Sacred Scripture. The Threefold Word is a collection of Divine revelations given over a two thousand year period, ending in 1771 when the last of the books of the Writings were published by Swedenborg. This began the new age of the Second Coming which is the revelation of God in His Divine Rational.

Now with these Divine Rational truths, we can elevate our consciousness to phase 3, which is the highest possible for human beings. This is where the genuine human being begins to exist, and lives to eternity, endlessly progressing in phase 3 thinking and feeling. All thinking exists only when the feeling is within it. Thinking without feeling is useless and falls back into phase 2 and phase thinking. Thinking with feeling is called willing. Whatever we intent or will is achieved by means of thinking. The love in the feeling unites with the truth in the thinking, and the two together give us this or that level of thinking and consciousness.

Level 3 feeling is celestial and heavenly, and marries itself to phase 3 thinking. The Writings refer to this union as the Marriage of Good and Truth, or the "celestial marriage." The offspring of this marriage is celestial consciousness. This is the consciousness we have when we feel and think at level 3. This feeling and thinking is nothing else than our reception of Divine Good and Divine Truth. We have completely left behind our own ego, our own self-intelligence and self- reliance. We have left behind reasoning about truth and have replaced it with perception of truth.

As each of us receives the same Divine Love and Divine Truth in a unique way, we each have a different awareness of God. In this celestial state of mind we are unwilling to will, think, and act from ourselves. We are only willing to receive the Lord's Will, and to marry it to the Lord's Understanding in our celestial-rational mind, and therefore all our external actions and external life around us, becomes a heaven to eternity.

17.9 What is the ennead matrix or the nine zones of spiritual development?

To understand rationally what is said above, is to think in phase 3 (zones 7, 8, and 9 on the

Moses, Paul, and Swedenborg

ennead matrix). But at phase 1 and 2, we feel like rejecting it.

The three phases of consciousness each have three sub-phases, and the 3x3 matrix creates an ennead or form of nine. The sub-states have the same names for each of the phases. They are the Old Testament state, the New Testament state, and the Third Testament state. The nine zones of the ennead matrix therefore constitute a map of consciousness showing the path from zone 1, the bottom of the consciousness to zone 9, the top of consciousness.

Here is the ennead matrix of spiritual development presented before in this book:

ENNEAD MATRIX OF RATIONAL SPIRITUALITY (9 zones of development)	Old Testament State (initial)	New Testament State (intermediate)	Third Testament State (mature)
Swedenborg Phase 3 (Particularism) (celestial mind)	7	8	9
Paul Phase 2 (Personalism) (spiritual mind)	4	5	6
Moses Phase 1 (Sectarianism) (natural mind)	1	2	3

Zone 1 is an initial state for every human being. It begins when we first hear about God and are able to think about Him. Zone 1 consciousness is the dividing line between animal cognition and human thinking. Since we first hear about God through the socialization process in childhood, our idea of God is sectarian rather than universal. Children associate God with their religion, tradition, and ethnicity. I was socialized into thinking of God as Jewish. Therefore, in my mind, 99.9 percent of human beings did not have God, since they were not Jewish. It is similar with other religions and cultures.

This initial phase of total sectarianism is followed by an intermediate phase (zone 2). I call it the New Testament state. It manifests itself as adolescent idealism. We are suddenly imbued by a passionate sense of universalism, internationalism, and pluralism. In religious behavior it shows itself as ecumenism and the desire to reach across denominations and even to other religions. In this state of thinking and feeling humanism becomes as important

Moses, Paul, and Swedenborg

in the mind as religion. This intermediate state is succeeded by the Third Testament state of sectarianism (phase 1).

Although we still recognize divisions and separations, we see them in a new light that minimizes their spiritual fundamental importance. We are freed from the dogma of our religion and sense that there is something higher. Our mind has been prepared to make the great leap from phase 1 thinking (zone 3) to phase 2 thinking and feeling (zone 4).

This new basis of our consciousness is grounded in the idea of a Personal God rather than a universal God. Prior to this (while we operate in zones 1, 2, 3), we see God as the God of our people, of our sect, but now (zone 4) we see God as the God of the individual. This means that for the first time we can have a relationship with God that is not dependent on our religion or ethnic group. We make a further step when we rely less on the literal meaning of what we are taught (zone 4) and more on the spirit of it (zone 5). We must face our own character and examine our thoughts, feelings, tendencies, asking God, "*Lord, do I do these bad things you talk about in your Holy Word?*"

By this greater deepening and internalization (zone 5), we prepare ourselves for the next higher state of consciousness (zone 6). Our relationship to God becomes a reciprocal relationship of mutual responsibility. God is responsible for taking care of me and my life, and He has declared in His Word that He loves us, which means that He feels responsible for us like a shepherd takes care of the sheep to make sure they are fed and safe.

At the same time we feel the reciprocal responsibility we have to Him, so that we not sin against Him by ignoring His Commandments. We experience shame and guilt before Him because we know we love sin and daily wallow in it. We get angry at our brother, we rage against our neighbor, and we neglect to properly take care of ourselves.

As a result we feel shame, remorse, and condemnable. Yet we overcome this by dedicating our lives to God, study His Word, and declare Him to others that He may be loved by all.

Zone 6 consciousness is not a fully happy one because it is filled with mystery and contradictions of doctrine. Our understanding of God and spiritual things like sin, heaven, hell, commandment, angel, devil, is so limited that we know nothing about the most important things of our spiritual future except that if we love the Lord and are decent to our neighbor, our spiritual future will be well off somehow, and if we do not, our spiritual future will be bleak.

Moses, Paul, and Swedenborg

Not knowing the details of our future and how God operates to get us there, leaves us in a state of confusion, doubt, and spiritual anxiety. These problems and difficulties are solved when we make the great leap from zone 6 to zone 7. They are solved to some extent, but not yet completely. The jump to zone 7 is accomplished when we first hear about True Science concepts from reading or instruction, either formal or informal. In this initial state of thinking in phase 3, we are bound to the literal meaning of the Writings (zone 7). This allows us a much higher perspective on spirituality than what we had in earlier phases, states, and zones.

But the literal meaning of the Word refers to natural-rational correspondences. This is a scientific view of particular spiritual phenomena but the view is outward, not inward. Our understanding of these spiritual things is natural because we use our own intelligence from the natural mind to fill in the picture, as it were.

But as soon as we accept the idea that True Science is about our own states of development, we begin to see a deeper applied meaning to the concepts and principles. Our theoretical meaning of the concepts of True Science (zone 7) is now advanced to the deeper state (zone 8) in which we can perceive inward spiritual-rational meanings within the outward natural-rational meanings of the literal text. This new perception is called enlightenment (zone 8).

One sees a new spiritual light within the natural things all around us and in the Word of God. This spiritual light comes to our awareness when we apply the principles of True Science to our own thinking and feeling. We read the Writings acknowledging it as Divine Truth, and we see the information in it as scientific revelations about our own states of spiritual development. As we progress in our regeneration we are brought to higher states of consciousness and enlightenment.

We now can perceive a still more interior light, a more brilliant light by far, and this comes into our conscious awareness by means of celestial-rational correspondences we can perceive in the literal meaning (zone 9). This is at last the beginning of our becoming a genuine human being called an angel. In this final state of thinking and feeling we are given everything that is humanly possible to have – but gradually, increasing daily to eternity.

Moses, Paul, and Swedenborg

17.9a What is spiritual enlightenment?
17.9b What is spiritual regeneration?

The Writings use the word "enlightenment" to refer to the perception of spiritual meanings in the literal meaning of the Threefold Word. The Writings explain that the Word of God is written in a special style that is unlike that of any book originating in the self-intelligence of human beings. The Old Testament, the New Testament, and the Writings constitute the Threefold Word that God authored through the minds of Moses and the old prophets, through the minds of the Gospel writers, and through the mind of Emanuel Swedenborg (1688-1772). God's purpose in giving the Threefold Word is to bring Divine Truths to the minds of human beings on this planet. By means of these Divine revelations, anyone can elevate the mind into the celestial sphere where their heaven is. This is how the human mind was created, to be in sync with Divine Truths, and to use these truths in our mind to think and will and higher levels than would be possible without divine Truth in our understanding.

When we rely exclusively on natural truths, and abstract principles based on them, we are locked in the natural mind, in its order that reflects the physical world. This order is an outside existence and reveals nothing about the inner world within itself, which is what keeps it up as the bones of the skeleton keep up the organs of the body. Remove the skeleton and you have a clump of organs, not a capable living body.

Remove the spiritual world within the natural, and you have nothing but a heap of materials that soon disintegrate into nothing, for they are not real or permanent. What keeps the physical world up and going is the spiritual world within it. No one can discover or invent this reality when thinking solely from abstractions based in the natural order of things.

So this is why the Word is necessary, to bring this knowledge of reality to us, without which we form theories that are unreal fantasies. Only spiritual truths can develop our spiritual and celestial mind and consciousness. And spiritual truths come from nowhere except the revealed Sacred Scripture that God brings to every civilization. A new Word is given at the beginning of each civilization.

The Writings detail the history of four prior civilizations to this one, which began on June 19, 1771. This civilization is called the Second Coming and is to endure forever. NO new civilizations can be given since the human race is now completed in its creation, having received the final portion of the Divine Word. This Last Testament, as the

Moses, Paul, and Swedenborg

Writings are called, is the scientific revelation of the Lord's Divine Rational Mind, by which He creates and manages the universe.

But understanding Divine Truth is not enough. It does not stay permanently in our mind. It's like a pot with a hole in it – the water escapes and the pot is empty. In order to plug the hole, as it were, we must love that which we understand. The only way to love some spiritual truth is to apply it to oneself, one's life, one's mental development and states. Truth is what jacks consciousness up. Truth is what needs to be appropriated to ourselves by willing that truth. There is no other way to appropriate truth except by willing it. This is a universal law. As we read the Writings, figure it out, understand it rationally, rearrange our mind according to it, we have the Divine Truth with us in our rational understanding. Now as we walk around all day, doing our thinking and willing, choosing and reacting, we have the Divine Truth in our rational understanding. Now all we have to do is use it, apply it, in order to love it and be enlightened by it. Unless we apply it, we are not enlightened, we do not love it.

Enlightenment is the perception of spiritual truths which we perceive when reading the literal meaning of the Word and apply it to our willing and thinking. The degree or intensity or height of our enlightenment is proportional to the degree to which we apply the divine Truth in rational understanding, to the willing and thinking we do all day long every day of our lives here on earth. This is called enlightenment and regeneration, and progresses until the end.

17.10a What are the laws of space and time in the spiritual world?
17.10b Are there devils and angels there?

When we awaken in the world of spirits a few hours after the death of the physical body, we are conscious of ourselves not unlike when we awaken from a deep sleep and gather our wits together – Where am I? What day is this?. We see our spirit-body and it feels like the body we had on the planet. We look around us and we see people similar to the people we last saw on earth. It's easy to think that you are still on earth, though you can't figure out where you are and how you got there. But this state of confusion quickly passes and gives way to other emotions and thoughts.

Swedenborg witnessed thousands of people being resuscitated in his 27 years of dual

Moses, Paul, and Swedenborg

citizenship. Everyone is resuscitated in a standard manner by attending angels, who are inhabitants of the heavens who volunteer to come down to the world of spirits and provide that loving service. To every individual regardless of who they are or which planet they come from. All this proceeds through a Divine order by Divine laws and through the participation of many others who are already adapted to life in the spiritual world.

The attending angel-physicians or nurses appear to peel off some thin veil on the face of the resuscitating individual. Upon this the person opens the eyes and becomes conscious. This process takes a little while, and the attending angels have the power and perception to control the thoughts and feelings of the resuscitating person. They keep the mind of the person calm and serene, keeping out all thoughts or emotions that interfere. When the person becomes conscious and begins to function and walk around, other attendants take over, spirits and angels who have the function of guiding the new arrivals so they can have certain specific experiences that brings out their interior loves.

This takes some days, weeks, or months, but not more. Eventually, the individual has become completely changed. The former surface personality traits and airs or pretenses are now gone. What now rules the individual are the interior loves that make themselves known. These loves now take over, completely. The chief of these loves arranges all other loves beneath itself, and what isn't compatible is discarded. Now the person is governed by the chief love with no other consideration capable of standing in its way. And such as this love is, such does the person become.

If it is an infernal or evil love, all good loves are discarded and the person becomes that evil love. The individual then sinks down into the bottom of the mind where the hells are. After this, there is no return, because the infernal love rules. Should this infernal love be brought near truth, it instantly turns it into its opposite. Should this love be brought near good or heaven, it feels like the individual is being suffocated and a terrible dread seizes the person which lasts until the individual is back in hell where they regain their familiar life in sub-human insane consciousness. But if the chief love is a good love, it discards all evil loves that are incompatible with it, and the individual rises in consciousness to the top of the mind where they enter heaven and its consciousness.

When we reach this final phase of resuscitation and preparation, we enter a society which is our home to eternity. There are no mistakes or errors or change of mind. God supervises every step of this process and He makes no mistakes. Our place in the spiritual world, whether heaven or hell, is permanent. And in fact, all inhabitants have an assigned dwelling for themselves, which is given them when they enter the society or city.

This place of final destination to eternity is determined by God alone. God brought this individual there, step by step, from the second of birth on the planet, to this particular city and spiritual society, either celestial or infernal. While we are still attached to the physical body on earth, our spirit-body remains in the world of spirits, which is in between heaven and hell. Under the permission of the Lord, people from heaven can come down to the world of spirits, while some people from the hells can come up. This "traveling" back and forth is for two purposes.

One is to assist the new arrivals in their resuscitation process and in its completion in identifying the ruling loves. The other is to influence the mind of the individuals on earth by acting into their spirit- body which is in the world of spirits. The Lord assigns two angels and two devils to each individual on earth so that their mind can remain in equilibrium or freedom of choice. Without the angels the evil spirits would corrupt every person and lead them to the hells where they are. This is their greatest delight. The angels' greatest delight is to take the individual to the heaven where they are.

In the spiritual world the surroundings are instantaneous projections or creations, that come and go, reflecting the individual's state of feeling and thinking. On earth the surroundings are fixed no matter what mood we're in, but not so in our dreams, where the surrounds reflect the content of the dream, which reflects the mood or feeling states of the dreamer. In the spiritual world the surrounds are made of spiritual substances, not material as on earth. The mind's feelings and thoughts are also made of spiritual substances. You can see therefore the great power the mind has there. It has the power to create the surrounding environment.

Only those who are in a similar state of feeling and thinking can therefore share the environment. If an individual should arrive in the world of spirits having feelings and thoughts completely different from anyone else, that individual would be all alone with never any company or communication possible with anyone else. What a horrible fate. But everyone arrives into the world of spirits from some planet with some cultural background, and therefore can form a spiritual community with other like minded people.

In general, people from different planets do not see each other in the spiritual world because their mentality or genius is so different, especially if the planets are in different galaxies. Swedenborg was able to "travel" to spiritual societies made of people from planets of different galaxy from ours, and this traveling was done by his change of mental state under the supervision of attending angels guided by the Lord.

Walking or locomoting is only a visual appearance since people in the spiritual world have a fixed location relative to everybody else. So when people meet, they appear to have walked or flown to a common place such as a building or garden. But in reality no locomotion has taken place and the people remain in their original fixed position, as determined by their basic mental type. The Writings say that some people develop the skill of appearing in more than one society simultaneously, and those around them are not aware of this.

Apparently they use these skills to deceive others, and this is permitted them for the sake of further spiritual growth by those whom they deceive. Deception is by means of persuasive ideas and simulations. There are people who arrive with a good character but with an undeveloped rational intellect. They take longer to be prepared for their final destination, and in the meantime, they may be deceived by some for their learning and eventual benefit. The Writings provide many more details about this subject.

The inhabitants of the hells are called devils, satans, genii, sirens, and other names which reflect their specific types of evils and insanities, of which there are too many to number. The inhabitants of the heavens are called good spirits, angelic spirits, and angels, and they too are too many to be numbered. To God, the entire heavens make up one Angel and the entire hells make up one monster. In other words, the hells and the heavens each act as one, even though they are so vast and getting vaster.

17.11a What's the difference between sensuous and rational consciousness?
17.11b Is spirituality closer to mysticism or to rationality?

It is easy to confirm by observation what the Writings say about the levels of the natural mind, and more difficult to confirm what's being said about the spiritual and celestial mind. The latter confirmation comes in due course with regeneration. But at the beginning of our reformation as an adult we can confirm that our natural mind has three levels of operation – corporeal, sensuous, and rational. We can recognize our corporeal thoughts and emotions by observing our sensorimotor habits and pleasures like eating, sleeping, hugging, kissing, stroking, scratching, belching, etc. These are corporeal because our natural mind at the bottom (facing downward and outward), is open directly to the sensory organs of physical sensations.

But when we begin to think about these corporeal activities we may feel that we need to exert control over them in accordance with expectations, norms, standards, or principles. This management of our corporeal self, or self-management, requires a level of thinking above the corporeal and is called the sensuous level. It is still identified closely with the senses but more in terms of information and abstraction.

Sensuous thinking and feeling is above the corporeal, which doesn't think but only senses. The sensuous level of thinking is able to order things into categories and to evaluate and measure them. But there is a level above sensuous thinking in the natural mind and it is called the rational level of thinking and feeling. This is the highest portion of the natural mind and has the peculiar quality of being able to face either downward towards the sensuous, or upward towards the spiritual mind which is a discrete degree above the natural mind.

In the natural mind and conscious awareness we possess therefore two types of consciousness, one belonging to the operation of the corporeal and sensuous mind, the other belonging to the natural-rational mind. The first consciousness is called sensuous and is fully developed in our infancy period of development, long before the rational is developed later in childhood and adolescence. We gain experience and receive instruction so that we are able to develop first our ability to abstract concepts from the sensual, and later, our ability to use rational categories rather than categories abstracted from natural order. Rational order is different from natural order. Rational order cannot be discovered solely from abstractions of the sensual. God organizes the rational in the natural mind to correspond to spiritual order. When this rational looks down to the sensual and corporeal, it sees only the natural, and sometimes a deeper natural, but sees nothing and knows nothing of the spiritual.

But when the rational looks up to the spiritual mind, it can see and understand spiritual ideas and rationality. The natural-rational is therefore an intermediary between the natural mind proper and the spiritual mind proper. The rational thus partakes of both the natural and the spiritual. It is a property of the human mind that it can become aware of its own operations of thinking and feeling.

In fact, the spiritual mind is opened by spiritual-rational ideas or truths, and the celestial mind is opened by celestial-rational ideas or truths. There are therefore in existence three levels of the rational in human beings. The lowest level is called the natural-rational level of thinking and feeling. The second level is called the spiritual-rational level of thinking and feeling. The third level is called the celestial-rational level of thinking and feeling. These three levels of thinking and feeling define the levels and phases of the development of consciousness in the human race.

Sensuous consciousness is external while rational consciousness is internal. What is external is natural and what is internal is spiritual. This is a universal law of True Science. Everything that exists has an external and an internal, and without this it cannot be created. This law applies in the largest and in the smallest case. The created universe has an external called the natural world and an internal called the spiritual world.

All things natural such as a planet, a tree, a grasshopper, an electron, have an external made of material elements and space, and they each have an internal made of spiritual substances without space. The human mind has an external made of material elements called the natural mind and it has an internal made of spiritual substances called the spiritual mind.

The natural and the spiritual are in discrete degrees, which means that there is no possibility of direct contact or communication, but only synchronous interaction governed by the laws of correspondence. In all cases, the external and the internal of anything must act together, simultaneously or synchronously. There is no action or subsistence and existence without this synchronous action by correspondence.

Similarly for consciousness to exist it must have an external and an internal that act together synchronously by the laws of correspondence. The external of consciousness is called sensuous consciousness and its internal is called rational consciousness. While we are developing in infancy, childhood, and adolescence, our natural mind is operational and conscious, and from this we have sensuous consciousness. This gives us conscious awareness of the order of the natural world and builds up our memory databases of information about our planet and its objects and laws of operation.

These sensorimotor, cognitive, and affective representations of our experiences will form the basis of our life in eternity, either heaven or hell. In other words, our consciousness in the bottom of our mind as well as at the top, is based in the content of our natural mind. Hence it is that the house, city, and landscape around us in hell and in heaven are like those on the planet, but only in external appearance. These appearances in correspondences of the thoughts and emotions. Every thought and every feeling or intention has its corresponding natural representative. These correspondences therefore determine what is around us.

On the planet this process is inhibited by materialism (absorbed by matter), but it operates fully in the spiritual world where there is no matter, time, or space. This inhibition effect is necessary on the planets to allow people with different and incompatible thoughts and emotions to live together in society. This condition is necessary for the growth of the natural mind. But in the spiritual world, further growth of the natural mind is no longer possible, and spiritual societies are therefore organized by means of similarity and compatibility of thoughts and emotions. This is necessary to allow societies to exist, for in the spiritual world different states create unavailability or denial of access and co-presence.

While the natural mind is being grown on the planet, the internal of it, which is called the spiritual mind, is operated by God through the vertical community and influx. Spirit societies are brought near or farther from our spirit-body in the world of spirits and this method is used by God to lead us in every moment of our life, awake and asleep. Every thought and every emotion that the natural mind experiences must originate from the vertical community to which God ties us moment by moment.

You can see how complicated this system is since the external material world of events around us that provide the content of our thoughts and emotions in the natural mind, must match perfectly the internal spiritual world of events within us that provide the correspondences for our thoughts and emotions. Only God, in His infinite Wisdom, Intelligence, and Rationality could manage this task.

And even more astonishing, the complexity of the task increases to infinite levels when you remember that the population of the heavens and the hells is constantly increasing, that the number of inhabited planets is multiplying at the rate of the speed of light, and so also the population of the human race in the created universe – and all this endlessly forever! That all this is under God's total control is also shown by the fact that of all these numberless planets, this one is the only one that has developed an industrial, mechanical, and technical civilization. This is the only planet that has written revelations from God. This is the planet God chose and prepared for His Incarnation.

The human race on this planet has a genius or quality that inclines towards materialism,

Moses, Paul, and Swedenborg

abstraction, and rationality more than the races on the other planets. Hence our natural-rational mind is developed by science, industry, and culture to greater extent than those on other planets. This unique quality of our race allows us to evolve a rational consciousness that is more developed and more complex or abstract. The human races on the other planets have a more keenly evolved sensuous consciousness. From these two sources of humanity, God builds up the level of consciousness of the entire human race from all the planets.

We fulfill an important function for the other races by contributing a more advanced level of rational consciousness to the sum total, and they contribute to our evolution by benefiting us through their more evolved sensuous consciousness. This interactional sharing mutually and reciprocally between all the varieties of human races is part of humanity's evolution of consciousness.

Swedenborg had occasions to discuss God with spirits originating from other planets. Everyone in the spiritual world regardless of their natural origin, speaks a common language that is innate to spirits. We begin to talk in this language spontaneously and unconsciously as soon as we awaken from the resuscitation process.

All consciousness to subsist and evolve in any human being must have an external called sensuous consciousness and an internal called rational consciousness. True Science reveals that if you remove rational consciousness in our mind, we are not capable of sensation, thinking, and feeling. The lowest corporeal sensation, such as looking at an object, or touching it, or smelling it, is completely inhibited and made void unless rational consciousness is also given. This shows itself in our awareness by recognizing the stimulus and perceiving its meaning. Or else, by puzzling over the stimulus if it is not recognized. Either way, recognizing it or puzzling over it, are operations of rational consciousness.

Our rational consciousness evolves through three phases or levels of operation called natural consciousness, spiritual consciousness, and celestial consciousness. Each of these are segregated by discrete degrees and interact by correspondences across the three portions or levels of the mind – natural mind, spiritual mind, and celestial mind. Natural-rational thinking is performed by means of natural-rational correspondences. Spiritual-rational thinking in the spiritual mind is performed by means of spiritual-rational correspondences.

Celestial-rational thinking in the celestial mind is performed by means of celestial-rational correspondences. Natural-rational correspondences are acquired externally by means of experience, instruction, and scientific revelations in the Word of God. Spiritual-rational correspondences are acquired internally by enlightenment from God while we apply the natural-rational correspondences of scientific revelations to our own mental states and decision making in daily living situations.

When we study the Threefold Word as True Science we acquire principles of life called doctrine. These tell us about God and other spiritual subjects such as sin, regeneration, and influx. These topics are discussed and presented in a natural human language in the form of natural-rational correspondences. This is called the literal meaning of the Threefold Word. This is a theoretical knowledge that raises our consciousness temporarily, while we are reading and studying.

But as soon as we apply this knowledge and understanding to our daily willing and thinking, we become conscious of the spiritual-rational correspondences that are correspondentially within the natural-rational correspondences. This new higher rational consciousness is called enlightenment. The process then continues to the next discrete level when we receive celestial enlightenment, the highest category that humans are capable of.

From then on we continue evolving our celestial-rational consciousness to eternity. Along with this continuing evolution of rational consciousness there must of course be a matching evolution in sensuous consciousness. It is from this that the environment of heaven gets more and more wonderful on a daily basis, while the environment of hell gets more and more bleak. In other words, we continue to rise, or we continue to fall, and this with no ending.

17.12 How does True Science view religious rituals and faith?

Rational spirituality is the venue created by God to save us from the Fall. This event refers to an evolutionary changeover in the human race. The early civilizations on earth prior to the Fall consisted of celestial humans. Their will and understanding operated in lockstep. They were united minds. They could not have evil in the will and truth in the understanding. Nor could they have good in the will and falsity in the understanding. Therefore everything they needed to know came into their consciousness from celestial influx. Whatever their affection or curiosity wanted to know, their understanding and intelligence was instantly

Moses, Paul, and Swedenborg

filled with the information or answer. But in the course of time some of them embarked on a willful course of separating their will from their understanding.

They invented fantasy characters and gods, and misused their celestial intelligence by learning how to simulate and deceive. Eventually all the generations of that civilization became tainted with this anti-human tendency. When there were no more united minds left, the human race had Fallen. This means that people lost their enlightenment. They were no longer able to sense the light of the spiritual Sun. The human race on earth was plunged into spiritual darkness.

The physical brain evolved as a result of the ending of the united mind. The subsequent generations had a split-brain, divided down the middle, with a right hemisphere reflecting the independent will, and a left hemisphere reflecting the independent understanding. The split-brain race with a divided mind was able to contain evil in the will and truth in the understanding, and also, good in the will and falsity in the understanding.

From a celestial civilization the race had fallen to the level of a spiritual civilization, which is one discrete degree lower. Celestial light is like the warm light of the bright sun on a clear spring day. Spiritual light is like the cold light of the full moon on a clear winter night. From this comparison, you can see how far the race had fallen! Swedenborg witnessed how the inhabitants of the various heavens see the Lord and the spiritual Sun around Him.

The inhabitants of the celestial heavens see the Lord surrounded by the spiritual Sun which is many thousands of times brighter than the noonday summer sun at the tropics on earth. And yet this intense Light does not in any way feel uncomfortable to the inhabitants, but instead is deeply comforting and joyous to them. They have this Sun in front of them no matter which way they turn or walk. Its Light is Divine Truth and the Heat within this Light is Divine Love. As they look upon this Sun their mind is thus filled with love and truth from within, from within their inmost. Thus they are intensely moved by it.

On the other hand, the inhabitants of the spiritual heavens see the Lord surrounded by the spiritual Sun which appears to them like the light of the full moon at night. What a tremendous difference! The consciousness of God in our spiritual mind is like the moon at night, whereas the consciousness of God in our celestial mind is like the sun in the middle of the day. Not a single idea which a celestial angel is conscious of in clear light can ever be understood by an angelic spirit in the spiritual heaven. When the inhabitants of the celestial heavens discuss a subject with each other, the inhabitants of the spiritual heaven are affected by the conversation in such a way that they become conscious of the spiritual-rational ideas that correspond to what the angels were talking about. The angels in the celestial heavens operate from their celestial mind whole the angelic spirits in the spiritual heaven operate from their spiritual mind (their celestial mind not being opened).

Such then was the great distance of the Fall that having operated from the celestial mind the race now began to operate from the spiritual mind. The mixed mind of the new split-brain Fallen race now required a method of regeneration. This was a Divine medical procedure whereby the disunited mind could be made united again. It consists of these progressive steps. First, since communication with the celestials was cut off, a different method of instruction became necessary. This was done through Divine scientific revelations given through selected and prepared individuals who were able to write down their visions into a collection called Sacred Scripture.

Second, the independent understanding is to be filled with Divine Truths from the study of Sacred Scripture. This was possible now because the understanding was independent of the will. The will was born filled with evils, but the understanding was empty at birth and could be filled with truths. Third, The understanding now filled with Divine Truth, was able to be conjoined with a new will that was a gift from the Lord's Own Proprium or Personality, that He implants unconsciously into the natural mind, a discrete degree within it. Now the understanding conjoined to the new will makes a new person with new feelings and thoughts. This is called the process of regeneration.

Regeneration is not an easy procedure. It requires conscious voluntary cooperation on our part. There are various methods and styles of cooperation in our regeneration. The psychology of cooperation is a science that is sorely needed today. How do we cooperate with the Lord in our own regeneration? The effectiveness of our regeneration is limited by our cooperation. And this requires struggling with temptations. The will is regenerated by means of temptations. The Lord brings different types of temptations to each person every day. There are natural temptations, spiritual temptations, and celestial temptations in that successive order.

The scientific explanation of temptations is that it is a process of cognitive reappraisal under affective pressure. For instance, I know I should stop writing and go interact with the cats. This is the time they expect me to feed them and play with them. So I feel guilty postponing it. It bothers me. It puts me under affective stress. It's a temptation to postpone it. My conscience and convictions, my love for the cats, is in doubt, hanging in the balance.

Moses, Paul, and Swedenborg

My sense of self is threatened. What kind of a person am I who neglects his cats? (pause here.) OK. I'm back. I fed the cats and I played with them. Meanwhile while I was doing that I felt like stopping and resuming my writing.

Such are temptations. They are attacks on our loves and on our truths. We struggle, look to the Lord, ask for help, and we conquer. Once we conquer, the Lord is able to snip the umbilical cord that tied us the this or that society of hell. It is their representatives, raised momentarily to the world of spirits, and brought near to our spirit-body, that instigated the temptation. It was their weakness, their evil delights, their insane falsities that I was filled with during the temptation process. It works as long as I have no awareness of their presence or of the source of my experience and attribute the feelings and thoughts to myself.

This is then the method by which the split-brain race is regenerated and by which their divided mind becomes united and whole again.

Consider the Table below regarding how True Science views faith.

	RITUAL FAITH (phase 1)	**MYSTICAL FAITH (phase 2)**	**RATIONAL FAITH (phase 3)**
Method of Salvation	Sacrifices	Sacraments	Regeneration
Level of Doctrine	Incantation	Prayer	True Science
Required Charity	Donations	Tithing	Uses

How True Science Views Faith

There are three essentials of faith. First, faith gives a method of salvation. Second, faith gives doctrine for the understanding. Third, faith prescribes forms of charity that we must perform. Faith exists in our natural mind at three representative levels – corporeal level, sensuous level, and rational level. At the corporeal level of thinking and feeling our faith consists of rituals of faith, rather than faith itself. We know that these rituals are about God and faith, but the level of thinking about God and faith is corporeal.

Moses, Paul, and Swedenborg

This is evident from reading the Old Testament. At the sensuous level of thinking and feeling our faith consists of mystical faith, not yet true faith itself. We know that this faith is about God, but the level of thinking about God is sensuous. This is evident from reading the New Testament. At the rational level of thinking and feeling our faith consists of rational faith, which is true faith itself. We know that spirituality is rational, and the level of thinking about God and faith is rational and scientific. This is evident from reading the Writings.

Consider the method of Salvation provided by God at each level of faith. Every individual steps through the same sequence that characterizes the evolution of consciousness in the race. In the "Old Testament states," our faith overlaps completely with outward behaviors. As children this is how we become socialized in our family and religious group. We know that there is God, but we think of Him as a Divine Monarch who demands that we follow prescribed rules, like sacrifices and taboos, and punishes us if we fail. When we move up a representative discrete degree in rational spirituality, we enter the "New Testament states."

We think of more inward things that are supernatural rather than natural. Instead of animal sacrifices and prohibitions, we rely on symbolic sacrifices like the Sacraments and on God's presence with each individual as the Holy Spirit "dwelling" in us. Because this level of faith is mystical, it is seen in obscurity and confusion. To compensate for this lack of clarity of comprehension, one focuses on the strength of one's "blind faith." Salvation is granted to anyone whose faith is sufficiently strong. In the "Third Testament states," our faith is rational and scientific.

We can see that the method of salvation cannot be sacrifices or sacraments, but must be something that changes our character from hellish to heavenly. This method is called regeneration and is a lifelong process of struggling with temptations, overcoming them, and desisting from former ways of thinking and feeling. This progressive regeneration of character prepares the mind for heavenly life. This is the only salvation possible.

Consider now the level of doctrine. In ritual faith our doctrine consists of incantations. Every religious denomination begins by instituting ritual incantations that are proper or peculiar to the group – singing, repeating in unison, repeating a certain number of times, using particular intonations accompanied by characteristic gestures and postures, singly or in group. These rituals of faith are considered holy and sacred.

Congregations that move beyond the ritual faith, establish a mystical creed that is repeated during prayer worship. These doctrinal things are considered beyond the level of thinking of

Moses, Paul, and Swedenborg

most adherents, and is left mostly to priests, ministers, and scholars. But they cannot penetrate the mystery but only pose more baffling questions about the mystery. Again, congregations that move to the next step – rational faith – dissolve all the prior mysticism with True Science from the Threefold Word.

Finally, consider the required charity in the three levels of our faith. In ritual faith, we think that donations we give to the poor or those in need, adds to our spiritual merit, and if we accumulate enough merit, we gain higher status and honors relative to others with less merit. As we move up to mystical faith we realize that performing prescribed outward behavior does not contribute to our merit because what we have is from God and what we share others as charity is also His. Nevertheless, even if our salvation does not depend on performing charitable acts, we ought to share at least Ten Percent of our annual income or wealth with those less fortunate than us. This is seen as a matter of individual conscience. At last, as we move into rational faith, we realize that everything we do is our charity towards the neighbor as long as we do something useful to the neighbor or society at large. This is called performing "uses."

17.13 What is the Science of Correspondences?

Thinking and willing refer to two basic spiritual operations ongoing in the human mind. The mind's two organs are the will and the understanding. In modern psychology, the "will" is identified with the affective domain of behavior, and the "understanding" with the cognitive domain of behavior. Affective behavior refers to the operation of the organ of the will. Cognitive behavior refers to the operation of the organ of the understanding. The human mind contains three discrete degrees or levels of organic operation – the natural, the rational, and the spiritual. The rational level of operation serves as an intermediary between the natural and the spiritual.

The three levels operate synchronously by the laws of correspondences that regulate the operation of discrete degrees. We are born with a dual existence, one temporary, the other permanent or eternal. Our mind is permanent, immortal, or eternal, while our physical body is temporary and mortal. Our mind is housed in a spirit-body that is functionally and spiritually tied to our physical body. When we are born, we have two bodies, one physical in the natural world, the other spiritual in the world of spirits. Though tied to the physical body, the spirit-body is not in the natural world but in the world of spirits.

When we are born, the spirit-body begins its immortal existence in the world of spirits, while the physical body begins its temporary existence in the natural world. Thus, we are citizens of a dual universe, one part of us natural, the other spiritual. Thinking and willing are operations of the will and understanding, these being the two organs of the mind. You can see therefore that thinking and feeling (or willing) are not operations in the physical brain, but operations in the spiritual organs of the will and understanding.

Thoughts and feelings are spiritual objects and substances, and therefore cannot exist in the natural world of material mass and space (brain). Thinking and willing are mental operations -- activity that is carried out by spiritual organs in the spirit-body located in the world of spirits. The activity of the brain is merely a physical representative of the activity in the organs of the understanding and the will.

What is a physical representative? All physical phenomena on this planet are representatives of spiritual phenomena in the spiritual world. The spiritual phenomenon must occur first in successive order, just like the cause must occur before the effect in successive order. If conditions on earth are mature or sufficiently prepared, then the spiritual cause will eventuate in a natural event. The physical phenomenon is called the cause of the natural event. The natural effect of the spiritual cause, is called a "physical representative" or natural representative. The natural event, being the effect, "represents" the spiritual event, which is the cause. This is the successive order by which God manages the dual universe.

From Himself through His Divine Rational Mind, the Divine Human Person creates and regulates the dual universe, which would instantly collapse into chaos and vanish from existence, were He to withdraw Himself from any region of the universe, or all of it. This is the rational meaning of omnipotence and omnipresence. The Divine Human Person may be called the only True Scientist from whom all true science originates. He has revealed that He manages the dual universe by means of rational laws that can be scientifically described and understood by human beings.

These new scientific revelations given to the human race are the Writings of Swedenborg. There we find an explanation of the laws of correspondences by which God produces physical events by means of spiritual states or enabling conditions. Correspondences are the enabling conditions of life and power. That knowledge with the ancient civilizations used

Moses, Paul, and Swedenborg

to be called the Science of Sciences, and also, the Science of Correspondences. Such knowledge was considered sacred. With the Fall, this science was lost.

The Lord in His Second Coming in the Writings of Swedenborg has now revealed once more this Science of Sciences. His Divine Rational Mind uses this True Science to effect phenomena in the universe, which was outwardly created through Divine Truth. Hence it is that spirituality is rational, and that the way to God is by rational faith. The science of God is True Science that He reveals.

Clearly, there cannot a be a true science of God that our natural-rational mind manufactures. Whatever we think or feel about Divinity is to be strictly avoided. We must never rely on our own reasoning regarding God or anything spiritual whatsoever. Our own reasoning, which is natural, would impose a natural order on the spiritual idea we are trying to understand. Therefore our understanding must remain natural, and a natural understanding of God or spiritual things, is not spiritual, not truly rational, but just merely natural.

Therefore any knowledge about God or spirituality must be obtained from Divine revelation. This is the method God has created for interacting with the conscious human mind. There is no other method of spiritual development or growth of consciousness. The Threefold Word is the source of all scientific knowledge about the Science of Correspondences. No other source is to be used or it will mix the two and the lower will destroy the higher in our mind. We then condemn ourselves to no spiritual growth, and consequently, to an eternity of hell. Such is the medical reality of the Fallen human race.

Rational faith is not something our rational mind manufactures, for that would be a false abomination called the "proprium of man" which, since the Fall, is the insanity of the love of self. One cannot exaggerate the importance to the human race of the revelation once again, of the Science of Correspondences. It is the grammar of True Science. And the future of humanity rests on True Science. All the prior generations are but few to all the future generations. And these endless generations to come will rely on True Science and benefit from it so that a paradise on earth can form the nursery of heaven, rather than a hell, as it is now.

To understand correspondences, consider the synchronous regulation that takes place between the operation in the spiritual organ of understanding and the operation in the physical organ of the brain. Whenever there is activity in the spiritual organ of understanding in the spirit-body, there is a parallel resultant activity in the physical organ of the brain in the physical body. The direction of interaction is always from the spiritual organ to the physical organ, in the same way as it is between cause and effect.

It is not possible to have an effect before a cause, and so it is not possible for any operation in the physical brain to occur prior to its enabling condition in the spirit-body to which it is connected by correspondences. These connections are discrete, that is, functional by correspondence. The effect in the lower degree (natural) is only as an indexical representative of the prior operation in the spiritual organ of understanding. The properties or characteristics of the brain activity match exactly in indexical representation, every characteristics of the thinking activity in the organ of the understanding.

It has been revealed that the right brain hemisphere more closely indexes the activity of the will, while the left brain hemisphere indexes the activity of the understanding. Within these general characteristics there are specific and singular characteristics so that the pattern of every brain activity moment by moment is unique because the thinking and willing sequence of life is unique, with never a single thought or feeling repeating itself exactly to the endless eternity. This feature of activity reflects, represents, or indexes God's infinity.

It's very important to realize that the indexing or representing of something spiritual by something natural, is not a one to one relationship of equivalence, but many to one. The natural and the spiritual are in discrete degrees relative to each other. This means that there is no continuity or overlap between them, but only representative indexing. An analogy might be to think of the index at the end of a book and the text of the book.

The index at the end is short in comparison to the book itself. The index cannot contain the information and knowledge that the book contains. The index is an inferior venue for communicating knowledge. You need to use text to communicate knowledge. So the index only represents or indexes the book, but itself does not contain the knowledge in the book. The activity of thinking in the spiritual organ of the understanding is like the text of the book that contains the knowledge.

But the activity of the physical organ of the brain is like an index to the activity in the understanding. Obviously, we could not reconstruct the book from the index! Similarly we could not reconstruct the thinking in the organ of understanding from the activity of the brain as measured by electrical recordings of brain activity during thinking.

For instance, a brain CAT scan is like an index from which one cannot reconstruct the text.

Moses, Paul, and Swedenborg

The text or understanding organ is spiritual, and spiritual objects are far more complex than natural objects. Thinking is far more complex than the brain so that the brain can reflect our thinking only as an index reflects the rest of the book. The spiritual world is a discrete degree richer and higher than the natural world in terms of information, knowledge, and all its spiritual and celestial phenomena.

While we are attached to the physical body on earth, our conscious awareness is restricted to the natural and rational levels of operation in our spirit-body. The natural mind is capable of representing all the discrete levels of the spiritual mind by establishing sub-levels, one above the other, and these sub-levels mimic or represent the discrete levels of spiritual-rational and celestial-rational. Our consciousness can therefore ascend through spiritual development of our rational understanding while we are here on earth.

The higher the spiritual development we attain here on earth, the higher will be our life when we leave this world. The essential purpose of our temporary sojourn here on earth is to prepare our will and understanding for higher consciousness in the afterlife. This preparation is first, by means of reformation of the understanding through the Threefold Word, and second, by regeneration of one's character through cooperation in our temptations.

Selections from the Writings on correspondences appear below in Section 19.8.

17.14 Can it be shown that genuine spirituality is rational and scientific?

Scientific has relation to science. Rationality is a type of mental operation. "Scientific" and "rationality" are closely connected. Science uses rational mental operations to gather observational facts and to formulate abstract accounts and explanations for those facts. Remove rationality from science and you've eliminated the existence of science, just like you've eliminated language if you've removed grammar. Intelligence and wisdom are closely related terms to rationality and science. The goal of science is to produce rational explanations of reality that lead to understanding the universe and how to control its phenomena. Studying science is a necessary component of education and the acquisition of rationality in adult life.

The uppermost portion of the human mind is called heaven and the lowest portion is called

Moses, Paul, and Swedenborg

hell. Science and rationality characterize the heavenly operations while the hellish ones are salient through their opposites -- superstitious and irrational mental operations. As we become more and more scientific in our thinking we gradually climb to the top of the mind where heaven is and where our rationality is in its purest form. The heavenly life is a rational life.

Angels are the most rational, the most scientific in their thinking about the universe and its phenomena. The purer the form of our rationality the closer it images the Divine Rationality called Divine Wisdom or Divine Truth. The source of this Divine Truth is the spiritual Sun from which streams out "spiritual light," which is a spiritual substance called Divine Truth within which is a celestial substance called "spiritual heat." Spiritual heat is a substance called Divine Love or Divine Good.

The universe is a dual universe since it has been created in discrete degrees – spiritual and natural. There is a natural or physical world and a spiritual or substantive world. The underlying framework of this dual universe and its every created object or quality, is the infinite uncreate substance streaming out of the infinite spiritual Sun as a ray, flux, or ceaseless stream. This substance is pure rationality or pure truth within which is pure good or love. Good and love are used interchangeably, and likewise with truth and wisdom (or "rationality").

Both Divine Good or Love, and Divine Truth or Rationality, are infinite substances in God. God as the Divine Human Person, can be seen amidst the spiritual Sun by the inhabitants of the heavens. In other words, when we climb in consciousness to the top of our mind, we can behold the Divine Human Person amidst the spiritual Sun from which streams out the foundation substances of all created things in the dual universe. What a sight that will be! Quick, how do I get there? The short answer is: By being good!

Clearly then, God is the True Scientist. Therefore, genuine rational spirituality is the mental operation by which our consciousness climbs to heaven where we are in the immediate influx of the Divine Human Person, by which we are made immortal and capable of living to eternity in a joyous and blissful conjugial state called being angels. Genuine rationality begins when we acknowledge that there is one infinite omnipotent omnipresent God and that God is the Divine Human Person. Next, we can acknowledge that this Divine Human Person is Rationality itself and the source of all rationality in the human mind.

The method by which we progress in rational spirituality is to study Divine scientific revelations contained in the Threefold Word. By this means we have at hand information about the spiritual world which is inaccessible to our physical senses. Yet this information is essential to form a rational and scientific understanding of reality – the dual universe, God's scientific and rational laws of managing it, and our immortal journey from physical to rational to spiritual to celestial.

Consider what happens without the scientific information about the dual universe that has been revealed to us in the Threefold Word. Without this factual knowledge of the spiritual world and how it interacts with the natural world, scientists are compelled by their method to reject whatever information comes to them about God and the spiritual world. Materialistic science is atheistic because of its inability to count as real the factual data from Divine revelation. Scientists operate by the assumption that only the material world exists and therefore facts that are not measurable by physical means are not facts, not part of science. This attitude and assumption forces atheism on every new scientist who obtains a Ph.D. in the academic world.

As a result of this attitudinal hegemony, the majority of scientists in the Western nations take up a schizoid position regarding the reality of God, heaven, spirit, and the afterlife. On weekends when they attend Church, and evenings when they engage in family religious activities, including Bible reading, the scientists act like believers. They are the same people who practice atheistic science during the rest of the week in their job and profession. In my own case, I lived this kind of schizoid mental life for most of my life and professional career.

As a scientist in the academic world of Psychology, I felt challenged to tie in my professional career with my personal interest in spirituality and theology. Our national and influential professional organization called the American Psychological Association (APA), issues guidelines regarding ethical behavior of scientists, and they include warnings against the promotion and use of what it calls "pseudoscientific" methods and concepts. It does not identify God and religious life by name, but the list of what is generally considered pseudoscientific includes magic, superstition, ghosts, visions, inner voices, miracles, supernatural influences, God, Divine revelation, angels, devils, immortality, afterlife, spiritual world, truth, consciousness.

As a young Ph.D. in my twenties, these were the very things I was deeply interested in. I found out that the only legitimate method of investigation that I was allowed regarding these topics was the method of materialistic measurement. Unless it was measurable by a material operation, it was not science and should not be represented to the public as science without incurring ethical violations of professional standards.

This indiscriminate and dictatorial requirement led me, and others, to investigate the usual aspects of psychological dimensions of human behavior in the area of religion. I joined the sanctioned sub-group of the APA called Psychologists for the Study of Religious Behavior -- Division 21. I familiarized myself with the research and theory in that segment of our science of psychology. Read articles and textbooks and attended conferences.

But my involvement did not last and my interest did not survive. The research consists in giving people questions to answer about their beliefs and faith, or attitude scales to fill out, or observing how many times they go to Church services and how involved they get in Church related activities, and the like. This is not what I was interested in. Other psychologists were studying the brain activity during meditation, prayer, out of body experiences, hallucinations, or experiences that people classify as supernatural such as miracles, visions, ecstatic union with God, dreams, apparitions, psychic powers, prediction of the future, talking with spirits, etc. Again, this is not what I was fundamentally interested in.

These topics only skirted around what I felt I wanted to find out. And so I could not continue to invest my time and effort in these existing research topics in "transpersonal psychology." They did not bring clarity to my understanding. I did not comprehend the world better.

Not finding what I wanted in the science literature, I cast my line of exploration into the hazy literature of theology, symbolism, mythology, Eastern philosophy, theosophy, and even some science fiction. I was interested in the content of these things, but I was dissatisfied with the method. I remained a scientist at heart. I was unable to give my mind over to the authority of someone else. I remained totally skeptical and floated around outside the circle of followers of these things. I insisted on believing nothing that I did not understand in a rational way. Why should I trust myself to anyone's intellect? It made no sense to me. My intellect was as good as anyone's, I felt.

And so I kept searching compulsively, hoping to find, having no other choice but to continue looking. Meanwhile I was leading a schizoid life like my colleagues, continuing my activities of research in psychology, research that led to reports that were acceptable for publication in the sanctioned journals. Of course, these publications never mentioned any of the topics that I was investigating from my personal interests. This went on until 1981 when I discovered the Writings of Swedenborg in our university library.

18. Discovering the Writings of Swedenborg

Now things changed in a fundamental way. At last I did find what I had been hoping for. The Writings (about 30 volumes) were written by a Swedish scientist (1688-1772) who rejected the materialism of science of his day, which was the science of Descartes, Leibniz, Kant, and Newton. Though these authors acknowledged God in their Prefaces (as did Darwin a few years later), the rest of their work did not mention God again, or how the supernatural interacts with natural phenomena, as it is revealed in the Bible they were familiar with.

Though they were men of religion by culture, their science was atheistic. In their mind, although God created the universe, He sort of left it to its own devices in the form of Natural Laws. I find this amazing, frankly, since it's completely illogical to say that God is omnipresent (in the Preface of their books), and in the text to say that God has taken an exit from the natural world and left to run by itself on the natural laws that He created. How can omnipresence be retained in that case?

The only rational position is to say that "God is omnipresent" means that He is at the intimate center, or inmost presence, of everything, of every object, of every quality, of every energy, of every power, force, rationality, or love. God is the very source and cause of these effects. Remove God from the inmost portion of these effects, and what do you have? Nothing. No effects. Zero. Non-existence. That's what omnipresence means when thought about it rationally. As Swedenborg had done years before he started to have dual consciousness. He published several scientific volumes on natural science – cosmology, chemistry, metallurgy, physics, optics, algebra, anatomy. Swedenborg's Principia (1734) and Newton's Principia (1726) make a wonderful contrast between materialistic science (Newton) and dualist science (Swedenborg).

Newton and Einstein allowed their science to mimic atheism even though they were believers, as stated in their own testimony, often the Preface to their theories. Swedenborg's fierce intellectual integrity and rational intelligence led him to formulate a different science, a theistic science that focused directly and explicitly on the chain of command from the one omnipotent God to the rock formation, or the flowering of a plant. In

Moses, Paul, and Swedenborg

Swedenborg's theistic science, the spiritual was connected to the natural by God's laws of order, and the two acted together as cause and effect. His rationality saw that it is the spiritual world where God is that is the cause of the natural world where we are.

Hence one could not scientifically describe a particular natural phenomenon on this earth without showing how it is an effect of a spiritual phenomenon that is its cause. He also saw that the Word contains Divine scientific revelations about the rational laws by which God creates, maintains, and manages the dual universe. His rationality also showed him that there must be a spiritual Sun in the spiritual world that is living from God and from which all things are made of, such as the natural sun which is dead. He discovered some of the laws of correspondence by which the spiritual and natural phenomena interact and depend on one another. He showed how these laws are revealed in the Old and New Testaments.

Remarkably, after these rational discoveries, Swedenborg at age 57 was granted dual consciousness to prepare him to write the volumes of the Writings as the scientific revelations of what is the Divine Rational of the Divine Human Person. This Third and last portion of the Threefold Word unveils all the mysteries of religion that had been unknown to all the prior generations of humankind. Now any individual, regardless of culture and religion, can read these revelations and develop thereby a rational intellect that is spiritually enlightened regarding the means and ends of creation, religion, heaven and hell, regeneration, and salvation.

With his new dual consciousness Swedenborg was able to be aware and be active in the spiritual world while he was pursuing his ordinary daily tasks in this world. He kept copious daily notes in the style of a careful, and even meticulous, investigator. Swedenborg the scientist had 27 years of dual consciousness, from age 57 to 84, during which he wrote and published the Writings in Latin between 1745 and 1771.

He conducted systematic interviews with large samples of the inhabitants of heaven and hell, and performed various empirical and experimental investigations, assisted by the inhabitants of the highest heavens who have the ability to perceive the thoughts and affections of those who are below them in spiritual development, and even to temporarily bring them forward or backward in development. They can also block out certain memories or knowledges, or empower their reasoning ability. These changes are temporary so that the people involved always fall back on their former state, which is their chief love. This cannot be altered by anyone to eternity. Nevertheless these temporary changes of spiritual state induced by angels who assisted Swedenborg, served him well in allowing him to experimentally and clinically explore their behavior and reactions. These types of data are most valuable since no scientist on earth has ever had consciousness.

Now you can see why I said above that this is what I had been looking for so compulsively for decades. Now at last I was not confronted with someone's tedious authority filled with speculative fantasies about God, heaven, hell, sin, prayer, universe, afterlife, growth, Divine laws of operation, scientific revelation, angels, devils, the mind, rationality, spirituality, truth, love. These are the topics that Swedenborg handles rationally and scientifically. Never before in the history of science has this been attempted.

The Writings of Swedenborg fully satisfy the scientist in me. For the first time I was able to read and know spiritual truth, explained rationally because God was rational. This really impressed me. I did not know that God was rational. I did not know that God was a Scientist, managing the universe by rational laws, like a Divine Engineer in charge of running everything around. My prior idea of God, from tradition, culture, and imagination, was that He was mystical, not logical. I had thought of God as something fuzzy, indefinable, hidden in fog and distance across the past and future.

But Swedenborg the Swedish scientist presents God as a definite particular Person, known in history, and known by the highest angels he talked to, who on occasions have seen Him face-to-Face, and at all times see Him amidst the spiritual Sun. His infinite Divine Love for the human race is so burning and intense that they come out of Him as a celestial Aura or Emanation that becomes visible to the inhabitants of the highest heavens, as the spiritual Sun. You, dear reader, and I can see this spiritual Sun whenever we ascend in rational spirituality to the top of our mind called the highest heaven. He, the Divine Human Person, wills to appear to each mind.

He wills to elevate the upper portion of each mind to Himself. His purpose for willing this, He has revealed in the Writings, for it is He who is the real Author of the Writings, through Swedenborg's as-of self authorship. You need to know this from your own perception, for otherwise it is not believable, just because I assert it, or Swedenborg asserts it, or if anyone you read asserts it. That would only serve you as a child, which is a wonderful age when spiritual truths are learned through a celestial influence. Children need to hear this assertion, that the real Author of the Writings is the Lord.

But as we grow in maturity and rationality, we put aside our childhood perspective of God and the world, and we put on an adult's perspective, one that over the years, more and

Moses, Paul, and Swedenborg

more reflects our own adult reasoning and preference. Now in this new individualized or personalized perspective we hear of this assertion, or we remember it from childhood, and we end up doubting it, or qualifying it in a way that it loses its pristine purity and absolute value. Hence it perishes in our mind. How sad. How sad.

Hence it is that there is no choice but to undergo reformation of one's adult perspective and basis for reasoning about everything. Our search for truth then begins. For me it lasted from my early twenties to my early forties. Then I found the Writings in our university library. No detail is managed by anything else than the Lord's Laws of Providence and Permissions. Thus it was that I was searching in the library for a Bible commentary because I had been feeling an intense desire to love it and understand it more.

Accompanied by my conjugial wife, who shared the same passionate desire, we jointly came upon a shelf filled with books that were bound in the same collection. There were about thirty of them, written by one author Emanuel Swedenborg. My first impression was, *"How can one man write so many books about the Bible?"* We did not hesitate. I checked out Warren's *Compendium* of the Writings, which was on the next shelf, because it would give me selections from the entire collection of books. My wife checked out Volume 1 of the Arcana Coelestia (Heavenly Secrets).

From that day in 1981, nothing could keep me away from daily reading of the Writings. It was the most exciting reading I could find. Nothing whatsoever came near it in competition. Wouldn't you feel that way too? I mean, assuming you accepted it for what it is with no suspicions or doubts, namely, that it is the Lord God of the universe talking to you in conscious way, no different from Him being present in your room and teaching you something about His universe.

And He tells you that you play a unique and important role in the universe, which is why He has created your soul in this particular unique way. I mean what would keep you from that room where He comes to visit you and talk to you? Would you not surely return to that room every day at the same time so that you can be in His Presence and hear Him speak to you? The movies couldn't keep you away, not even a business deal, and certainly not another book. So this is what I mean that nothing could keep me away from reading the Writings since that first day I met Him.

Hence it is that as an adult, during our reformation, we go to Him and hear Him speak. And we make Doctrine of Life from what He says. In other words, using our academic skills for

Moses, Paul, and Swedenborg

learning, we strive to understand the rational statements and descriptions in the Writings. With our knowledge of spiritual things accumulating in our understanding we gain the ability to redefine our previous concepts, ideas, and values so that they are congruent with the Doctrine of Life in our understanding. Eventually all of our ideas are cleaned and purified from nondualism and other influences that abound around us and partially form our intellect before we have reached the state of reformation sometime in adulthood.

Now we are ready to begin the lifelong process of regeneration. We are spiritually enlightened because we have undergone reformation. We now have a new rational perception of spirituality. We now are consciously aware of the Holy Spirit. We now read the Writings daily with worship, humility, and fear. It is the same Lord as before, but we are closer to Him. He is more impressive in this closer state. Our spirit feels awed and humbled. Yet since He is Pure Love, we cannot be anxious or afraid for long and He grants us Divine familiarity. This is when for the first time True Science is born in our mind.

Now the Lord is Co-present in conscious awareness as we move around in our daily tasks. The more we advance to the wisdom of innocence of old age, the less and less minutes we spend daily in rational unconsciousness of His actual co-Presence. We begin with one hundred percent of daily rational un- consciousness of His actual co-Presence. We end with *one hundred percent of daily rational consciousness of His actual co-Presence.*

At this point we are ready to be transferred to heaven. But until then and in the meantime, we must strive to achieve this goal by all the means of intelligence and ingeniousness that we can muster for the task – the most important task on earth. Thus is the heavenly preparation we undergo through regeneration.

As I began to read the Writings on a daily basis, I for the first time in my professional career, had access to a scientist's direct observations of the process of dying, the process of resuscitation from death a few hours later, the process of entering heaven or hell, the process of change once there to eternity. For the first time as a psychologist I gained access to the anatomy of the human mind, its organs, its discrete levels, its sequence of development mapped out in minute detail. I

read the medical descriptions of the human personality or spirit, laid open from within. For the first time I was able to see the objective difference between evil and good properties of the mind. Good vs. evil was not a religious or philosophical bias but a physiological mechanism or operation of the mind. I learned about the physiology of the spirit and about

Moses, Paul, and Swedenborg

spiritual geography. The secret of dreams was exposed and explained as a process. Symbolism in art was uncovered and described. Undiscoverable history of the past generations was made known by the people themselves who lived them while they were on earth. I gained inside empirical knowledge of some of the actual motives and reasonings of historical figures like Aristotle, the Virgin Mary, King David, Luther, Newton, as told to Swedenborg by these very people.

Clearly, Swedenborg was not just given dual consciousness and left helpless. Every minute detail of his experiences was managed by Divine Providence to allow him to write the volumes of the Writings in such a way that they will actually be the last complementary portion of the Threefold Word, in which every sentence, phrase, and word is Divinely managed and contains infinite truths to be endlessly extracted by the forever increasing population of the immortal human race.

18.1 The Holy Spirit --
Rational Consciousness of God's Co-Presence

From these considerations you can now see that spirituality is both rational and scientific. The amazing thing to remember is that the highest form of spirituality is heaven, which is also the highest form of human rationality. This is amazing in view of the many things I have read about "mystical union" with God which is represented by some people as opposed to doctrine or intellectual knowledge of God ("Logos"). Now I see that these claims to mystical union and ecstatic

religious states belong to the realm of sensuous consciousness of the Divine, and this form of consciousness has ceased upon this earth after the giving of the Holy Spirit, as described in the New Testament. From then on, as revealed in the Writings, the Holy Spirit was to be the sole conscious connectivity possible between God and human beings on earth. This mode of connectivity clearly belongs to rational consciousness, not sensuous consciousness.

It is most important to understand this distinction. The New Testament tells us that everything that was made was made through the Word or Logos. The Writings tell us that "the Word or Logos" means Divine Truth. Therefore, all created things are created by means of truth, which as already explained above, is an actual substance streaming forth from the spiritual Sun as spiritual light.

Clearly, "truth" and "rationality" are closely related terms. Further, "truth" and "rationality" are both related to "science" and to "rational explanation of observable phenomena," that is, to reality. Since all truth is from the spiritual Sun, which is the emanation from the Divine Human Person, it is fully clear that this Divine Human Person, i.e. God, is Divine Rationality Itself, or Divine Wisdom, or Divine Truth. Therefore also, the One True Scientist from whom all True Science issues and descends into the consciousness of humanity. The vehicle for this conscious transmission is the Threefold Word. Hence, the Threefold Word is the source of True Science.

No other source exists or is possible, according to *the Writings*. Rational consciousness of God, or rational spirituality, is achieved by internalizing the Threefold Word as Doctrine of Life. This means that we first rearrange our thinking in accordance with our understanding of the Threefold Word. This is called acquiring Doctrine of Life from the Threefold Word. When this Doctrine is in our conscious understanding, we are spiritually enlightened beings. This is the first step and is called the reformation of the understanding. It is a physiological process in the spiritual organ that operates our understanding.

The first step of reformation and spiritual enlightenment is not yet our salvation, which requires the second step. This second step is called the regeneration of the will. This too is a physiological process in the spiritual organ where the will operates. The reformation of the understanding must reach a completed stage before regeneration of the will can begin. This regeneration is induced and accomplished by God, but His action is restricted and limited by the extent of our voluntary cooperation.

This cooperation involves struggling against temptations that God brings us face to face with on a daily basis for many years. The essential purpose for which He grants us those years here on earth, is to regenerate our will, not to contribute to society by accomplishments or inventions. These are uses we should do along the way, but the central purpose is not to contribute those uses but to regenerate the self. Obviously this must be the case since without regeneration all is lost. Ending up in the hells of our mind is called spiritual death. Everyone is immortal in the spirit-body, after casting aside the temporary physical body.

Ending up in hell is the worst nightmare that can befall us. Such is the savagery and rage of our mind at the corporeal level at the bottom of our mind. When our consciousness is habituated to the level of thinking and feeling at the bottom of the human mind, we are far more savage and cruel that wild beasts who live by catching each other, tearing each other apart, limb by limb, and consuming our rage by obliterating everything about the victim. Such is the ferocity and slyness of life in hell, where all people meet face to face, whose thinking and willing operates at the lowest level.

Eternal experience in hell has been hinted at by the Lord in the New Testament, and fully described by the Lord in the Writings. Clearly He wants us to have a clear idea and representation of what it would be like to be an inhabitant of the hells in our mind. An accurate knowledge of our hells is necessary for the rational mind to be able to reject that state of life and consciousness. The states of hell in our mind are powerfully attractive and delightful. It is impossible to exaggerate the importance of knowing this revealed truth – namely, that the inherited evil we each receive regardless of background, religion, or planet, is hidden, or more accurately said, hides itself from awareness. And still more accurately, or scientifically, we can say that they hide themselves from our awareness!

Wait a second – What do you mean "they hide themselves from our awareness." Sounds creepy. Who are they?

18.2 Dual Citizenship --
Horizontal and Vertical Community

It has been revealed in the Writings that we are never alone. We are dual citizens and we belong to two different cultures or societies – one natural, with our physical body and legal identity, the other spiritual, with our spirit-body and spiritual identity. You know very well the laws of your external horizontal community or citizenship. It is your country, and for some people, your religion, and for still others, the lifestyle you idolize. This is your horizontal community, and exerts itself through your physical body.

You also have a vertical community, which exerts itself through your spirit-body. Swedenborg saw the spirit-body of those who are still connected to a physical body on earth. They are seen by everyone in the world of spirits who are already detached from earth, and you will see the spirit-body of those still on earth after you move on. When observed in this way, the spirit-body of earthlings appears quiescent and non reactive. This is because consciousness of the spirit-body is not permitted while still an earthling.

Moses, Paul, and Swedenborg

It would be confusing, I imagine, to have the simultaneous sensory input from the spirit-body and from the physical body. At any rate, this would harm the development of rational consciousness, which is the very purpose of regeneration, which is salvation, that is, a consciousness that lives at the top of the mind through thinking and willing heavenly things only. There is also an aura of scent around the spirit-body of earthlings that deters the inhabitants of the world of spirits to approach, thus insuring that no input into the conscious mind may come directly from the world of spirits.

The outward apparent quiescence of the spirit-body of earthlings contrasts with the inner active operations going on in the spirit-body which houses the mind. This activity in the spiritual mind remains completely unconscious. The activity is operated, not by sensory input from outside the spirit-body, but by rational input from within. This rational input originates from the vertical community to which we belong. The Lord has revealed that it is He Himself who operates the universal networking of our vertical community. You can understand this better through an analogy. Consider your telephone. All people around the globe form a network with each other by acquiring and paying for, a telephone account or number. Anyone from anyplace can access anyone else who is

on the network. You can call your wife in the car with a cell phone, or someone in India, or any place, even off the planet, and on the moon (though this line is not yet active!). The Lord wills that the entire human race should form one network. This inter-communication of the entire race, past and present, on the planets or in the heavens and the hells, is an amazing new scientific revelation of enormous importance for our societies on earth. I have coined the phrase "vertical community" to designate this mental networking in the human race.

This is what meant when I said that "we are never alone." Our physical body may appear to be alone, away from our horizontal community, when we are in a prison, or an uninhabited island, or on a boat lost in the middle of the ocean. But wherever and however we are in relation to the horizontal community, we are never far or near from the vertical community, but always fully in it, when we walk, talk, dream, think, reason, desire, enjoy, hate, or fear. The Lord wills that every individual on earth and in the spiritual world, remain connected to others all the time.

It has been revealed that if this connection were broken for a moment, the entire race would perish. The Lord's operation of the vertical networking has been revealed. He operates by bringing into contact an individual somewhere on earth, with a society somewhere in the spiritual world. Note this: our horizontal community is mixed and diverse in many ways due to cultural, religious, and personality differences. If you travel to a new city or country you will see people who differ in many ways, some of whom you may enjoy being with, others whom you would do anything to avoid. But societies in the vertical community are organized differently.

One's membership in a spiritual society is not determined by geographic location – as in horizontal communities, but by mental state. Those who have very similar mental states belong to one particular society, and no one can live in a spiritual society when they have mental states that clash with the predominant mental states of that society. This is not surprising from our experience with horizontal communities, where we live, work, and spend time with people who have similar mental states to ours, and we avoid as much as we can, coming into contact with people who are in an antagonistic state to ours.

When we cannot avoid the contact, we experience unpleasantness, fear, discomfort, need for relief, and even panic and agony. These emotions are familiar to us. We experience them through the action of the Lord bringing this or that spiritual society in communication with our unconscious spiritual mind. The result of the interaction descends by correspondence into our natural mind where we can become conscious of their presence in our mind.

How utterly amazing and even baffling, at first!

For example, the thought occurs that we are then merely robots. Our thoughts and feelings are not ours after all. We are nothing but radios or television sets or computers in a biological form. Etc. But this is vain thinking. If we go back to the True Science of the Writings we can have the real answer – the concept of "as-of self."

18.3 As-of Self – First Fruits of Rational Consciousness

The revelation of the vertical community is pretty important, as we have seen, but equally important and astonishing is the revelation of the as-of self. Our consciousness is elevated when we understand the rational idea that God is omnipotent. The logical consequence of this idea is that no other power exists. In other words, wherever there is power, it is God's power. For example, our heart is beating. This takes power. Where is this power? Is it in the

Moses, Paul, and Swedenborg

burning of calories by the action of the cells in the heart muscle? No, because how could the burning of calories generate power? Where does that power come from? The inherent motion of the atoms within the molecules? No, because where would that power come from? Clearly God cannot give His power, or any power, to someone or something else than Himself. If He gave power away, He would no longer be omnipotent.

So there is no logical or rational way of having power belong to anything but to God.

This being the actuality and reality, where is the power that keeps the operation of thinking and willing going in our organ of the mind? This power cannot be from ourselves. We cannot supply the power for the brain or the mind. Now this: Where does the power come from for making decisions, choosing between right and wrong? Choosing is a mental operation, and an operation takes power. The fact is that God is the only one who can supply the power to our mental operations and to our feelings. A feeling is an operation in the organ of the will. This takes power.

So God supplies the moment by moment power it takes to do our willing and thinking. So now the question arises again: If God is behind the power of my choosing between good and evil, how can I be held responsible for that choice?

The answer can only be understood through the concept of the as-of self that the Lord has given humanity for its salvation. It is indeed the actuality that we have no power for anything, including making decisions or being prudent, or being good or evil, but God gives us the appearance that we have power of our own. This is not a genuine reality but an appearance of reality. God allows us to experience that we make our own choices that we have our own power to think this or that, or to lift the finger or not. But in fact we do not have this power.

The inhabitants of the heavens told Swedenborg that their greatest joy is to acknowledge that they have zero power of their own and that all power they exhibit is the Lord's alone. Yet, even as they know this and think it, the sensation they have is that they are acting from themselves. This is what gives them the sense of heavenly freedom and wisdom. And they said the second they think that they are moving or thinking from themselves, they fall out of their heaven, down into hell. Those who are in hell all believe that they have their own power and are acting from themselves, vehemently denying the idea that they have their power from God.

And so, these are the two explanatory concepts we need to ascend in consciousness: First, knowing that only God has any power or life, and second, knowing that we think by means of the vertical community.

God leads and manages our thinking and willing first, by supplying the power for the operation, and second, by supplying the content of the operation. The content of thinking and feeling, which is their quality, is supplied by the spiritual societies that the Lord brings into contact with our unconscious spiritual mind. If we feel rage it's because the Lord has connected us to a hellish society that has rage as its chief love. If we feel compassion it's because the Lord has connected us to a heavenly society that has compassion as its chief love. In this way, moment by moment, day and night, the Lord connects us to particular societies of our vertical community, supplying the content and quality of our experiential life – our thinking and willing.

Now the obvious question arises: Well, if God supplies the power, and the content, and manages all the details, why does He need to connect us to hellish societies, why not only to heavenly societies.?

The revealed explanation is that God manages our as-of self from the background, without showing it to our conscious awareness. Therefore He sets limits on how much He can control it one way rather another. In other words, if He connected us only to heavenly societies, how would we feel? We would feel like we are dying, that we do not want to live in such agony. This actually was demonstrated to Swedenborg numerous times, namely, when inhabitants from the hells were assisted by angels so that they could be elevated to the upper regions of their minds. When they came into contact with the heavenly societies they fell into a swoon and life was ebbing out of them. In terrible agony, they begged to be allowed to return to their former state.

God therefore imposes limits on His management procedures of our mental activities, being careful to supply us with the right amount of this and that, so that we can retain the motivation for living, and consequently for improving and regenerating. And in fact, with the new revelations, we can actually map out the societies with which we are brought into contact. This tells us what our unconscious needs are that the Lord allows us to retain, namely, the need for certain evil delights without which we feel that life is leaving us. The Lord keeps bending and managing our mental operations through the vertical community, with a view to gradually cutting off the communication with evil societies. This indeed is the process of regeneration, which He performs for us, to the extent that we are willing to cooperate.

18.4 Self-Witnessing – The Psychology of Cooperation

God has revealed the medical process by which He regenerates every person in the universe. We have discussed the vertical community and the as-of self and the two chief mechanisms of regeneration. The third component we must add to the first two, is the concept of "temptations." People think of temptations as something private and personal, deep in the heart, hidden from view. One is pulled in two opposite directions, one moment giving in, another moment resisting and going back. People might see the beads of sweat and the shaking of the hands, but that's all, they cannot see the temptation you experience within.

But of course you are never alone, and in your temptations, there is actually a whole crowd of people present, participating. It makes sense in view of what we've discussed already. What is a temptation but a syndrome of events in an episode. Step by step we undergo the course of the temptation – seeing something, thinking something, smelling something, imagining something, concocting something, intending something, wishing, fearing, avoiding, feeling irresistibly attracted, feeling obsessed, compelled from within, and so on. It is a very active state of mind with lots of mental operations.

But of course, as discussed, mental operations cannot take place except in a chained connection in the vertical community. Many societies have to be brought into contact with our unconscious spiritual mind in order to accomplish these sequenced mental events in our natural conscious mind. The Lord brings certain societies nearer to us, even for just a moment, then switches the connection to another society, perhaps also just for a moment, and so on, until the sequence of steps of each temptation runs itself through.

There is a way of becoming aware of this sequence of steps in temptations. The Writings command regular self-examination as a method for becoming aware of the evils in our temptations. A form of self-examination that I have practiced for years is the self-witnessing method, described in Volume 3 of *A Man of the Field* available here: https://web.archive.org/web/20161226165154/http://www.soc.hawaii.edu:80/leonj/nonduality.html

Why are we required to perform self-witnessing or self-monitoring activities? In order to identify the thoughts and feelings that we habitually have in the course of a day, every day, throughout our adult life. Once identified, the mental operation must be tagged by applying our understanding of Doctrine of Life from the Threefold Word. The bottom line of this application must be the final decision: Is this from heaven or from hell? When I was in training as a psychologist I was given the value that it is unintelligent to think in black and white terms, either or morality, on any subject.

Besides "prejudice" another example frequently mentioned is the Church where everything is either good or evil, with nothing in between. This training philosophy attempted to destroy the categorical dualism of good vs. evil, absolute truth vs. relative truth, guilty vs. innocent, right vs. wrong, heaven vs. hell, devil vs. angel. I believe that this has not changed in the academic world and that today the claim that spirituality can be rational and scientific, would be rejected without receiving full examination. To those who already despise absolute dualism as a scientific claim, it is hardly possible to give a full, fair, and impartial, or scientific, examination of the nearly 30 volumes of the Writings, or even of this one book.

The Writings discuss a mechanism of protection called "the Cherubim" which is in place to protect people from being spiritually injured by the *Threefold Word*. All sorts of people in every generation read portions of the *Threefold Word* – students, scholars, general readers, professional clergy, scientists, atheists, people from other religions, educated and uneducated, movie directors, poets, cultists, and so on. None of these categories of readers read the *Threefold Word* for the purpose of regeneration. None of them receive access to the spiritual meaning of the Threefold Word.

Without this access, the only meaning they are aware of is the surface literal meaning. This meaning is about spiritual topics, but talks about them in natural meanings. Our comprehension of spiritual topics is therefore not spiritual but merely natural. We learn these terms, but we do not see them rationally or spiritually -- God, heaven, sin, punishment, angel, miracle, sacrifice, prayer, hell, resurrection, forgiveness. Everyone reading the Threefold Word is allowed to have natural ideas about these spiritual topics, but only one category of readers are allowed to have a rational-spiritual perception of the meaning contained or implied in the literal sentences.

This category of people are those who read the Threefold Word as a method to be regenerated. They know that the Lord commands us to regenerate our character, and it is the condition for entering His Kingdom of Heaven. Because they apply what they read to their life, to their thinking and willing all day long, they are enlightened and given perception of the spiritual meaning of the sentences in the Threefold Word. This enlightenment allows

Moses, Paul, and Swedenborg

us to go further and further in our regeneration by cooperating with the Lord in particular ways, rather than general ways.

The most general way of cooperating with the Lord is to make a confession of all our sins and ask for forgiveness, usually accompanied by some ritual of giving, bathing, or praying. The Lord in the Writings tells us that this is not good enough to allow us to regenerate. When I was young growing up in an orthodox Jewish family in Transylvania in the 1930s, it was strongly impressed upon us children how important it was to prepare adequately for the Day of Atonement ("Yom Kippur Day"). This was once a year according to the lunar calendar, and when Yom Kippur fell on a Saturday or "Shabbos," the overlapping holiness was so great that it could not be described.

One prepared oneself for the fateful day by long prayers, by fastings, by walking without shoes, and by sitting on the floor instead of a chair. These physical acts had to be accompanied by specific prayers. When the Day of Atonement arrives, the whole people (or tribe) gathers in a few worship houses early in the morning, and they stay together until late afternoon when they go home and have a feast. But during the Day of Atonement everybody has to show up in the synagogue, read the confessions of the people together out loud, and silently to yourself. These confessions are written in Hebrew and Aramaic and I never knew what they were as we all recited them by phonetic reading, which we are taught to do since age 3.

Besides the recitations we also had to beat our chest each time we recited an evil deed, though we did not understand the language. Finally, we had to kneel a lot during that day, and also, cry a lot. Crying and sobbing out loud was a specialty of some people, I noticed. They were very loud and convincing. The purpose of public crying, sobbing, and beating of the chest, is to convince God that we are being sincere. When I became an adolescent I flatly refused to go to the synagogue on Saturdays and celebration Holidays.

To avoid a fight with my mother, who herself did not go but felt I should, I would go to the movies for a few hours than go back home, pretending I was in the synagogue. I'm not proud of my rebellion. Yet I also feel that I was moved to rebel by the Lord so that I remain free to keep climbing the ladder of rational spirituality. I believe that I was willing to be led by the Lord, even if unconsciously at that time, because of my love for rationality. He secretly led my mind until my early forties, when I started to recognize Him consciously and rationally, as I read the *New Testament*, and later, *the Writings*.

64

Moses, Paul, and Swedenborg

God secretly leads every individual's mind, regardless of background or belief. Those who are willing, are ultimately led by Him to heaven. Swedenborg reports that the heavens are vast and populated with multitudes of people called "angels." All of them while on earth, were evidently willing to be led there by the Lord. Nothing has helped me stay the course as much as the spiritual discipline of daily self-witnessing. As we do this on a daily basis for many years, our character is gradually being regenerated by the Lord. This is salvation because this is the only way God has provided that we acquire a character that is capable of sustaining life in heaven. In other words, this method of regeneration is the only way by which our consciousness can be raised to the top of our mind and maintained there to eternity.

(Note: I have written a chapter called the *Doctrine of the Wife For Regenerating Husbands*. It is available here:
https://web.archive.org/web/20150628033659/http://www.soc.hawaii.edu:80/leonj/wife.html

To look for God by the vehicle of sensuous consciousness is not a method of regeneration as specified above. We cannot regenerate by meditating or by trance, by experiencing "ecstatic union" with the Divine, by communicating with "more evolved" beings, by sacrificing, by worshipping, by touching sacred objects, by pious fervor, by ritual, by witnessing or performing "miracles," and so on. These are all methods of *sensuous consciousness* that cannot regenerate the Fallen inherited human character of evil.

The Holy Spirit was given for regeneration. "Holy Spirit" means Divine Truth or the *Threefold Word*. The *Threefold Word* is the *Holy Spirit* that was given for acquiring *rational consciousness* of God. By studying and understanding the *Threefold Word* rationally and psychologically we are taking in the *Holy Spirit* to be active in us. This means that the thinking operation in the organ of the understanding is being rearranged, or reformed, so that second by second, our mind is in the stream of truth as we think about this or that, and reason, and make choices. This is rational spirituality.

Today God's direct co-Presence is within our conscious rational mind, not the sensuous mind as in former civilizations. This is why rational spirituality is the developmental pathway to conscious closeness to God. It is this closeness that defines the quality of love and wisdom in our life of eternity.

Rational consciousness of God was initiated with the *Old Testament*, then brought to a new high level by the *New Testament*, and at last completed with *the Writings*. The *Threefold*

Moses, Paul, and Swedenborg

Word was completed in 1771, when the last book of the Writings was published by Swedenborg. The title was *"The True Christian Religion."* Many people since then have acknowledged the Writings as the Word of God, alongside with the Bible. They have formed a small but vigorous and thriving intellectual Christian community called the *New Church*. In their Church services and sermons, they use selections from the *Threefold Word*. In my opinion it is good and right that the New Church has been founded based on the Writings. But this is not the whole story.

The Writings have been given to all people regardless of religion and culture. What is going to unify the peoples of this earth? Love and truth, that is, God's love and truth. The Writings have been given as a source of truth. When this truth is acknowledged as Divine and we understand it rationally, the result is spiritual enlightenment. This spiritual enlightenment is nothing else than knowledge of True Science. The Writings give us scientific revelations about all the things of religion. The New Church school logo in Bryn Athyn Pennsylvania carries the phrase "Nunc Licet" from the last volume of the Writings. It is Latin for *"Now it is permitted,"* and is discussed above in Section 15.2 with a quote from *the Writings*. It refers to the end of mystery in religion. It redefines faith as truth. Rational faith is truth. Blind faith or mystical faith or persuasive faith is not truth.

18.5 What is God Talking About?

God now speaks to the human race through the Threefold Word. And what does He talk about? He talks about Himself and about us. He tells us why He created us, how He created us, why He allowed us to Fall into materialism, how He proposes to take us out of it, what awaits us if we cooperate and what awaits us if not.

Along the way God tells us about the dual universe at large, the many populated earths, the discrete degrees of all creation, the Divine Laws of Providence and Permissions by which the dual universe is maintained in good order, about the science of correspondences by which natural phenomena are produced, about the levels of the mind, the developmental steps of history, the relation between history, evolution, and personality, about the character and spiritual fate of animals, and much more. What would be an obvious name for these scientific revelations by God? True Science.

And so it is that the last work of the Writings is called *True Christian Religion*, which it is, but it is also True Science, which many have not yet realized. God has given us True Science as a source of endless scientific knowledge to be extracted by rational rules, correspondences, enlightenment, and regeneration. All four conditions must be present for anyone to see that the Threefold Word is True Science. True Science is the Divine Rational descending upon the human mind. No one can define True Science or discover its methods, except True Science itself. True Science is untainted by human error and limitation.

True Science is the Science of God – both from God and about God. A science about God that is not from God cannot be True Science. If anything from the human mind is added to True Science, it is immediately destroyed and is no longer True in our mind. We may think that what we add is True, but it is not.

True Science, or theistic science, or theistic psychology, remains of God from God in our mind when we understand it and take it in for regeneration.

When we take it in with this purpose, we would never dare add anything to it, and when we take it in for any other purpose, we are prevented from understanding anything spiritual. It is far better to understand nothing spiritual in the Threefold Word, than to understand something that is then misused or modified to suit oneself. This is called "profanation" and those who are unwilling to turn aside from what is sacred, though they despise it, precipitate themselves into the lowest hells of the human mind, where they suffer more than those in lesser hells above them. The Cherubim have been given to protect people from profanation by hiding from them any spiritual meaning or thought about the things discussed in the *Threefold Word*.

Any individual today, regardless of background, can read the Writings in the original Latin, or more likely in a translation, like I have, can comply with the four conditions just mentioned, and thereby obtain salvation and everlasting happiness in heaven. This is a guarantee because it is brought about by God through a scientific process that He has revealed to us as True Science in the *Threefold Word*.

Salvation is a Divine medical intervention that includes these four conditions or steps:

(1) rational understanding of the *Threefold Word* (which requires regular, long-term, and serious study)

(2) thinking by means of the revealed correspondences (as taught and illustrated in *the*

Moses, Paul, and Swedenborg

Writings)

(3) enlightenment by means of reformation (which is the reordering of everything in the mind to fit the requirements specified by *the Writings* exclusively with no other influences allowed)

(4) regeneration of character (which is a lifelong progressive struggle with temptations of three kinds – natural, spiritual, and celestial).

These conditions are provided for by God. He is a close partner in this process of regeneration, bringing temptations to us that we can handle, keeping others from us, timing everything in excruciating detail, day by day, minute by minute. Our task is to cooperate by exerting as-of self effort to resist the temptations we face, one by one, and to allow God to bring us to victory over them, one by one, in a progressive sequence of increasing rational spirituality.

The temptations are necessary for regeneration. This is because salvation must be something that we freely choose out of love for God. We lay everything aside and elevate this love for God higher than any other love. Without temptations we could not freely choose to leave hell behind and to set our course for heaven. Heaven is not a place to which we are admitted by permission. It is a state of mind which we achieve by freely choosing between our lower and higher self. That is, between heaven at the top of our mind, and hell, at the bottom.

We already have heaven in our mind. We do not need permission to be admitted, or meet certain external conditions. Heaven is already ours, already within us, as God reveals in the New Testament. And so is hell. We have the capacity to go to either state of consciousness, everyone of us who are called human beings. And so God has already done what is possible and perfect. Now He waits. He waits for each one of us separately to cooperate in regeneration, to suffer ourselves to step through the temptations God brings us to face, and to choose good and to reject evil. We must make this choice repeatedly in our thinking and willing all day long every day.

What does it take to bring ourselves to cooperate in the Divine medical process of character regeneration by means of the painful struggle against temptations?

True Science in our mind explains what we must do and what the process is. It explains what stands in the way – the love of self, which has many branches like the love of dominion, the love of possessions, the love of merit, the love of cruelty to all who do not favor us, against whom we are filled with hatreds and murders, the love of hurting and corrupting innocence, the love of hurting the institution of marriage, the love of hurting the Lord and all heavenly things.

All this together is called the love of self that opposes our cooperation in regeneration. There are also cultural influences, religious influences, philosophical influences, all of which oppose cooperation in regeneration. Evil loves in our will are married to falsities in our understanding that justify them. Evil loves cannot be married to truths. Truths can only be married to good loves which we are to acquire from regeneration.

The steps of our regeneration have been laid out in the Writings in amazing detail and intimacy. These developmental steps were created by the Lord when He was a Child growing up on earth. God incarnated so that He can unite the Human He acquired by supernatural birth to the Divine He already was from everlasting. By accomplishing this task of unition, God created a new entity that before this was not accessible to the human race, namely, the Visible Divine Human Person.

This Visible Divine Human Person has now revealed Himself in His Divine Rational Mind. This is True Science or the revelations of the Second Coming that ushers in the last new age that is to last forever. The Lord has now revealed in the Writings how He accomplished this unification process that produced the Visible Divine Human Person. In a remarkable recent book titled *The Path: The Inner Life Jesus Christ* (Rochester, MI: Fountain Publishing, 2002), New Church Rev. Geoffrey Childs traces an outline of what the *Writings* describe about the spiritual meaning of the stories of Abraham, Isaac, Jacob, and Joseph in the Book of Genesis of the *Old Testament*.

The *Threefold Word* is written in a special and unique sacred language whereby each phrase contains meanings within meanings that can be extracted endlessly by future generations. These meanings are scientific revelations arranged in rational order that represents the Divine Rational Thinking of the Divine Human Person. This is so important to us because everything around us – the world – and everything within us – thoughts and feelings, march to the beat of order imposed absolutely by the Divine Rational Thinking of the Divine Human Person.

This is a scientific fact. It is true reality. We know it from God Himself because it is His Rational Voice that Speaks to our consciousness when we acknowledge, read, and

Moses, Paul, and Swedenborg

understand the Writings of Swedenborg. No one can believe this on anyone's authority, and if they do, it is merely a persuasive belief that does not sink down into the permanent immortal character (located in the spirit-body in the world of spirits). One can only hold this view as a conclusion we come to from ourselves, each of us as individuals. God brings this view of Himself to every person on this planet, one way or another – this is discussed in the Writings.

Geoffrey Childs encapsulates and summarizes the sequence of mental development undergone by the Divine Child Jesus. There are almost no details in the New Testament about the Lord's Childhood days. The revelation of those events could not be revealed prior to the Writings of Swedenborg. It takes a rational understanding, prepared by education and science, to comprehend those Divine events and how they affect the human race. Consider this very idea in itself. It is the idea, first, that crucial types of mental events that punctuated the daily life of Jesus in His childhood, are recorded in the narrative in Genesis regarding Abraham, Isaac, Jacob, and Joseph, as well as their families and the history of events described in those portions of the Old Testament.

It takes a rational mind, trained in science and abstraction, to be able to understand what this means, and further, to be able to see the proof that is presented. But it doesn't take technical knowledge or expertise, nor a higher than average intelligence to be able to understand the vast majority of the Writings. I would say that today that level can be described as a high school graduate, which in Western countries refer to the majority of people.

As education of societies deepen, and science becomes more real, almost everybody in any human population will be able to understand most of the Writings, if not all of it. For regeneration it is enough that the person understand some of the Writings, and continue to persist in its study and application to one's daily thinking and willing.

Consider again the first fact I'm mentioning here regarding the "inner life of Jesus Christ." Namely that the developmental steps He underwent in His Childhood are recorded, or specified in detail, in the Genesis narratives of the four patriarchs. How can this be? All sorts of objections arise. Genesis was written by Moses a thousand years before the birth of Jesus of Nazareth. How could Moses record the mental life of Jesus? It doesn't make sense.

Indeed, it doesn't make sense to the natural-rational level of thinking. This is because there is nothing in the order of the natural in our mind that can justify or explain such a thing. If we move a level of thinking above this, we can turn it into something mystical rather than rational and scientific. We can say, for example, quoting the Lord, Well, to God all things are possible. Nevertheless, this type of blind faith does not allow penetrate to the inner character, and therefore we cannot use this mystical faith to elevate our consciousness of God all the way to heaven in our mind.

Then we can go to the final step above this, the level of thinking that is scientific and rational, that explains in abstract terms and with demonstrations, how it is that this is possible, and especially, how you can see for yourself that it is so. This is why the Lord calls it "Rational Faith" or "*Nunc Licet*" faith. Now "it is permitted" to "enter rationally" into the "mysteries of faith" – so sayeth the Lord in the Writings.

The *Threefold Word* is the connecting point of heaven and earth. Wherever ideas from the *Threefold Word* are in people's minds, there it is where the connection is maintained between heaven and earth. Without this connection, earth is lost, and without earth, heaven is lost. The connection between heaven and earth serves to transmit Divine Truth consciously, and Divine Good unconsciously. In other words, we pick Divine Truth from the Threefold Word in our understanding when we acknowledge it as Divine Truth in our mind. Every single such Divine Truth concept that we place in our understanding, is filled by God with Divine Good.

This is an amazing process. The ideas of truth in our mind, when they come from the Threefold Word only, are capable of acting as "cognitive vessels" that hold affective powers. It is up to us to read, understand, and hold the Divine Truth from the Threefold Word. There is no other way in creation to produce these cognitive vessels or receptor organs for good. The goods that we receive in this way are the powers of virtue, the joys of love, and the enlightenment of wisdom.

We receive Divine Truth in our conscious understanding and there it operates in our daily thinking and willing. Divine Truth is useless for salvation unless we make to it to operate on our daily thinking and willing. Once Divine Truth is in our mind, and honored there, the Lord can insert into our will numberless and measureless goods that empower us for a higher life.

Note that in this process both the truth and the good in our mind is not ours but His. We act as-of self, as He wills that we not be conscious of His influx of good into our mind. As a result, our sensuous consciousness of our thinking and feeling, experiences the process as our own, despite the fact that our rational consciousness acknowledges and understands how it is actually not our own.

Isn't this an amazing process? How intimately the Lord's Mind and our mind are intertwined! How closely we work together to achieve who we are, who He wants us to be, and angel increasing in love and wisdom to eternity.

18.6 Christianity Demystified

The Lord in the Writings has revealed that His life on earth was spent in fashioning a developmental sequence for the human mind that will take it from its fallen evil state to heaven. This was the purpose for the Lord's Incarnation as a Child on this earth. This Child was of course unique and different from human boys and girls, since their soul is a unique offshoot of the father's soul. But the soul of the Jesus Child, born of a virgin woman, was not an offshoot of a father. The soul of Jesus was Jehovah, the Creator God of the universe known as Father.

Jesus was not an offshoot of the Father. He was the Father. It makes a discrete difference whether you think that Jesus, also called the "Son of God," was an offshoot of the Father, or was the Father Himself. This idea is difficult to accept because difficult to comprehend when thinking naturally about it, that is, materialistically. Then your thinking and reasoning follow a natural order, and from a natural order perspective, the "Son of God" is not the Father, but another Divine Person.

As already discussed in the book, to have more than one Divine Person who is omnipotent God, is not a rational or scientific idea. It is a mystical idea. To remain rational, we must equate Jesus and Jehovah, if we consider both to be God. In that case Jesus is one Name for God, Jehovah is another Name for God. Of course there are great spiritual secrets hidden in this equation, which you can obtain by studying the Writings.

For now, it is sufficient to understand that God Himself came to His people as Jesus. Of course, this created a special condition in Jesus, as ably reviewed in the Geoffrey Childs book. When Jesus was born His first days and weeks were not enlightened as to who He was on the inside. His higher self was God, but His lower self did not know it.

Moses, Paul, and Swedenborg

Then at one point, while He was still an Infant, His Higher Self broke through to His consciousness and He became aware of who He was. With the ensuing years of growth the young Jesus understood His mission and His Inner Self, which He referred to as His "Father."

Already as a young Child, Jesus burned with the desire to accomplish His mission. The fate of the entire human evolution depended on His full success. He experienced enormous and unbelievable temptations of anxiety and agony during those times when He became unconscious again of His Higher Self.

Throughout His life on earth the Lord alternated between periods of consciousness and unconsciousness of who He was. He never forgot who He was or why He came, even in his periods of unconsciousness of the Father. Rather, He lowered His consciousness to the human thinking operation of the natural-rational mind. He entrapped His consciousness in that level of the mind, where He then suffered unbelievable agony. Why did He do this? We must have a rational and scientific explanation or else we hesitate to accept it.

The Lord entrapped His consciousness in the natural-rational mind in order to create natural-rational solutions to the puzzles in life that keeps us in a fallen state. The actuality is that the fallen human race is also entrapped in the natural levels of the mind. This is what the Fall is – being unable to rise to rational consciousness of duality, of the spiritual. Hence the Lord had to fashion a mental way out of our dilemma.

It had to be a way that we can understand and accept. And so by His infinite Love and pity for our suffering, He humbled Himself by bending the heavens and coming out into the natural world as a helpless Child, whose physical body and natural mind was like the physical body and natural mind of the rest of us. He assumed this lowered state of thinking and willing so that He could come up with a reasoning process that would satisfy our human understanding. Once we understand it rationally, we can accept it and we can love Him for it, and this reciprocal love He is able to make us increasingly happy to eternity.

In His states of self-entrapment at the human level of thinking and feeling, Jesus was confronted by the entire hells. The hells and the heavens had been advised as to the birth of Jesus, the Messiah, the Savior of Humankind. The inhabitants of the heavens were joyful, though concerned about the Lord trapped on earth. The inhabitants of the hells were gleeful, filled with a new sense that their hatred for God could now be vented on the entrapped Jesus. Now Jehovah, as the Higher Self of Jesus, connected the natural mind of

Moses, Paul, and Swedenborg

Jesus to the hells in the way that He connects each of us today in our vertical community, as already discussed.

Jesus thus underwent a series of temptations throughout the days He was on earth. This series was precisely timed and created by God so that in Jesus, it retains a permanent form, which then can be stepped through by anyone, thus saving the human race from hell.

So this is what Jesus was doing while on earth. He was "binding the hells" which means that He was fashioning the rational arguments and ideas that all human beings can understand as a way of resisting our hell and rising above it. Recall that hell is not some place in the spiritual world or purgatory. It is within every human mind, just like heaven is. Hell is the level of thinking and feeling in the corporeal mind when it is separated from the higher rational and spiritual mind.

The human race was in hell, and since the Fall, every person at birth is in hell as to the will. Jesus had to engineer a way out of hell for us, a way out of the bottom of the mind where we were stuck in our thinking and willing. Today we are still in hell at birth and remain there until we reform our understanding and regenerate our will. The inner life of Jesus on earth was the method by which God used to create a pathway for the consciousness out of the corporeal level where it had gotten stuck. But we can step through the steps of rational spirituality that Jesus stepped through in His struggles against the hells while in a state of "exinanition" or entrapment in a lower form of consciousness.

Quoting from *The Path*:

> In the story in Genesis, Isaac did not know that he himself was to be sacrificed: "Behold the fire and the wood; and where is the lamb for a burn-offering?" (Gen. 22:7) These words touch our hearts. In the celestial sense, they go even more deeply. The young Divine rational, in a state of limited truth, asks the Divine itself, "Where are those in the human race who are to 'be sanctified' or who are to be saved? (see AC 2805). Where are the good people that I may save? I don't see any."
>
> All of the Lord's temptations focused on human kind – here on the youthful Jesus' tender love for us. But His rational mind is still in very limited truth – a state in which things are not clear to Him. In His outward confusion, He cannot see how humankind can be rescued. He despairs.
>
> (...)A picture of this is the boy Isaac, bound upon the altar, with his father, raising a

Moses, Paul, and Swedenborg

knife to kill him. His [Jesus'] rational level is bound (AC 2813, 2814).

Imagine the love and fear in Isaac. He loved his father. Yet his father was about to sacrifice him! (...) Looking from the appearances in this still limited rational (AC 2814), and with the hells viciously attacking, the youthful Jesus feels helpless. He lies upon the wood of the altar, bound and apparently about to be destroyed. (...) Jesus feels terrible despair. But, instead of yielding in this despair, He endures, and a miracle happens. First, "whatever was from the merely human" rational level dies (AC 2818). What despaired in Him dies. In its place is born a higher rational, a Divine rational, that can clearly see the possibility of salvation for all people. This part of Him becomes "the Son of God," the Divine Human.

(...)What takes place of former doubts within Jesus, a new level in the Divine Rational glorified, this can save us. Now from His Divine Human in His glorified rational level, He can see the possible reception within humankind and begin to offer salvation. A true rational replaces one that was bound, Isaac is freed from the altar. (...)The inmost love of the boy Jesus is moved with delight, because those He feared would be lost can now be saved!(...)The Lord provided a ram for the sacrifice. The ram represents all those of the spiritual church or genius. To sacrifice the ram here means to sanctify – to save. By the glorification of His Divine rational, the Lord is now able to save all those who are spiritual from the time of this glorification onwards. In addition, this same degree of glorification opens salvation to all the good people in the world who are represented by the families of Nahor in Haran, mentioned at the end of Genesis 22. These are all the good Gentiles on earth.

Jesus liberates the spiritual people and sanctifies them. That is, as the ram was freed from the thicket, so spiritual people are given the means to escape from mental and spiritual entanglement in merely earthly knowledge. The Lord shows them the way to their rebirth, to their reformation and regeneration. This way is first shown in the New Testament, but then is fully unfolded in the Writings of Swedenborg. The "glory in the clouds" is revealed (HH 1), and now the era of true science is gradually dawning. The two foundations of truth (SE 5709), the Word and nature, will meet and support each other. (Geoffrey Childs, The Path, 74- 77).

(end of quote)

Now how does Rev. Geoffrey Childs know these details? It's because he is actually merely

Moses, Paul, and Swedenborg

summarizing and following in an outline form what the Writings present in the 12-volume *Arcana Coelestia* where the narrative of the four patriarchs as given in the *Old Testament*, is explicated in their internal sense by means of the code of correspondences in which they are written. In other words, you need to accept and understand the idea that the *Threefold Word* is written by correspondences.

This is another great scientific revelation that will accelerate the progress of science. The *Arcana Coelestia* go through a word for word and verse by verse analysis of the Books of *Genesis* and *Exodus* in the *Old Testament*. In this analysis the correspondences are revealed. I discussed this topic in prior sections, though not extensively. When you study the correspondences you can begin to see the Divinity of the *Threefold Word*.

It's important to realize that the same correspondences apply throughout the Old and New Testaments, even though they were written independently by dozens of writers over many centuries. None of these writers had any inkling that what they were writing down were in the code of correspondences. The prophetic authors were just writing down what they could see in their visions, or the narratives of the historical events they participated in. Unbeknownst to them, God insured two things. First, that those events, names, numbers, and places actually occurred historically and are accurate facts. Second, that only those events and visions were recorded that corresponded to the mental pathway that Jesus was going to fashion in Himself centuries later.

The enormity of this coincidence is not believable. It has to be understood rationally and scientifically as to how Jesus accomplished this amazing event. I quote portions of the text from Swedenborg's *Arcana Coelestia*:

> Verse 1 "And Jehovah said to Abram, Go away from your land, and from the place of your nativity and from your father's house, to the land which I will cause you to see." [Genesis 12]

The events described here and in what follows took place in history as they are recorded, yet the historical events as described are representative, and every word carries a spiritual meaning. This is so in all of the historical parts of the Word, not only in the Books of Moses but also in those of Joshua, Judges, Samuel, and Kings, all of which books contain nothing else than historical narratives.

But although they are historical narratives in the sense of the letter, in the internal sense there are arcana of heaven lying hidden there. These arcana cannot possibly

76

be seen as long as the mind keeps its eye fixed on the historical details, nor are they disclosed until the mind removes itself from the sense of the letter.

(...)From this one may recognize that the vessels are one thing and the essential elements within the vessels another. The vessels are natural, and the essential elements within the vessels are spiritual and celestial. In the same way the historical narratives of the Word, as with each individual expression in the Word, are general, natural, indeed material vessels that have spiritual and celestial things within them. These things never come into sight except through the internal sense. (AC 1407)

(...)'Go away from your land' means the bodily and worldly things from which He was to depart. This is clear from the meaning of 'land', which is varied depending on the person or thing to which it refers, as also in Genesis 1 where 'land', or 'earth', likewise meant the external man, and elsewhere, 82, 620, 636, 913. The reason why here it means bodily and worldly things is that these belong to the external man. (AC 1411).

Because the subject here is the Lord these words contain more arcana than anyone can possibly conceive and make known. For here in the internal sense is meant the Lord's first state after He had been born. Because that state is a very deep arcanum any intelligible explanation of it is hardly possible. Let it be said simply that He was like any other human being, except that He was conceived from Jehovah, yet born of a woman who was a virgin, and that by birth from that virgin He took on all the weaknesses that are common to all. These weaknesses are bodily, and are referred to in this verse in that He was to depart from them in order that celestial and spiritual things might be brought into view for Him.(AC 1414)

> (...)Verse 14 "And Jehovah said to Abram after Lot had been separated from him, Lift up your eyes, now, and look from the place where you are, towards the north, and towards the south, and towards the east, and towards the west."

'Jehovah said to Abram' means that Jehovah so spoke to the Lord. 'After Lot had been separated from him' means when the desires of the External Man had been removed so that they did not obstruct. 'Lift up your eyes, now, and look from the place where you are' means the Lord's state at that time from which He was able to perceive things to come. 'Towards the north, and towards the south, and towards the *east, and towards the west' means all men, as many as there are in the entire universe. (AC 1601)*

'Towards the north, and towards the south, and towards the east, and towards the west' means all men, as many as there are in the entire universe. This is clear from the meaning of these four directions. In the Word north, south, east, and west each have their own particular meaning. 'North' means people who are outside the Church, that is to say, who are in darkness as regard truths of faith; and it also means the darkness residing with the individual. 'South' however means people who are inside the Church, that is to say, who are in light as regards cognitions; and likewise it means the light itself.

'East' means people who lived in the past; and it also means celestial love, as shown already. 'West' however means people who will live in the future, and likewise people who do not have love. What they mean is clear from the train of thought in the internal sense. But when north, south, east, and west are all mentioned together, as they are here, they mean everybody living throughout the whole world, as well as those who lived in the past and those who will do so in the future. They also mean the states of the human race as regards love and faith. (AC 1605)

'Pharaoh' is the natural in general which has now become inactive, leaving everything to the celestial of the spiritual, which is 'Joseph'. The seven years of the abundance of corn in the land of Egypt are the factual knowledge to which good from the celestial of the spiritual can be attached, while the seven years of famine are subsequent states when no good is present within factual knowledge except that coming from the Divine celestial of the spiritual, which is received from the Lord's Divine Human. A detailed explanation of this is given in what follows below. (AC 5192)

"And bring me out of this house" [Genesis 40] That this signifies deliverance from evils, is evident from the signification of "bringing out," as being deliverance; and from the signification of a "house," as being good (see n. 710, 1708, 2048, 2233, 3128, 3652, 3720, 4982); and therefore in the opposite sense, evil. Hence it is plain that deliverance from evils is signified by the words, "bring me out of this house," and this also follows in its order from the things which precede.

When faith is received in the exterior natural (which is here treated of, see n. 5130),

Moses, Paul, and Swedenborg

> *correspondence is effected (n. 5131), and charity is received (n. 5132), and thus communication is effected with the interior natural (n. 5133), which is then delivered from the evils whereby the celestial represented by Joseph (n. 5086, 5087, 5106) was alienated; which alienation is signified by his being "carried off by theft," as presently follows. Moreover, when the natural is being regenerated by means of charity and faith, it is delivered from evils; for evils are then separated, and are cast out from the center where they were before, to the circumferences, whither the light of truth from good does not reach. In this way are evils separated in man, and yet are retained, for they cannot be entirely destroyed.*
>
> *But with the Lord, who made the natural in Himself Divine, evils and falsities were utterly cast out and destroyed; for the Divine can have nothing in common with evils and falsities, nor be terminated in them, as is the case with man; for the Divine is the very being of good and of truth, which is infinitely removed from what is evil and false. (AC 5134)*

(end of quote)

These quotes give you examples of how the Old Testament verses can be analyzed by means of the code correspondences so that their spiritual meaning is brought into the open. This is how we know all the details of the mental developmental steps of Jesus. These are the steps that every human being can now take in order to vanquish the hells within themselves through the development of rational spirituality. The mental struggles of the young Jesus were foreseen by the Lord from the beginning of creation. The Lord then brought about the historical events in the lives of the four patriarchs, and then had these events recorded through the visions of Moses.

Then came the Boy Jesus who read the Old Testament in His native Hebrew and Aramaic. Jesus was given to discover from within his spiritual mind that the Old Testament details were representative of His task that lay ahead and for which He Incarnated. This Divine Task was to create a new evolutionary mechanism for the medical regeneration of the Fallen human mind.

The Boy Jesus was far more advanced in intellectual development than any man, young or old, because His spiritual mind became conscious at an early age. These details are unfolded in the coded story of Abram receiving the call from Jehovah. This represents the moment of enlightenment of Jesus who was then still an infant. He became conscious in

Moses, Paul, and Swedenborg

His spiritual mind, which no human being on earth is able to do. It's only when we become a spirit in the afterlife that we become conscious in our spirit-body that houses the spiritual mind.

Of course this gave the Child Jesus a direct source of information about God, Himself, salvation, and the Word. Every time we read in Genesis that Jehovah spoke to Abram, later Abraham, the coded decipherable message in correspondences is that the external natural mind of the Boy Jesus was in a state of enlightenment so that He could be consciously aware of His spiritual mind. This spiritual mind is called His "internal man" and it is Jehovah.

The Lord Jehovah, Creator and Father, incarnated as the Babe Jesus. This Divine human being had then to discover who He was and why He was separated from Himself. In other words, Jesus throughout His life on earth, went through a series of alternating mental states between being trapped in the natural mind, which was merely human, and being enlightened in His natural mind by the operation of His spiritual mind within it, which was Divine Human. When He was trapped in the merely natural mind, He was in a state of "exinanition" in which He humbled Himself and admitted temptations into Himself by wrestling with the hells so as to gain victory over them.

Victory over the hells meant that they were separated and isolated so that the good people destined for entrance into heaven were able to delivered or freed from their dire influence that kept them out of heaven. They are the spiritual people who believe in heaven and hell, and in loving the neighbor, but who are filled with all sorts of false beliefs and persuasions. As long they were holding on to these false persuasions, they could not enter heaven where truth is required.

Through these false persuasions of the good people, the evil could hang on and torment them, preventing from heavenly life. The Lord thus freed all these people by admitting temptations into His mere human and ordering the hells. The Lord accomplished these events even as a young Boy growing up in Nazareth, where He let no one know what His real work was until the final events of His days on earth. At that point His work was nearly completed and His disciples were enabled to hear Him.

18.7 Forming the New Church Mind in Ourselves

Moses, Paul, and Swedenborg

When I consider my generation I can see that a few of us have been given a special opportunity to be forerunner minds of the future. A minor fraction of one percent of the earth's population has had to meet two conditions to be in this evolutionary shattering group of forerunner minds. First, to have received sufficient science education to be able to comprehend a high school or college textbook. Second, to come across the Writings and being willing to read the majority of it (about 30 volumes). You can see how few people would fall into this group.

But now consider this: Having read most or all of the Writings, how many are left who then can say, This is the Word of God. You can see that there are few of those. They are the enlightened ones. And finally, how many among them are willing to exclude everything in their mind – thoughts and feelings – that are not in accord with the heavenly order described in the Writings? Even more than this, how many of those left are willing to change their inner character to comply with this heavenly order as described in the Writings? Those who are left in this forerunner group have a New Church mind. If you're interested in the details of how to acquire that lofty consciousness, you may want to consult my book titled *A Man of the Field – Forming the New Church Mind in Today's World* available on the Web at: https://web.archive.org/web/20161226165154/http://www.soc.hawaii.edu:80/leonj/nonduality.html

What about future generations? It makes sense to think that God, through omnipotence and omniscience, inevitably brings out the goals He has set. In the Writings, God has laid out for humanity both the goal and the means of the future. The future of the human race is endless, and God provides numberless new planets in the vast and explosively expanding galaxies, as nurseries for human beings.

Every individual on the numberless planets is created a unique person with a mind in an immortal spirit-body capable of living in heaven to eternity. This is God's goal in creating the physical universe – to support life for human beings on their way to becoming angels in heaven. God's method is to prepare the individual on some earth and then transfer the person to heaven with the physical body left behind to disintegrate. Further, God has revealed the reason He wants to get endless numbers of unique persons to heaven. And this reason is Divine Love.

God explains His Love in the Writings. It is defined as the desire to make others happy from self. In other words, He is possessed of an eternal and ceaseless desire to make human beings more and more happy by giving them the Goods that He possesses from infinite

Moses, Paul, and Swedenborg

eternity. These Goods are called celestial blessings and they operate only in the uppermost portion of the human mind. All

we need to do is to elevate our consciousness of God to this uppermost level of our individual mind, and stay there forever. This is heaven. And the only way to get to this wonderful state of our mind and consciousness, is by developmental steps in our rational spirituality (as discussed in this book). This is a central idea of the Writings.

This amazing Divine Love that God has revealed to our rational mind, works things from the background, unseen. Do you know what is the visible front that operates and manages everything that Love intends as a goal? God has revealed it – it is Divine Truth, also called, Divine Wisdom. In other words, God creates and manages everything by means of His infinite omniscient Divine Wisdom or Truth, with His infinite omnipresent Divine Love as the dynamic force and power by which truth works every phenomenon in the dual universe.

You can understand this when you remember that you yourself, being an image of God, work things around you by means of your intelligence that is empowered by the motivation to reach certain goals or intentions. You're motivated by some goal and you carry out a plan that your intelligence fashions for that goal. God's goal is an increasingly populous heaven for the human race.

Swedenborg was granted to have a sensuous consciousness of the entire heavens. He was put into a spiritual state that appeared to take him into a far view of the heavens, and he visually saw its shape -- like one sees the continent below in an earth satellite. It was the image of a beautiful angel. In other words, the numberless heavenly societies, cities, mountains, and regions of the heavens, were arranged in the perfect and intact human form. While Swedenborg was visiting many of these societies he tells the reader what their location is.

For example, "in the region of the right eye" or "in the uterus" or "in the pancreas," etc. The Writings have a name for this spiritual map of the human mind. It is: the "Grand Human" or the "Grand Man." It represents the spiritual idea that God is building a Grand Human or Angel, out of the numberless unique individuals, and that to God all of humanity is always going to appear as one, integrated as one. This is because in God, infinite things are a one.

Further, the character of the heavens is such that the happiness of those in that state should be the maximum they can support, without being destroyed. In order to achieve this goal, God finds a way to increase the happiness of everyone in the heavenly state, that is,

Moses, Paul, and Swedenborg

to increase it progressively every day so that today is always going to be grander than yesterday. One of the scientific methods God uses to bring this remarkable phenomenon about, is to structure the Grand Human into a spiritually networked vertical community.

An analogy might be to think of the formation of regional libraries in the United States and elsewhere. A number of university libraries pool their catalogue into one and make it available to all the members of each library by mail loan and online access. This means that anytime a new book is purchased by any of the pooled libraries, all the members of each library are enriched by being able to borrow that book. The treasures and increase of each, is mutually shared by all. This is the method God uses to increase the happiness of each individual in heaven.

Every time an individual anywhere climbs to the top of the mind called heaven, all individuals who are also at the top of their mind, will experience in increase in their happiness. Since there are numberless individuals from numberless planets entering that state every day, you can see how large the increase of happiness is in heaven every day. Such is the amazing Love and Wisdom of God!

So now you know a lot about God, what He is doing and why. And you also know your individual fate – that you are immortal and that you will determine whether you climb to the top or fall to the bottom of your mind. *Quo Vadis*, my friend? Choose now, and live in the grand palaces of the Grand Human. Climb to the top of your consciousness and human potential, and enter that state of immortality and beauty. God wants you there.

God is taking you there. Only one thing – you need to want to get there by the method God gives, and no other, whether your own or someone else's. The spirit wants it, but the flesh hates it. This is our dilemma. Our rational consciousness wants heaven, but our natural consciousness denies heaven. It is the battle of hell – the arrogance of the love of self, vs. heaven – the rational love of wanting to obey the Threefold Word.

This is the Divine plan and method, therefore it will be the end result of the human race. True Science is destined to live in the understanding of all humanity. The Lord in the Writings refers to the new humanity as "*New Church*," and calls it the "*Crown of Churches*." In other words, the evolution of the human race is now completed. We now have in place an uppermost portion of the mind called the "celestial-rational" level of thinking and willing. When we suffer ourselves to obey the Heavenly Doctrines in the Writings, our consciousness rises to that uppermost portion of our mind, to which the Lord now refers to

Moses, Paul, and Swedenborg

as the "New Heavens."

When Swedenborg completed the writing and publication in 1771 of the last volume of the Writings called *The True Christian Religion*, the New Heavens were created by means of the Divine Rational Truth that was revealed in the Writings. Henceforth, anyone regardless of background, can ascend to this New Heaven formed by God in everybody's mind. All it takes is to follow the medical procedure whereby God regenerates our character, which is the lifelong process of struggling against falsities in our understanding and evils in our character. These evils are attached to us from inheritance since the character of the father's soul, and its content, is transmitted to the child's soul, both boy and girl.

Further, these inherited evils are cumulative over the generations since every generation adds its new collection of evils acquired through a life of disobedience to God's order. Hence you can see how numerous are the evils in you and me, after so many generations since the Fall of the celestial civilization on earth (as discussed above). This cumulative evil is overwhelming, entering in every desire, intention, and motive that we have all day long. This internal evil is not readily apparent since we are required to hide our evils so that we may participate in social life.

We may for instance be filled with rage and imagine all sorts of retaliation and torture of our enemies and the people we don't like. Yet we may keep this to ourselves for fear of punishment or sanctions in one form or another. Similarly with what we think. We may have all sorts of beliefs and justifications that we don't talk about because we want to avoid disapproval. We learn therefore to simulate and deceive, and to hide with secrets. Thus we appear normal on the outside, but are actually insane on the inside.

This spiritual insanity is also a lack of rationality. People lead mixed lives in that they love something good at one point, and a minute or even second later, they love something evil. I noticed this in myself with amazement. For instance, I'm eating. I want to stop because I love good things like health, self-control, dapper appearance. I swallow and rest for a moment. I feel the desire to eat returning with intensity. It' feels like a dictatorial voice and power. I eat some more because I love that evil. I try to specify it in my mind. It wants to hide, stay out of conscious awareness. It is an evil delight I have not given up. It rules over me as a result, and it will continue to do so, until I suffer myself to overcome in temptation.

Countless such events every day demonstrate that we are inexorably tied to the hell societies that motivate these delights in us. This is how they get their kicks. This is how God connects all of humanity into a vertical community so that each's is communicated to all, and all to each. The only way I can be saved from those ties is to associate myself with good loves from heaven. Further, the evil in us always corrupts the good we may also have, unless we shun the evil by the power of the truth we have internalized in the understanding.

Another example. We are making a quick stop at the automatic teller machine at my local bank. I stop behind someone's car who parked while accessing the automatic teller. My wife steps out and stands in line. I'm keeping the car running. I love the cool air of the air conditioner and I can't keep it on if I turn the engine off. So I give in to my evil delight of doing what pleases me regardless of how it affects the bystanders. With exhaust running, I feel guilty. I think that I should turn off the engine or move to another location. I'm influenced by a good love as I want to take care of others. I see my wife getting up to the machine. I decide to wait. I give in to the love of evil, the love of self.

And so it goes, day in, day out. This is the level of operational work we must perform for regeneration -- self-monitoring of thoughts and feelings, self- assessment in the light of the Threefold Word, putting aside of the evil love and espousing the good love. God does the rest, and we end up being regenerated, ready to climb into our heaven. And remember that your soul mate, the love of your life, your conjugial spouse, will be with you. This is a certainty of Divine revelation.

18.8 On Discrete Degrees and Correspondences

Quoting Swedenborg:

> *Correspondences have all force, so that what is done on earth according to correspondences has power in heaven; for correspondences are from the Divine. Those who are in the good of love and of faith are in correspondences, and the Divine effects all things with them... All miracles in the Word were effected through correspondences. The Word is so written that every minute thing therein corresponds to the things in heaven; hence the Word has Divine force, and conjoins heaven and earth. (AC 8615:3)*
>
> >>>

Moses, Paul, and Swedenborg

The Most Ancient Church, which was celestial, looked upon all earthly and worldly, and also bodily things, which were in any wise objects of the senses, as being dead things; but as each and all things in the world present some idea of the Lord's kingdom, consequently of things celestial and spiritual, when they saw them or apprehended them by any sense, they thought not of them, but of the celestial and spiritual things; indeed they thought not from the worldly things, but by means of them; and thus with them things that were dead became living. (AC 1409)

>>>

The things thus signified were collected from their lips by their posterity and were formed by them into doctrinals, which were the Word of the Ancient Church, after the flood. With the Ancient Church these were significative; for through them they learned internal things, and from them they thought of spiritual and celestial things. But when this knowledge began to perish, so that they did not know that such things were signified, and began to regard the terrestrial and worldly things as holy, and to worship them, with no thought of their signification, the same things were then made representative. Thus arose the Representative Church, which had its beginning in Abram and was afterwards instituted with the posterity of Jacob. (AC 1409)

>>>

It is hardly credible that the numbers included in such details, since these belong to a historical narrative, have a spiritual meaning. That is, five thousand, the number of people, has a spiritual meaning; so does five, the number of leaves, as well as two, the number of fishes. A hundred, and likewise fifty, the numbers of people sitting down together, each have a spiritual meaning; and so lastly does twelve, the number of baskets containing broken pieces. Though it may seem incredible, every detail holds some arcanum. Every single thing occurred providentially, to the end that Divine realities might be represented by them. (AC 5291)

>>>

Third Memorable Relation

The next day an angel came to me from another society and said, "We have heard in our society that on account of your meditations about the creation of the universe you were summoned to a society near ours, and there told things about creation which the society then assented to, and have since remembered with pleasure. I will now show you how all kinds of animals and vegetables were produced by God."

He led me away to a broad green field and said, "Look around." And I looked around, and saw birds of most beautiful colors, some flying, some perched upon the trees, and some scattered over the field plucking little leaves from roses. Among the birds were doves and swans. After these had disappeared from my sight I saw not far from me flocks of sheep with lambs, and of kids and she-goats; and round about these flocks I saw

herds of cattle, young and old, also of camels and mules, and in a kind of grove, deer with high horns, and also unicorns.

When I had beheld these things the angel said, "Turn your face towards the east." And I saw a garden containing fruit trees, as orange trees, lemon trees, olive trees, vines, fig-trees, pomegranates, and also shrubs bearing berries.

The angel then said, "Look now towards the south." And I saw fields of various kinds of grain, as wheat, millet, barley, and beans, and round about them flower beds containing roses of beautifully varied colors; but toward the north I saw thick groves of chestnut trees, palms, lindens, plane trees, and other trees with rich foliage.

[2] When I had seen these things the angel said, "All these things that you have seen are correspondences of affections of the love of the angels who are near." And he told me to what affection each particular thing corresponded; and moreover, that not these only, but also all other things that presented themselves to their sight were correspondences, as houses, the articles of furniture in them, the tables and food, the clothing, and even the gold and silver coins, as also the diamonds and other precious stones with which wives and virgins in the heavens are adorned. "From all these things," he said, "the character of every person in respect to love and wisdom is perceived by us. The things in our houses that are of use remain there permanently; while to the sight of those who wander from one society to another these things change as their associations change.

[3] These things have been shown to enable you to see, in a special example, the entire creation. For God is love itself and wisdom itself; the affections of His love are infinite, and the perceptions of His wisdom are infinite; and of these each thing and all things that appear on earth are correspondences. This is the origin of birds and

beasts, forest trees, fruit trees, crops and harvests, herbs and grasses. For God is not extended, and yet He is present throughout all extension, thus throughout the universe from its firsts to its lasts; and He being thus omnipresent, there are these correspondences of the affections of His love and wisdom in the whole natural world; while in our world, which is called the spiritual world, there are like correspondences with those who are receiving affections and perceptions from God.

The difference is that in our world such things are created by God from moment to moment in accordance with the affections of the angels. In your world they were created in like manner in the beginning; but it was provided that they should be renewed unceasingly by the propagation of one from another, and creation be thus continued.

[4] In our world creation is from moment to moment, and in yours continued by propagation, because the atmospheres and earths of our world are spiritual, and the atmospheres and earths of your world natural; and natural things were created to clothe spiritual things as skin clothes the bodies of men and animals, as outer and inner barks clothe the trunks and branches of trees, the several membranes clothe the brain, tunics the nerves, and the inner coats their fibers, and so on. This is why all things in your world are constant, and are renewed constantly from year to year."

To this the angel added, "Go and tell the inhabitants of your world what you have seen and heard, for hitherto they have been in complete ignorance about the spiritual world; and without some knowledge about it no one can know, nor even guess, that in our world creation is a continuous process, and that it was the same in yours while the universe was being created by God."

[5] After this we talked about various matters; and at length about hell, that no such things are seen there as are seen in heaven, but only their opposites; since the affections of the love of those there, which are lusts of evil, are opposites of the affections of love in which angels of heaven are. Thus with those in hell, and in general in their deserts, there are seen birds of night, such as bats and owls; also wolves, panthers, tigers, and rats and mice; also venomous serpents of every kind, dragons and crocodiles; and (where there is any herbage) brambles, nettles, thorns, and thistles, and some poisonous plants grow: and at times these disappear, and then nothing is seen but heaps of stones, and bogs in which frogs croak.

Moses, Paul, and Swedenborg

All of these things are correspondences; but as has been said, they are correspondences of the affections of the love of those in hell, which affections are lusts of evil. Notwithstanding these things are not created there by God; nor were they created by Him in the natural world, where like things exist. For all things that God has created and does create were and are good; while such things on the earth sprang up along with hell, and hell originated in men, who by turning away from God became after death satans and devils. But as these terrible things began to be painful to our ears, we turned our thoughts from them and recalled to mind what we had seen in heaven. (TCR 78)

>>>

Only he who knows how degrees are related to Divine order can comprehend how the heavens are distinct, or even what is meant by the internal and the external man. Most men in the world have no other idea of what is interior and what is exterior, or of what is higher and what is lower, than as something continuous, or coherent by continuity, from purer to grosser. But the relation of what is interior to what is exterior is discrete, not continuous. Degrees are of two kinds, those that are continuous and those that are not. Continuous degrees are related like the degrees of the waning of a light from its bright blaze to darkness, or like the degrees of the decrease of vision from objects in the light to those in the shade, or like degrees of purity in the atmosphere from bottom to top. These degrees are determined by distance.

(...)[3] Until one has acquired for himself a perception of these degrees he cannot possibly understand the differences between the heavens, nor between the interior and exterior faculties of man, nor the differences between the spiritual world and the natural world, nor between the spirit of man and his body. So neither can he understand the nature and source of correspondences and representations, or the nature of influx. Sensual men do not apprehend these differences, for they make increase and decrease, even according to these degrees, to be continuous, and are therefore unable to conceive of what is spiritual otherwise than as a purer natural. And in consequence they remain outside of and a great way off from intelligence. (HH 38)

>>>

From this ordering of creation it can be seen that the coherent linkage from first things to last is such that taken together they make up a single unit; in this prior cannot be separated from posterior, just as cause cannot be separated from the effect produced by it. Thus the spiritual world cannot be separated from the natural world, nor this from the spiritual. In the same way the heaven where the angels are cannot be separated from the human race, nor the human race from that heaven. It has therefore been provided by the Lord that one should perform services for the other, that is, the heaven of angels should perform services for the human race, and the human race for the heaven of angels. (LJ 9:[3]).

\>\>\>

One who knows nothing about discrete degrees, that is, degrees of height, can know nothing about the state of man as regards his reformation and regeneration, which are effected through the reception of love and wisdom of the Lord, and then through the opening of the interior degrees of his mind in their order. Nor can he know anything about influx from the Lord through the heavens nor anything about the order into which he was created. For if anyone thinks about these, not from discrete degrees or degrees of height but from continuous degrees or degrees of breadth, he is not able to perceive anything about them from causes, but only from effects; and to see from effects only is to see from fallacies, from which come errors, one after another; and these may be so multiplied by inductions that at length enormous falsities are called truths. (DLW 187)

\>\>\>

Everything created must needs be from an Uncreate. What is created is also finite, and the finite can exist only from the Infinite. (DLW 44)

\>\>\>

A knowledge of degrees is like a key for opening the causes of things, and for entering into them. Without that knowledge, scarcely anything of cause

can be known. For without it, the objects and subjects of both worlds appear so simple as though there were nothing in them beyond that which meets the eye, when yet the things that appear are as one to thousands, indeed, to myriads, compared with the things which lie hidden within. The interiors which do not lie open can by no means be disclosed except by a knowledge of degrees. (DLW 184)

Moses, Paul, and Swedenborg

\>\>\>

On the other hand, degrees that are not continuous, but discrete, are distinguished like prior and posterior, like cause and effect, and like what produces and what is produced. Whoever looks into the matter will see that in each thing and all things in the whole world, whatever they are, there are such degrees of producing and compounding, that is, from one a second, and from that a third, and so on.

[3] Until one has acquired for himself a perception of these degrees he cannot possibly understand the differences between the heavens, nor between the interior and exterior faculties of man, nor the differences between the spiritual world and the natural world, nor between the spirit of man and his body. So neither can he understand the nature and source of correspondences and representations, or the nature of influx. Sensual men do not apprehend these differences, for they make increase and decrease, even according to these degrees, to be continuous, and are therefore unable to conceive of what is spiritual otherwise than as a purer natural. And in consequence they remain outside of and a great way off from intelligence.

One thing is formed from another, and the things so formed are not continuously purer and grosser ...

Until the difference between what is interior and what is exterior according to such degrees is perceived, neither the internal and external man nor the interior and exterior heavens can be clearly understood ...(HH 38)

\>\>\>

The interiors of man are distinct according to degrees by means of derivations, and according to these degrees are also the lights. The internal sensuous, which is nearest the sensuous things of the body, has the most gross light. This light it has been given me to discern by much experience, and I have noticed that whenever I sank into this light, falsities and evils of many kinds presented themselves, and even things scandalous against heavenly and Divine things, besides things filthy and foul. The reason is that this light rules in the hells, and by means of it chiefly do the hells flow into man. When a man is in this light, his thought is in nearly the same light as that in which is his external sight, and is then almost in the body. (AC 6310)

\>\>\>

Moses, Paul, and Swedenborg

Every human being has been so created that Divine things that are the Lord's may come down through him even to the lowest things of natural order, and from the lowest things of natural order may return to Him. Thus the human being was created to be the means through which the Divine was linked to the natural world, and the natural world linked to the Divine. (AC 3702).

>>>

Miracles have not been done from causes sought out from nature ... Miracles related in the Word were done by means of influx from that prior world into this posterior one, ... by means of bringing such things as are in the spiritual world, into corresponding things in the natural world, so that the things which come forth actually in the spiritual world are actually brought into such things in the natural world as correspond. (Invitation 60)

>>>

Correspondences have all power ... what is done on earth according to correspondence, avails in heaven, because they are from the Divine. All miracles recorded in the Word were done by means of correspondences. (AC 8615.3)

>>>

There is a correspondence of sensuous with natural things, a correspondence of natural with spiritual things, a correspondence of spiritual with celestial things, and finally a correspondence of celestial things with the Divine of the Lord; thus there is a succession of correspondences from the Divine down to the ultimate natural.

[2] But as an idea of the nature of correspondences can with difficulty be formed by those who have never thought about them before, it may be well to say a few words on the subject. It is known from philosophy that the end is the first of the cause, and that the cause is the first of the effect. That the end, the cause, and the effect may follow in order, and act as a one, it is needful that the effect should correspond to the cause, and the cause to the end.

But still the end does not appear as the cause, nor the cause as the effect; for in order that the end may produce the cause, it must take to itself administrant means from the region where the cause is, by which means the end may produce the cause;

and in order that the cause may produce the effect, it also must take to itself administrant means from the region where the effect is, by which means the cause may produce the effect.

These administrant means are what correspond; and because they correspond, the end can be in the cause and can actuate the cause, and the cause can be in the effect and can actuate the effect; consequently the end through the cause can actuate the effect. It is otherwise when there is no correspondence; for then the end has no cause in which it may be, still less an effect in which it may be, but is changed and varied in the cause, and finally in the effect, according to the form made by the administrant means.

[3] All things in general and in particular in man, nay, all things in general and in particular in nature, succeed one another as end, cause, and effect; and when they thus correspond to one another, they act as a one; for then the end is the all in all things of the cause, and through the cause is the all in all things of the effect.

As for example, when heavenly love is the end, the will the cause, and action the effect, if there is correspondence, then heavenly love flows into the will, and the will into the action, and they so act as a one that by means of the correspondence the action is as it were the love; or as when the faith of charity is the end, thought the cause, and speech the effect, then if there is correspondence, faith from charity flows into the thought, and this into the speech, and they so act as a one, that by means of the correspondence the speech is as it were the end.

In order however that the end, which is love and faith, may produce the cause, which is will and thought, it must take to itself administrant means in the rational mind that will correspond; for without administrant means that correspond, the end, which is love or faith, cannot be received, however much it may flow in from the Lord through heaven. From this it is plain that the interiors and the exteriors of man, that is, what is rational, natural, and sensuous in him must be brought into correspondence, in order that he may receive the Divine influx, and consequently that he may be born again; and that it is not well with him till then. This is the reason why here by "when it is well with thee" is signified correspondence. (AC 5131)

(end of quote)

18.9 On Personality, Sacred Scripture, And the Afterlife

Quoting Swedenborg:

> *The eye sees the universe, and the mind thinks about it, first that it was created and afterwards by whom it was created. The mind that thinks from the eye thinks that it was created by nature; but the mind that does not think from the eye thinks that it is from God; while the mind that takes the middle path thinks that it is from an Entity of which it has no idea, for it perceives that something cannot exist from nothing. (D. Wis. 12)*

> *The human rational as to truth is of such a nature that it cannot understand what the Divine is, for the reason that that truth is in appearances; and therefore that which it cannot understand, it does not believe; and by that which it does not believe it is not affected. (AC 2203)*

> *The Word is not understood except by a rational man (WH 7)*

> *The human rational as to truth is of such a nature that it cannot understand what the Divine is, for the reason that that truth is in appearances; and therefore that which it cannot understand, it does not believe; and by that which it does not believe it is not affected. (AC 2203)*

> *A sensual man finds it impossible to believe that such is the state of man after death, because he cannot comprehend it; for a sensual man must needs think naturally even about spiritual things; therefore, anything that does not appeal to his senses, that is, that he does not see with his bodily eyes and touch with his hands (as is said of Thomas, John 20: 25, 27, 29) he denies that it is. (HH 461)*

> *A man's mind is his spirit (DP 296).*

> *Seeing that men after death are in the interior memory (which has belonged to their rational) therefore those who in the world have been preeminently skilled in languages, cannot call forth even one syllable of them; and they who have been preeminently versed in the sciences cannot call up anything of their knowledges, and*

are sometimes more stupid than others. But whatever they have imbibed by means of the languages, or of the sciences, this they bring forth into use, because it has formed their rational.

The rational they had so procured is that from which they think and speak. He who has imbibed falsities by means of the languages and sciences, and has confirmed himself in them, reasons from nothing but falsities; but he who has imbibed and confirmed truths, speaks from the truths. (AC 2480)

[3] The human rational - that is to say, the rational formed from images of worldly things received through the senses, and later on from images of things analogous to actual worldly ones, such as are received from factual knowledge and from cognitions - virtually laughs or mocks if it is told that it does not live of itself but only appears to itself to do so.

It likewise laughs if it is told that the less anyone believes that he lives of himself, the more he is truly living, that is, the more wise and intelligent he is, and the more blessed and happy. And it also laughs if it is told that that life is the life which angels possess, especially those who are celestial and are inmost or nearest to the Lord; for these know that nobody except Jehovah alone, that is, the Lord, lives of himself.

[4] This rational would also mock if it were told that it has nothing of its own, and that its possessing anything of its own is an illusion or an appearance. Still more would it mock if it were told that the more it is subject to the illusion that it possesses anything of its own the less it in fact possesses, and vice versa. It would likewise mock if it were told that whatever it thinks and does from what is its own is evil, even though it was good [in its effect], and if it were told that it has no wisdom until it believes and perceives that all evil comes from hell and all good from the Lord.

This is a conviction, indeed a perception that exists in all angels, yet they possess selfhood or a proprium in fuller measure than all others. But they realize and perceive that their selfhood comes from the Lord, even though it seems to be completely their own.

[5] This rational would again mock if it were told that in heaven the greatest are those who are least; that the wisest are those who believe and perceive that they themselves are the least wise; that the happiest are those who wish the greatest happiness to others and the least to themselves; that heaven consists in wishing to

be below everyone else, but hell in wishing to be above everyone else; and that consequently the glory of heaven does not hold within it anything at all of that which the glory of the world holds.

[6] This rational would similarly mock if it were told that in the next life space and time do not exist at all but states in accordance with which there are appearances of space and time, and that life becomes more heavenly the further removed it is from the things that belong to space and time and the closer it comes to that which is eternal - for that which is eternal has absolutely nothing within it that is received from the notion of time or anything analogous to it. In the same way would the rational mock at countless other things it could be told.

[7] The Lord saw that such things were present in the merely human rational and that this rational therefore mocked Divine things. He did so from the Divine spiritual, which is meant by the words 'Sarah saw the son of Hagar the Egyptian', 2651, 2652. The fact that a person is able from within to have insight into the things residing with him that are below is well known from experience to those who have perception, and also to those who have conscience, for they see clearly enough to reproach themselves for what they think.

This exemplifies how regenerate persons are able to see what their rational prior to regeneration is like. In man's case however such perception is received from the Lord, but in the Lord's case it was Self-derived. (AC 2654)

How important it is to have a right idea of God can be seen from the fact that the idea of God forms the inmost element of thought in all who have any religion, for all constituents of religion and all constituents of worship relate to God. And because God is universally and specifically involved in all constituents of religion and worship, therefore without a right idea of God no communication with the heavens is possible. So it is that every nation in the spiritual world is allotted its location in accordance with its idea of God as a person; for in this idea and in no other lies an idea of the Lord. (DLW 13)

The difference between the natural, the spiritual, and the celestial is such, that there is no ratio between them, for which reason the natural can in no wise by any approximation approach towards the spiritual, nor the spiritual towards the natural; hence it is that the heavens are distinct. This it has been given me to know by much experience; I have often been sent

among the spiritual angels, and I then spoke with them spiritually, and then, retaining in my memory what I had spoken, when I returned into my natural state, in which every man is in this world, I then wished to bring it forth from the former memory and describe it, but I could not, it was impossible; there were no expressions, nor even ideas of thought, by which I could express it; they were spiritual ideas of thought and spiritual expressions so remote from natural ideas of thought and natural expressions, that they did not approximate in the least. (De Verbo 3).

Man cannot discover a single Divine truth, except by approaching the Lord immediately (INV 22)

All things of nature are like sheaths around spiritual things (TCR Additions 1)

From the fact that greatest and least things are forms of both kinds of degrees, there is connection between them from firsts to lasts, for likeness conjoins them. But yet there can be no least thing which is the same as any other. Consequently, there is a distinction of all the singulars and of the veriest singulars. There can be no least thing in any form or among any forms the same as another for the reason that there are like degrees in greatest things, and greatest things consist of least things. When there are such degrees in greatest things, and in accordance with those degrees, perpetual distinctions from top to bottom, and from centre to circumference, it follows that there cannot be any lesser or least of these, in which are like degrees, which are the same as any other. (DLW 226)

God is omnipresent from the firsts to the lasts of His order. God is omnipresent from the firsts to the lasts of His order by means of the heat and light of the spiritual sun, in the midst of which He is. It was by means of that sun that order was produced; and from it He sends forth a heat and a light which pervade the universe from firsts to lasts, and produce the life that is in man and in every animal, and also the vegetative soul that is in every germ upon the earth (TCR 63)

How the rational faculty may be cultivated shall also be told in a few words. The genuine rational faculty consists of truths and not of falsities; whatever consists of falsities is not rational. There are three kinds of truths, civil, moral, and spiritual. Civil truths relate to matters of judgment and of government in kingdoms, and in general to what is just and equitable in them. Moral truths pertain to the matters of

Moses, Paul, and Swedenborg

everyone's life which have regard to companionships and social relations, in general to what is honest and right, and in particular to virtues of every kind. But spiritual truths relate to matters of heaven and of the church, and in general to the good of love and the truth of faith.

[2] In every man there are three degrees of life (see above, n. 267 [in HH]). The rational faculty is opened to the first degree by civil truths, to the second degree by moral truths, and to the third degree by spiritual truths.

But it must be understood that the rational faculty that consists of these truths is not formed and opened by man's knowing them, but by his living according to them; and living according to them means loving them from spiritual affection; and to love truths from spiritual affection is to love what is just and equitable because it is just and equitable, what is honest and right because it is honest and right, and what is good and true because it is good and true; while living according to them and loving them from the bodily affection is loving them for the sake of self and for the sake of one's reputation, honor or gain.

Consequently, so far as man loves these truths from a bodily affection he fails to become rational, for he loves, not them, but himself; and the truths are made to serve him as servants serve their Lord; and when truths become servants they do not enter the man and open any degree of life in him, not even the first, but merely rest in the memory as knowledges under a material form, and there conjoin themselves with the love of self, which is a bodily love.

[3] All this shows how man becomes rational, namely, that he becomes rational to the third degree by a spiritual love of the good and truth which pertain to heaven and the church; he becomes rational to the second degree by a love of what is honest and right; and to the first degree by a love of what is just and equitable. These two latter loves also become spiritual from a spiritual love of good and truth, because that love flows into them and conjoins itself to them and forms in them as it were its own semblance. (HH 468)

The Rational is predicated solely of the celestial and spiritual Natural (9Q2)

The human commences in the inmost of the rational, AC n. 2106 (AC 2666)

The only source of wisdom is from Divine truths analytically arranged by means of

Moses, Paul, and Swedenborg

the light which falls on them, coming from the Lord. Nor is there any other source of human intelligence, if it is truly intelligence. (TCR 350)

(In this earth, more than in other earths, there are sciences and arts quite unknown elsewhere: [the following] sciences, to wit, the physical sciences in general, chemistry, medicine, optics, astronomy, geometry, and philosophy, whereof they know nothing at all elsewhere; [the following] arts, for example, the smelting of metals, the art of sculpture, of painting, music, the art of constructing ships, carriages, magnificent buildings and palaces out of stone and marble, and mirrors; besides very many arts, which are for use and pleasure. Not only are they [in this earth] skilful in these, but they also have communication, by means of ships, with distant regions; and the gains of different regions are distributed to others.

Similarly with the arts, and also with the sciences. These, when invented and known by one person, are communicated, by means of books and writings, to all others; and the things which are known in one region are likewise communicated to those who are in another; and those things which the ancients knew, are also known to posterity; for writings remain.

For which reason also, and especially, the Word and the truths of faith, could be given in this earth, because [they could be known] in many [places] at the same time, and successively through the ages; and so could be multiplied, which could not happen elsewhere.) (SE 4663)

Since they wondered that such things can be described in writing, I spoke with them concerning our earth: that such things are known in our earth; and that, so far as is yet known, it is not so in other earths; also, that in this earth are sciences, which are increased by being capable of inscription in writings, and so left to others and to posterity, and that hence are many arts in this earth, as for example, the art of constructing ships, and many other things.

It was granted me to tell them the reason; [namely], that, from the earliest times, those in this earth wished to be wise in such things, and that this was represented by the tree of knowledge in paradise; and that, because they had eaten thereof, therefore they cannot be made healthy [spiritually] by other means than by sciences, thus by the scientifics which are of faith.) (SE 4663)

(It was then told me, by the angels, that the Lord willed to be born in this earth,

where divine truths are handed down by means of writings even from the earliest times, because, in this manner, the truths of faith could here be multiplied and preserved better than with others: but, with others, these truths are only learnt from parents, and so retained in the memory, and then very many things perish in the lapse of time; but, here, it is not so.

Thus, also, the angels of heaven are able not only to be perfected from the Word, but also to perceive blessedness and happiness of life: for the Word, read in this earth, passes, by correspondences, even into heaven, as was shown. Thus, also, can the truths of faith be communicated to the angels of other earths. This is the reason that the Lord willed to be born here, and to become, while he was in the world, the Divine truth, that is, the Word, and afterwards the Divine Good, that is, Jehovah.) (SE 4663)

As in the world it is quite unknown that there is a correspondence of heaven or the Grand Man with all things of man, and that man comes forth and subsists therefrom, so that what is said on the subject may seem paradoxical and incredible, I may here relate the things that experience has enabled me to know with certainty. (AC 3884)

Another reason that the natural mind reacts against the spiritual mind is that the natural mind consists not only of substances of the spiritual world but also of substances of the natural world, as was said above (n. 257), and substances of the natural world from their very nature react against the substances of the spiritual world.

For substances of the natural world are in themselves dead, and are acted upon from without by substances of the spiritual world. And substances which are dead, and are acted upon from without, resist from their own nature, and thus from their nature react. From these considerations it can be established that the natural man reacts against the spiritual man, and that there is a conflict. It is the same thing whether it is said the natural and spiritual man, or the natural and spiritual mind. (DLW 260)

They are called "drunkards" who believe nothing but what they apprehend, and for this reason search into the mysteries of faith. And because this is done by means of sensuous things, either of memory or of philosophy, man being what he is, cannot but fall thereby into errors. For man's thought is merely earthly, corporeal, and

Moses, Paul, and Swedenborg

material, because it is from earthly, corporeal, and material things, which cling constantly to it, and in which the ideas of his thought are based and terminated.

To think and reason therefore from these concerning Divine things, is to bring oneself into errors and perversions; and it is as impossible to procure faith in this way as for a camel to go through the eye of a needle. The error and insanity from this source are called in the Word "drunkenness." Indeed the souls or spirits who in the other life reason about the truths of faith and against them, become like drunken men and act like them (AC 1072)

Creation itself cannot be explained to human comprehension unless one removes from his thinking any thought of space and time. But if these are removed, it can be comprehended. Remove if you can, or as far as you can, thought of space and time, and keep your mind intent on an idea abstracted from these. You will then perceive there to be no difference between a large interval of space and an infinitesimal one, and in that case you cannot but have the same idea of the creation of the universe as of the creation of particular elements in the universe. (AC 155)

For such is the case with all truths Divine; if the rational be consulted respecting them, they cannot possibly be believed, for they surpass all its comprehension. For example: that no man, spirit, or angel, lives from himself, but the Lord only; and that the life of a man, spirit, or angel is an appearance of life in him; this is repugnant to the rational, which judges from fallacies, but still it is to be believed because it is the truth. (AC 1936)

Spirits from another earth were with me for a considerable time; and I described to them the wisdom of our globe, and told them that among the sciences pursued by the learned is that of analytics, with which they busy themselves in exploring what is of the mind and its thoughts, calling it metaphysics and logic. But I said that men have advanced little beyond terms, and certain shifting rules; and that they argue concerning these terms-as what form is; what substance; what the mind; and what the soul; and that by means of these general shifting rules they vehemently dispute about truths. I then perceived from these spirits that when men inhere in such things as terms, and think concerning these matters by artificial rules, they take away all sense and understanding of a subject.

(...)[3] Learned men of our earth were present, and could not in the least

comprehend these things, although in the life of the body they had discoursed much on such subjects in a philosophical way; and when the spirits just referred to in turn perceived their thoughts, in that they inhered in mere terms, and were inclined to dispute on every point as to whether it is so, they called such things feculent froth. (AC 3348)

As in the world it is quite unknown that there is a correspondence of heaven or the Grand Man with all things of man, and that man comes forth and subsists therefrom, so that what is said on the subject may seem paradoxical and incredible, I may here relate the things that experience has enabled me to know with certainty.

Once, when the interior heaven was opened to me, and I was conversing with the angels there, I was permitted to observe the following phenomena. Be it known that although I was in heaven, I was nevertheless not out of myself, but in the body, for heaven is within man, wherever he may be, so that when it pleases the Lord, a man may be in heaven and yet not be withdrawn from the body.

In this way it was given me to perceive the general workings of heaven as plainly as an object is perceived by any of the senses. Four workings or operations were then perceived by me. The first was into the brain at the left temple, and was a general operation as regards the organs of reason; for the left side of the brain corresponds to rational or intellectual things, but the right to the affections or things of the will.

[2] The second general operation that I perceived was into the respiration of the lungs, and it led my respiration gently, but from within, so that I had no need to draw breath or respire by any exertion of my will. The very respiration of heaven was at the time plainly perceived by me. It is internal, and for this reason is imperceptible to man; but by a wonderful correspondence it inflows into man's respiration, which is external, or of the body; and if man were deprived of this influx, he would instantly fall down dead.

[3] The third operation that I perceived was into the systole and diastole of the heart, which had then more of softness with me than I had ever experienced at any other time. The intervals of the pulse were regular, being about three within each period of respiration; yet such as to terminate in and thus direct the things belonging to the lungs. How at the close of each respiration the alternations of the heart insinuated themselves into those of the lungs, I was in some measure enabled to observe. The

alternations of the pulse were so observable that I was able to count them; they were distinct and soft.

[4] The fourth general operation was into the kidneys, which also it was given me to perceive, but obscurely. From these things it was made manifest that heaven or the Grand Man has cardiac pulses, and that it has respirations; and that the cardiac pulses of heaven or the Grand Man have a correspondence with the heart and with its systolic and diastolic motions; and that the respirations of heaven or the Grand Man have a correspondence with the lungs and their respirations; but that they are both unobservable to man, being imperceptible, because internal. (AC 3884)

The Conjunction Of The Body And The Spirit In Man Is Through The Motions Of His Heart And Lungs, And A Separation Takes Place When These Motions Cease.

That this may be comprehended it is necessary for some things to be premised which may as it were bear a torch in advance. The truth will appear from the following propositions:

1. The spirit of man is equally a man.

2. It has equally a heart and pulsation therefrom, and lungs and respiration therefrom.

3. The pulsation of its heart and the respiration of its lungs flow into the pulsation of the heart and the respiration of the lungs with man in the world.

4. The life of the body, which is natural, exists and subsists through that influx, and ceases by its removal, thus by the separation.

5. Man then from natural becomes spiritual.

1. *The spirit of man is equally a man.* Of this you will find many proofs in the work on Heaven and Hell; also that every man as to his interiors is a spirit.

To this it may be added, that everything spiritual is in its essence man, thus everything of love and wisdom that proceeds from the Lord, for this is spiritual. Everything spiritual, or everything that proceeds from the Lord, is man because the Lord Himself, who is the God of the universe, is Man, and from Him nothing can proceed except what is like, for the Divine is not changeable in itself and is not *extended, and that which is not extended, wherever it may be, is such as it is. From this is the Divine omnipresence.*

Man's conception of an angel, of a spirit, and of himself after death, as something like ether or air without a human body, comes from the conception of the sensual learned, which is derived from the term spirit, as meaning the breath of the mouth, also from their being invisible, and never evident to the sense of sight; for the sensual think solely from the sensual- corporeal and from what is material, and also from certain passages of the Word not spiritually understood. Yet they know from the Word that although the Lord was a man as to flesh and bones, still He became invisible to the disciples, and passed through closed doors. They know also from the Word that angels have been seen by many as men, who did not assume a human form, but they manifested themselves in their own form before the eyes of their spirits which were then opened.

That man, therefore, may no longer remain in a fallacious idea respecting spirits and angels and his own soul after death, it, has pleased the Lord to open the sight of my spirit, and to permit me to converse face to face with angels and men that have died, and to observe them and touch them, and to say many things about the unbelief and fallacies of men who are still living. With these I have had daily association from the year 1744 to the present time, a period of nineteen years. From all this it can be seen that the spirit of man is equally a man.

[2] 2. The spirit of man has equally a heart and pulsation therefrom, and lungs and respiration therefrom. This shall first be confirmed by experience, and afterwards by reason.

By experience:-The angelic heaven is divided into two kingdoms, one called celestial and the other called spiritual. The celestial kingdom is in love to the Lord, and the spiritual kingdom is in wisdom from that love. Heaven is thus divided because love and wisdom in the Lord and from the Lord are two distinct things, and yet are united; for they are distinct as heat and light from the sun are, as has been said above.

The angels of the celestial kingdom, because they are in love to the Lord, have relation to the heart of heaven; and the spiritual angels, because they are in wisdom from that love have relation to the lungs of heaven; for the whole heaven, as has been said above, is in the Lord's sight as one man. Moreover, the influx of the celestial kingdom into the spiritual kingdom is like the influx in man of the heart into the lungs.

Thus there is a universal correspondence of heaven with these two motions, that of the heart and that of the lungs, in every one. I have also been permitted to learn from the angels that their arteries have a pulsation from the heart, and that they breathe the same as men in the world do; also that with them the pulsations vary with the states of love, and the respiration with the states of wisdom. They themselves have touched their wrists, and have told me so, and I have often perceived the respiration of their mouth.

[[2]] As the entire heaven is divided into societies according to the affections which belong to love, and as all wisdom and intelligence is according to these affections, so each society has its peculiar respiration distinct from the respiration of any other society, likewise its peculiar and distinct pulsation of the heart; therefore no one can enter from one society into another that is separated from it, nor can any one descend from a higher heaven into a lower, or ascend from a lower into a higher, without causing the heart to labor and the lungs to be oppressed; least of all can any one ascend from hell into heaven; if he ventures to ascend he pants like one in the agony of death, or like a fish lifted from the water into the air.

[[3]] The most general difference in respiration and pulsation is according to the idea of God, for from that idea the differences of love and of wisdom therefrom spring; and for this reason a nation of one religion cannot approach nations of another religion. I have seen that Christians could not approach Mohammedans on account of the respiration. The most easy and gentle breathing is enjoyed by those who have the idea that God is Man; and from the Christian world those who have the idea that the Lord is the God of heaven; while those who deny His Divinity, as the Socinians and Arians do, have a hard and rough breathing. As the pulsation makes one with the love of the will, and the respiration makes one with the wisdom of the understanding, therefore those who are about to come into heaven are introduced into angelic life by harmonious respirations; and this is effected in various ways; and from this they come into interior perceptions and into heavenly freedom.

[[4]] By reason:-The spirit of a man is not a substance that is separate from his viscera, organs, and members, but it cleaves to them in close conjunction; for the spiritual goes along with every fiber of these from outermosts to inmosts; and thus

with every fiber and filament of the heart

and lungs; consequently, when the bond between man's body and spirit is loosed the spirit is in a form like that in which the man was before; there is only a separation of spiritual substance from material. For this reason the spirit has a heart and lungs the same as the man in the world, and for the same reason it has like senses and like motions, and also speech; and there can be no senses or motions or speech without heart and lungs. Spirits also have atmospheres, but spiritual. How greatly, then, are those deceived who assign to the soul a special seat somewhere in the brain or in the heart, for the soul of man, which is to live after death, is his spirit.

[3] 3. This pulsation of its heart and the respiration of its lungs flow into the pulsation of the heart and the respiration of the lungs with man in the world. This, too, must be confirmed by experience and afterwards by reason.

By experience:-It is not known that during his life in the world man has a double respiration of the lungs, and a double pulsation of the heart; because it is not known that man in regard to his interiors is a spirit, and that a spirit is equally a man. But it has been granted to perceive sensibly that these two motions exist continually in man, and that these two motions of the spirit flow into the two motions of the body.

I was once admitted into these motions when certain spirits were with me, who from a strong power of persuasion were able to deprive the understanding of the faculty of thinking and at the same time to take away the ability of breathing. That this might do me no harm I was brought into the respiration of my spirit, which I then plainly felt to be harmonious with the respiration of the angels of heaven. And from this it was clear that heaven in general and every angel there in particular breathes; also that so far as the understanding suffers, the respiration also suffers; for the power to persuade that is possessed by some evil spirits in the spiritual world at the same time suffocates, consequently this power is called suffocative in reference to the body, and destructive in reference to the mind.

On one occasion it was also granted to the angels to control my respiration, and to diminish and gradually withdraw the respiration of my body until only the respiration of my spirit remained, which I then sensibly perceived. Moreover, I have been in the respiration of my spirit whenever I have been in a state like that of spirits and angels, and whenever I have been raised up into heaven; and oftentimes I have been in the spirit and not in the body, at other times both in the body and in the spirit. See the work on Heaven and Hell (n. 449) for an account of the removal of the animation of the lungs and of the body, while the animation of my spirit remained.

[[2]] By reason:-From these living experiences it can be seen that since every man enjoys a double respiration, one within the other, he has the power to think rationally and also spiritually from his understanding, and by this is distinguished from the beasts; also that as to his understanding he can be enlightened, raised up into heaven, and respire with the angels, and thus be reformed and regenerated. Moreover, where there is an external there must be an internal, and the internal must be in every action and in every sensation; the external supplies the general and the internal the particular, and where there is no general there is no particular.

For this reason there is in man both an external and an internal systolic and animative motion, and external which is natural an internal which is spiritual. And thus the will together with the understanding can produce bodily motions, and the understanding with the will can produce bodily sensations. General and particular pulsations and respirations exist also in beasts but with them both the external and internal are natural, while with man the external is natural and the internal is spiritual. In a word, such as the understanding is such is the respiration, because such is the spirit of man; and the spirit is what thinks from the understanding and wills from the will.

That these spiritual operations may flow into the body and enable man to think and will naturally, the respiration and pulsation of the spirit must be conjoined to the respiration and pulsation of the body, and there must be an influx of one into the other; otherwise no transfer is effected.

[4] 4. The life of the body, which is natural, exists and subsists through that influx, and ceases by its removal, thus by the separation.

A man after death is just as much a man as before death, except that after death he becomes a spirit-man, for the reason that his spiritual is adjoined to his natural, or the substantial of the spirit to the material of the body, so fitly and unitedly that there is not a filament or fiber or smallest thread of them in which the human of the spirit is not in union with the human body.

And as the life of the whole and the life of the parts depend solely on these two most

Moses, Paul, and Swedenborg

general motions, the systolic motion of the heart and the respiratory motion of the lungs, it follows that when these motions in the body cease, natural things, which are material, are separated from the spiritual things, which are substantial, because they are no longer able to do the same work together; and in consequence the spiritual which is the essential active withdraws from the particulars acted upon, which are natural, and thus the man becomes another man. This, therefore, is the death of man and this is his resurrection, about which some things from living experience may be seen in the work on Heaven and Hell (n. 445- 452, 453-460, 461-469).

[[2]] It is known that when respiration ceases man seems to be dead, and yet man is not dead until the motion of the heart also ceases, and this commonly takes place later. That until this the man is not dead is shown by the life of infants in the womb, and by the life of adults in swoon or suffocation, in which the heart maintains its contractions and dilations, while the lungs are at rest, and yet they live, although without sensation and motion, thus without any consciousness of life.

The reason of this is that the respiration of the spirit then continues, but there is no corresponding respiration of the body, and thus no reciprocation between the two vital motions, that of the heart and that of the lungs; and without correspondence and reciprocation there is no sensitive life, neither is there any action.

What is true of the natural life of man's body is true also of the spiritual life of his mind. If the will and understanding, or love and wisdom, do not act conjointly, no rational operation can take place. If the understanding or wisdom withdraws, the will with its love becomes as it were dead; nevertheless, it continues to live, though with no consciousness of itself, so long as the understanding only ceases to act, as takes place when memory fails.

But it is otherwise when the will or love recedes; then all is over with the mind of man, as all is over with him when the heart stops beating. That the separation of the spirit from the body generally takes place on the second day after the last struggle I have been permitted to know from the fact that I have talked with some deceased persons on the third day after their decease, and they were then spirits.

[5] 5. Man then from natural becomes spiritual. A natural man is wholly different from a spiritual man, and a spiritual man from a natural man; the difference is so great that they cannot be given together. One who does not know what the spiritual is in its

108

essence may believe that the spiritual is only a purer natural, which in man is called the rational; but the spiritual is above the natural, and as distinct from it as the light of midday from the evening shadow in the time of autumn. The distinction and the difference can be known only to one who is in both worlds, the natural and the spiritual, and who can change alternately from one to the other, and be in one and then in the other, and by reflection can look at one from the other.

From this privilege, which has been granted to me, I have learned what the natural man is and what the spiritual man is who is a spirit. That this may be known it shall be described briefly.

In all things of his thought and speech, and in all things of his will and action, the natural man has as his subject matter, space, time and quantity; with him these are fixed and permanent, and without them he can have no idea of thought and speech from it, and no affection of the will and action from it. The spiritual man or the spirit does not have these as subjects, but only as objects.

[[2]] The reason is that in the spiritual world the objects are altogether similar to those in the natural world; there are lands, plains, fields, gardens and forests, houses containing rooms, and in them all useful things; moreover, there are garments for women and for men, such as are in the world; there are tables, food, and drinks, such as are in the world; there are also animals both gentle and destructive; there are spaces and times, and numbers and measures. All these things have such a resemblance to the things that are in the world that to the eye they cannot be distinguished, and yet all these are appearances of the wisdom belonging to the understanding of angels, and perceptions of loves belonging to their wills; for these objects are created in a moment by the Lord, and in a moment are dissipated.

They are permanent or not permanent according to the constancy or inconstancy of the spirits or angels in the things of which they are the appearances. This is why these things are merely objects of their thoughts and affections, while their subjects are those things of which these are the appearances, which, as has been said, are such things as relate to wisdom and love, thus spiritual things. For example, when they see spaces they do not think of them from space; when they see gardens containing trees, fruits, shrubs, flowers, and seeds, they do not think of these from their appearance but according to the things from which these appearances spring; and so in all other cases.

Moses, Paul, and Swedenborg

[[3]] *In consequence of this the thoughts of the spiritual, and their affections also, are wholly different from the thoughts and affections of the natural, and so different that they transcend natural ideas and do not fall into them except in some measure into the interior rational sight, and this in no other way than by withdrawals or removals of quantities from qualities. This shows clearly that the angels have a wisdom that is incomprehensible and also ineffable to the natural man. As their thoughts are such so their speech is such, and so different from the speech of men that they do not agree in a single expression.*

The same is true of their writing; although as to its letters this resembles the writing of men in the world, no man in the world can understand it. Every consonant in their writing expresses a distinct meaning, every vowel a distinct affection. The vowels are not written, but pointed. Their manual employments, which are innumerable, and the duties of their callings, likewise differ from the employments and duties of natural men in the world, and cannot therefore be described in the terms of human language.

[[4]] *From these few instances it can be seen that the natural and the spiritual differ from each other like shadow and light. Nevertheless, there*

are, various differences; there are some who are sensual-spiritual, some who are rational-spiritual, and some celestial-spiritual, also there are the spiritual evil and the spiritual good. The differences are according to the affections and the thoughts therefrom, and the appearances are according to the affections. From all this it is clear that man from natural becomes spiritual as soon as the. lungs and heart of the body cease to be moved, and by this means the material body is separated from the spiritual body. (D. WIS 7)

Those who receive the light of intelligence from the Lord as a sun are those with whom the intellectual and its rational have been opened, and who have, in consequence, thought rationally about what should be believed from the spiritual affection of truth; while those who receive light from the Lord as a moon are those in whom the intellectual and interior rational have not been opened, but only the natural, and who in consequence have thought from the memory about what should be believed; and to think about this from the memory is to think only from such things as have been heard from a teacher or preacher, which they call truths and believe to be truths although they may be falsities, since they are not seen beyond the memory.

If such while in the world were also in the faith of charity, they are in the heavens under the Lord as a moon, for the lumen, from which is their intelligence, is like the moon's lumen in the nighttime, while the light from which is the intelligence of those who are in the heavens under the Lord as a sun is like the light of day.

(...) Their affection of knowing truth and doing good is, like themselves, natural, thus deriving more or less from the glory of being learned, and from reputation that looks to honors and gain as rewards, differing in this from such spiritual affection of knowing truth and doing good as those have who are in heaven under the Lord as a sun, for with these this affection is so separated from natural affection that the natural affection is under the feet.(...)

To this is to be added, that there are three heavens that are under the Lord as a moon, a higher, a middle, and a lower; or what is the same, an interior, a middle, and an exterior, but yet all who are in these heavens are natural. These heavens are interior, middle, and exterior, because the natural like the spiritual is divided into three degrees; the exterior-natural communicates with the world, the interior with heaven, and the middle conjoins.

Nevertheless, those who are in the heavens under the Lord as a moon cannot enter into the heavens that are under the Lord as a sun, because their interior sight or understanding has been formed to receive the lunar

light there, and not to receive the solar light. They are comparatively not unlike those birds that see in the night and not in the daytime, consequently when they come into the sunlight that those have who are under the Lord as a sun their sight is darkened. Those who are in these heavens are those who have been in charity according to their religious principle, or according to their faith; but such as are natural and are not in the faith of charity are in the hells under these heavens. (AE 708)

The preacher who was with me had no belief at all in the existence of planets other than our own, because in the world he had thought that the Lord was born solely on this planet and that without the Lord there was no salvation. He was therefore brought into a state like the one spirits enter when they appear on their planet as people - the one described above - and was then sent to that planet, not only to see it but also to talk to the inhabitants there. When this had been done, communication

Moses, Paul, and Swedenborg

from there was granted to me as well in order that I might in a similar way behold those inhabitants and also some things on that planet. Spirits and angels can talk to people, whatever language they speak, because their thought passes into the ideas in people's minds and so into the words they speak. (AC 10752)

A CONTINUATION ABOUT THE FIFTH EARTH IN THE STARRY HEAVEN.

It was afterward granted me to speak with these spirits about their own earth, for all spirits know about this when their natural or external memory is opened by the Lord, because they bring this memory with them from the world; but it is not opened except with the Lord's good pleasure. With regard to the earth from which they were, the spirits then said that when leave is granted they appear to the inhabitants of their earth and speak with them as men, and that this is effected by their being let into their natural or external memory, and consequently into thought such as they had when they lived in the world; and that at the same time the interior sight of the inhabitants, that is, the sight of their spirit, is opened, and in this way the spirits appear to them. They added that the inhabitants know not but that they are men of their earth, and only notice that this is not the case when the spirits are suddenly taken away from their eyes.

I told them that in ancient times it was the same on our earth, as with Abraham, Sarah, Lot, the inhabitants of Sodom, Manoah and his wife, Joshua, Mary, Elizabeth, and the prophets in general; and that the Lord appeared in the same way, and that until He revealed Himself those who saw Him knew not but that He was a man of the earth; but that now this rarely happens, lest such things should compel men to believe; for a compulsory faith, such as enters by means of miracles, does not cleave to the man, and also might be an injury to those with whom faith could be implanted through the Word in a state that is not compulsory. (AC 10751)

Thus, the reason that conscious rapport with spirits is never allowed on this earth any more is that such direct awareness takes away one's rational, hence one's spiritual freedom to choose. In the past the rational did not play that role in regeneration. The result is corporeal spirituality in the natural mind, while the spiritual mind remains closed. All who are in this state are infernal (AC 141).

Since the dispensation of the Second coming has now begun only the rational can support spiritual life. Either the rational must be opened here, or hereafter. When *arriving in the afterlife our mind (spirit-body) must have been grown into a form that can receive spiritual-rational truths which are more interior than the natural mind. But the natural mind must have suitable conceptual vessels to contain the spiritual-rational truths we receive by being instructed when we arrive in the afterlife (NJHD 51).*

(end of Swedenborg quote)

19. Further Exercises

19.1 Characterize the thinking and feeling levels of every day activities

This is the crux of the matter in spiritual development. Regeneration is another term for spiritual development. We begin our regeneration in adult life when we begin to think according to our own cognitive makeup and affective character. Every individual is unique. Though individuals will be born in numerous earths endlessly forever and accumulate in the spiritual world, no two individuals can ever be the same to endless time.

Such is the nature of God's infinity who produces every individual from birth to immortal eternity that He wills that every human being will be unique. What does this uniqueness consist of? In thoughts and feelings. In heaven and in hell the thoughts and feelings of each individual determine by correspondence what the outward environment will consist of. Hence every individual has a unique place allocated in the spiritual world in accordance with the thoughts and feelings that enliven that individual.

Since everything but everything depends on our thoughts and feelings would it not be an excellent idea to monitor them in ourselves?

If we do not know our thoughts and feelings, moment by moment, hour by hour, day by day, can we change them? Can we change our character? What is our character except the thoughts and feelings in our mind?

The process of self-witnessing our cognitive and affective life is a necessary focus for

Moses, Paul, and Swedenborg

regeneration. I discuss the details of this method in Volume 3 of A Man of the Field, available on the Web at: www.soc.hawaii.edu/leonj/v3ch1-nonduality.htmlFor now, let us focus on a few ordinary activities in everyday life such as eating, business, sexuality, entertainment, etc., as shown in the table below. Note that each everyday behavior can be performed in each of the 3 phases of consciousness. We will focus on thinking and feeling (or willing) since these two together determine the overt acts of the behavior to be witnessed.

Everyday Behavior	Phase 1 Thinking	Phase 1 Feeling	Phase 2 Thinking	Phase 2 Feeling	Phase 3 Thinking	Phase 3 Feeling
eating						
health						
sexuality						
religion						
business						
politics						
science						
entertainment						
etc.	See Text in Section 15.4					

Select a particular behavior, say eating, and witness your thoughts and feelings in the course of an eating episode. Use whatever techniques you need to obtain a sample of your thoughts and feelings while you are eating, or, anticipating eating, or preparing a meal or snack. You can make a recording of speaking your thoughts out loud, or you can take notes as you go along, minute by minute. You can only obtain fragments and samples of the constant stream of thoughts and feelings, but this is enough. Analyze the fragments you've identified. Characterize the level of thinking and feeling that it reflects. See the text in Section 15.4 for illustrations.

19.2 Explain the level of thinking in each religious tradition sampled below

Moses, Paul, and Swedenborg

The following are quotations found on the Web when I looked up "charity" in relation to the major religions, as indicated. Read each description and characterize its level of thinking and feeling in relation to the nine zones of the ennead matrix (discussed in Section 11 above).

At the end of the Exercise you will find my answer to each religious definition of charity. You can then compare what your answer was with mine.

19.2.a Charity and Buddhism

"Every pious Buddhist more or less carries out the meritorious deeds of dispensing charity, observing morality and practicing meditation. Out of these three, the Buddhists usually perform the charitable deeds daily. At every house of Buddhists, they offer food, water and flowers dedicated to the Triple Gems every morning.

Charity means donation or giving away one's own properties to others. There are three kinds of charity: giving material offerings (Amisa dana), giving sanctuary and protection to animals (Abhaya dana) and giving doctrinal lectures (Dhamma dana). The Advantages of Charity. Charity is praised by Buddha in many ways. It is:

- *the stairway to celestial realms*
- *the packet of provisions in the long cycle of rebirths*
- *the direct way to good destination*
- *the cause of becoming a ruler*
- *capable of producing luxuries and wealth*
- *capable of enjoying happiness*
- *capable of self-protection*
- *capable of civilizing the uncivilized*
- *capable of bringing success in everything"*

From: web.ukonline.co.uk/buddhism/charity.htm

19.2.b Charity and Christianity

Moses, Paul, and Swedenborg

"The obligation to perform acts of charity is taught both by revelation and by reason. Under the former head may be cited the words of Christ: "thou shalt love thy neighbour as thyself"; "as you would that men should do to you, do you also to them in like manner"; and particularly the description in St. Mathew (xxv) of the separation of the good from the bad at the Final Judgment. Reason tells us that we ought to love our neighbors, since they are children of God; since they are our brothers, members of the same human family; and since they have the same nature, dignity, destiny, and needs as ourselves. This love, or charity, should be both internal and external. The former wishes the neighbour well, and rejoices in his good fortune; the latter comprises all those actions by which any of the needs are supplied."

From: http://www.newadvent.org/cathen/03592a.htm

19.2.c Charity and Judaism

"Levels of Tzedakah (Charity): Certain kinds of tzedakah are considered more meritorious than others. How to give charity, from the most meritorious to the least meritorious:

Enabling the recipient to become self-reliantGiving when neither party knows the other's identityGiving when you know the recipient's identity, but the recipient doesn't know your identityGiving when you do not know the recipient's identity, but the recipient knows your identityGiving before being asked

Giving after being askedGiving less that you should, but giving it cheerfully Giving begrudgingly

Where and Who to give charity to, in order of priorities: Family and close relatives

Local Jewish communityJewish community in Eretz IsraelJewish communities worldwideLocal community in generalInternational assistance to needy people"

From: http://www.ahavat-israel.com/ahavat/am/charity.asp

19.2.d Charity and Islam

"The following are some of the many benefits mentioned in the Ahaadeeth for the one who gives his Zakaat:

Pleasure of Allah;Increase in wealth;Protection from losses;Forgiveness and blessing from Allah; Safety from calamities;

Protection from the wrath of Allah and from bad death; Shelter on the Day of Judgment;Security from seventy misfortunes;Shield from the fire of Jahannam;

Safety from grief."

From: http://www.islaam.org/Zakaat/zakaat_10.htm

19.2.e Charity and Hinduism

"The riches of the liberal never waste away, while he who will not give finds none to comfort him.The man with food in store who, when the needy comes in miserable case begging for bread to eat, Hardens his heart against him-even when of old he did him service-finds not one to comfort him.

Bounteous is he who gives unto the beggar who comes to him in want of food and feeble.No friend is he who to his friend and comrade who comes imploring food, will offer nothing.

Let the rich satisfy the poor implorer, and bend his eye upon a longer pathway.

Riches come now to one, now to another, and like the wheels of cars are ever rolling.To receive, even if sinless, is bad; and to give, Even without a heaven, is good.

Hunger, dread, disease, will never touch, One who shares his food. To eat alone what one has hoarded, Is worse than begging."

http://www.geocities.com/hinduismcharity

19.2.f Charity and Secular Humanism

> *"Volunteering can enhance your life. Research has shown that older adults who participate in volunteer activities have a higher energy level and greater self-esteem and satisfaction with life."*
>
> From: www.ucihealth.com/seniors/HelpOthers.htm
>
> *"Volunteering has many other intangible benefits. It can help you give back to society, break down barriers of misunderstanding or fear, explore personal issues, and even have fun."*
>
> From: www.collegeboard.com/article/0,3341,2-7-0-7813,00.html?orig=sub
>
> "Volunteering was my way of helping others but I'm a much happier person in myself as a result""Living in the country I often felt lonely and a bit isolated, but then I got involved in a community project - I'm never in the house now!"
>
> From: http://www.cvwb.org/benefits.htm

19.2.g Charity and New Church or New Christianity

Quoting Swedenborg:

> "I. The "first" of charity is to look to the lord and shun evils as sins.
>
> Ii. The "second" of charity is to do good to the neighbour.
>
> Iii. In a natural sense, the neighbour who is to be loved is a fellow citizen, also a society, small or large, also one's country, also the human race.
>
> Iv. The neighbour is to be loved in accordance with his spiritual good, and his moral, civil, and natural good therefrom; consequently it is good that, in a spiritual sense, is the neighbour to be loved.

V. Everyone loves the neighbour from the good of charity in himself; consequently the quality of anyone's charity is such as the charity he himself is.

Vi. A man is born to the end that he may become a charity; but he cannot become a charity unless he constantly wills and does the good of charity from affection and its delight.*

Vii. Every man, who looks to the lord, and shuns evils as sins, becomes a charity, if he honestly, justly, and faithfully carries out the work of his occupation or employment.

Viii. Signs of charity are all the things that are of worship.

Ix. Benefactions of charity are all the goods that a man who is a charity does, in freedom, outside the scope of his occupation.

X. Obligations of charity are all those things it behooves a man to do in addition to those set forth above.

XI. There are diversions of charity, which are various enjoyments and pleasures of the bodily senses useful for recreating the mind. Xii. Where there is no truth of faith, the church does not exist, and where there is no good of charity, religion does not exist.

XII. The "first" of charity is to look to the Lord and shun evils as sins.

It is well known that charity, or love towards the neighbour, is doing good to others. But how one should do good, and to whom, so that the charity may be charity, will be described in what follows. Everyone knows that no one can do good that is in itself good, except from Him who is Good Itself, or Good in Himself, that is, except from God. Moreover, it is possible for everyone to know that, so long as a man is in evil, and thus, through that evil, in company with the devil, he can do no other good than impure good, which outwardly has the appearance of being good, but inwardly is evil; which good is either pharisaical or done for reward. It will be necessary, therefore, to say first what a man should be, so that the good proceeding from him may be in itself good, thus the good of charity. (CHARITY 199)"

Moses, Paul, and Swedenborg

Now here are my answers so you can compare them to yours.

Answer to 19.2.a Charity for Buddhism

Here is the definition again:

> "Every pious Buddhist more or less carries out the meritorious deeds of dispensing charity, observing morality and practicing meditation. Out of these three, the Buddhists usually perform the charitable deeds daily. At every house of Buddhists, they offer food, water and flowers dedicated to the Triple Gems every morning.
>
> Charity means donation or giving away one's own properties to others. There are three kinds of charity: giving material offerings (Amisa dana), giving sanctuary and protection to animals (Abhaya dana) and giving doctrinal lectures (Dhamma dana).
>
> The Advantages of Charity. Charity is praised by Buddha in many ways. It is:—
>
> - the stairway to celestial realms;- the packet of provisions in the long cycle of rebirths
>
> - the direct way to good destination;- the cause of becoming a ruler;- capable of producing luxuries and wealth; - capable of enjoying happiness;- capable of self-protection;- capable of civilizing the uncivilized;- capable of bringing success in everything"
>
> web.ukonline.co.uk/buddhism/charity.htm

Charity as a pious act belongs to phase 1 consciousness. It is where we start in our journey to the top of our mind. As children we are taught charity in terms of giving gifts and sharing what one has with selective others. When we give to others in that way, we feel good afterwards, and we experience an increased sense of self-esteem and self-efficacy as a result of what we did for another. This level of involvement with charity is natural and moral, and a prelude to future steps. In this external phase of piety we expect that our charitable deeds will make us more meritorious in the eyes of authority figures and God.

Phase 1 thinking and feeling about charity revolves around external services we can perform for anyone in need of them, but especially, those that support and maintain community life and organization. External charity covers giving "material offerings," protecting animals, and giving away knowledge about religion or "doctrinal things." The benefits of this type of charity are said to include "provisions in the long cycle of rebirths," self-protection, success and happiness. These are things for the natural mind. Even what is mentioned about spiritual things – journey to "celestial realms" and "provisions" while getting there – are viewed in natural terms and natural needs.

When we begin to understand these natural things in a spiritual way, we make a distinction between the performance of charity as a social and moral act, and the motive for which it is done. We do things for natural motives (phase 1), for spiritual motives (phase 2), or for celestial motives (phase 3). Charity done for natural motives does not allow elevating our consciousness to spiritual and celestial levels. Nevertheless, it prepares us for that step. We cannot skip phase 1 thinking and feeling, and thus we begin our spiritual development by exercising charity from a natural or moral motive. Once we are in this phase, we can be prepared for escalating to the next step in consciousness (phase 2).

Charity can be done for natural motives or spiritual. Morality is done for natural motives. Shunning evils as sins is done for spiritual motives. Morality about the outward social personality, while spirituality is about one's character or inner loves. Hence being a moral person is not regenerating, unless we connect our morality to our spirituality. If we refrain from stealing because it is immoral, the desire to steal remains. But if we refrain from stealing because it is a sin against God, that is, destroys our heavenly life, then we connect spirituality to morality, and we regenerate.

Answer to 19.2.b Charity for Christianity

Here is the definition again:

> "The obligation to perform acts of charity is taught both by revelation and by reason. Under the former head may be cited the words of Christ: "thou shalt love thy neighbour as thyself"; "as you would that men should do to you, do you also to them in like manner"; and particularly the description in St. Mathew (xxv) of the separation of the good from the bad at the Final Judgment. Reason tells us that we ought to love our neighbors, since they are children of God; since they are our brothers,

members of the same human family; and since they have the same nature, dignity, destiny, and needs as ourselves. This love, or charity, should be both internal and external. The former wishes the neighbour well, and rejoices in his good fortune; the latter comprises all those actions by which any of the needs are supplied."

www.newadvent.org/cathen/03592a.htm

Christianity is defined by the New Testament, namely, that it is Divine Truth called The Word of God. In the quote above there is a connection made between revelation (or the Word of God) and reason, which refers to human reasoning, how we justify things and arrive at conclusions. This connection can be seen in phase 2 thinking, but not in phase 1 thinking. The connection between Divine revelation and human reason requires a spiritual understanding. It is not understandable from a natural perspective since the natural perspective defines and makes human reason, and it has no place for Divine revelation.

Or, if it admits Divine revelation (zone 1), it has a natural view of God and of the Word (e.g., sectarianism, meritoriousness). By tying together revelation and reason, we create a discrete relationship between the natural and spiritual. At first this relationship is seen in general and universal terms (zone 4, 5, and 6), but later, it is seen in particularistic and actualizing terms (zones 7, 8, and 9).

In the quote above, revelation about love and charity is given from the Lord's statements in the Gospel of Matthew. In other words, the Lord commands us to love others as much as we love ourselves. This is spiritual charity. We know it is spiritual because the Lord's commands it and whatever the Lord says is spiritual by definition (phase 2). But it is not enough to realize that God gives us commandments that we must obey (phase 1).

We must also realize that what God commands and says is rational, since truth is rational by definition. Note that the justification for altruism does not rely here on human reason, which would be phase 1 thinking. Instead, it relies on revelation that it sees as rational. It then explains why the commandment of altruism is rational.

Note what it is that elevates the consciousness from phase 1 to phase 2. It is not the idea that we must obey commandments (phase 1). It is not the idea that it is rational to be altruistic (phase 1). Rather, it is the idea that revelation is rational. This is what makes a duality of discrete degrees in our mind, namely, reason within which is revelation. In other words, our reasoning process is natural within which is something spiritual, namely, the revelation or Divine commandment. Seeing the spiritual within the natural creates phase 2 understanding and consciousness.

The quote above refers to the internal and the external. The internal is good will to the neighbor, which is spiritual charity, and the external is the service or gift that is needed by the neighbor. The two together create phase 2 consciousness of charity. Giving and helping without the internal good will is not spiritual charity but only natural charity.

Note that the justification or confirmation by human reason for the commandment of charity is also given in the quote above. Human reason tells us that every person deserves to receive human dignity from other people since all people share human needs and belong to each other as a community and as a race. This phase 2 justification of charity focuses on universalism and the community of the race. Later we step up to phase 3 consciousness when realize that spiritual charity can become celestial charity by thinking less of the person and more of the good in the person. This is the difference between Christianity and the New Christianity discussed below (Section 18.2.g).

Answer to 19.2.c Charity for Judaism

Here is the definition again:

> "Levels of Tzedakah (Charity): Certain kinds of tzedakah are considered more meritorious than others. How to give charity, from the most meritorious to the least meritorious:
>
> Enabling the recipient to become self-reliantGiving when neither party knows the other's identityGiving when you know the recipient's identity, but the recipient doesn't know your identityGiving when you do not know the recipient's identity, but the recipient knows your identityGiving before being askedGiving after being askedGiving less that you should, but giving it cheerfullyGiving begrudginglyWhere and Who to give charity to, in order of priorities:Family and close relativesLocal Jewish community
>
> Jewish community in Eretz IsraelJewish communities worldwideLocal community in

Moses, Paul, and Swedenborg

generalInternational assistance to needy people"

www.ahavat-israel.com/ahavat/am/charity.asp

In Hebrew Charity or Tzedakah has the same root meaning as Tzedek, which means Justice. At this level of thinking and feeling, the idea of charity is tied to the idea of justice. The result of this marriage of ideas is the third idea of meritoriousness. These three ideas – charity, justice, and meritoriousness – form a triangle of obscurity that holds the mind in phase 1 consciousness. The listing in the quote above is a rank ordering of meritoriousness achieved by the individual performing an act of charity.

For instance, we acquire but little merit for "giving grudgingly," more merit for "giving before being asked," and still more merit for giving anonymously. It is evident that this idea of charity is legalistic and performative, that is, ritualistic (phase 1). This is the initial phase of spiritual development. Children show much natural generosity that can be harnessed for rituals of charity during socialization practices. Children want to earn merit points and want others to praise them for their works of charity. And indeed we should.

Note also the ranking of merit regarding to whom we give. We get the most merit for giving charity to our family, less merit for giving to individuals of our religion, and still less credit (or merit) for unknown "needy people." Sectarian charity or giving is considered more holy than charity towards those of other denominations and religions. This attitude is characteristic of phase 1 thinking.

Then a step upward in thinking and feeling can be taken by learning that God is the power behind the giving hand and the willing mind. We cannot rightly take credit for the gift or the giving. Therefore we ought not be attached to meritoriousness since God must receive all the merit, and us none (phase 2 thinking and feeling).

Ultimately a third elevation of the understanding occurs when we realize that charity is nothing else than performing our uses in daily life (phase 2 thinking and feeling). If we pick up a piece of broken glass on the street or in the park, because we don't want anyone to be injured, we are performing charity. If we expend effort in improving our typing skills, that's performing charity, when our motive is to learn to do something useful to society, to self, and to others. If we refrain in our mind from thinking derogatory thoughts about someone, we are performing charity.

Moses, Paul, and Swedenborg

This type of phase 3 thinking sees that the motive to be useful is from God and is a heavenly state of mind. It also sees that charity defined as gifting, sharing, and helping is not spiritual when considered as performative acts. What makes these acts spiritual is to the motive to do them as uses. All acts are acts of charity when they are performed as uses. And they are not acts of genuine charity when performed for the sake of ritual, piety, merit, reward, conformity, or tradition – which are external natural things, not spiritual. *These external things are needed in society even if some people may do it for merit or reward.* The benefit to the community and individuals are external and are needed whatever the motive of the giver. But for the giver, it is the motive that decides whether the giving is spiritual charity.

Answer to 19.2.e Charity for Hinduism

Here is the definition again:

> *"The riches of the liberal never waste away, while he who will not give finds none to comfort him. The man with food in store who, when the needy comes in miserable case begging for bread to eat, Hardens his heart against him-even when of old he did him service-finds not one to comfort him. Bounteous is he who gives unto the beggar who comes to him in want of food and feeble. No friend is he who to his friend and comrade who comes imploring food, will offer nothing. Let the rich satisfy the poor implorer, and bend his eye upon a longer pathway. Riches come now to one, now to another, and like the wheels of cars are ever rolling. To receive, even if sinless, is bad; and to give, Even without a heaven, is good. Hunger, dread, disease, will never touch, One who shares his food. To eat alone what one has hoarded, Is worse than begging."*
>
> *www.geocities.com/hinduismcharity*

Phase 1 thinking justifies obligations by stating external consequences of meeting or not meeting those obligations. We can examine the stated consequences or justifications to see if they are external (phase 1) or internal (phase 2 and 3). Phase 1 justifications appeal to natural consequences. Phase 2 justifications appeal to spiritual consequences. Phase 3 justifications appeal to celestial consequences. The natural, the spiritual, and the celestial are the three levels of the mind, hence of spiritual development. In the above sample quote from Hinduism, the consequences of performing charity are listed – friends to comfort us, bounty and riches as reward, and protection from disease and want.

Note that the seeds of phase 2 thinking is embedded in phase 1 thinking. In the quote above, there is reference to "hardening the heart" and setting the eye upon "a longer pathway." Both of these are references to inner things while using outer symbols. We know from the Writings that the heart symbolizes the will to do good to someone, which is love, and a pathway symbolizes the understanding of truth and being guided by it.

Those in phase 1 thinking who are willing to reflect on these inner relations to charity, namely good and truth, are able to progress to phase 2 thinking and feeling, and eventually to phase 3 by going into the inner meaning of good and truth, which is doing good for the sake of good, and thinking truth for the sake of truth, both being for the sake of uses.

Answer to 19.2.f Charity for Secular Humanism

Here is the definition again:

> "Volunteering can enhance your life. Research has shown that older adults who participate in volunteer activities have a higher energy level and greater self-esteem and satisfaction with life."
>
> www.ucihealth.com/seniors/HelpOthers.htm
>
> "Volunteering has many other intangible benefits. It can help you give back to society, break down barriers of misunderstanding or fear, explore personal issues, and even have fun."
>
> www.collegeboard.com/article/0,3341,2-7-0-7813,00.html?orig=sub
>
> "Volunteering was my way of helping others but I'm a much happier person in myself as a result""Living in the country I often felt lonely and a bit isolated, but then I got involved in a community project - I'm never in the house now!"

Moses, Paul, and Swedenborg

www.cvwb.org/benefits.htm

Secular humanism is a philosophy of life that people hold who are opposed to religion and assume that the natural world is the only one that either exists or matters for the human race on the planet. It supports scientific materialism (phase 1) and defines spirituality by means of morality based in the human mind (phase 1). A classic problem to be solved by those who think within secular humanism is how to justify altruistic behavior such as charity or volunteering for unpaid community service.

The above quote makes an appeal for volunteering on the basis of the benefits we derive from such activity. For example, it "enhances your life" or increases "your energy level" and your "self-esteem." These are wonderful benefits for the natural mind and the physical body. A benefit listed for volunteering is the "breaking down of barriers" in society. Another is that its' "fun." The benefits listed appeal to motives that all citizens can strive for, whether they are moral or immoral in their life orientation and practice. This shows that the motive for volunteering in secular humanism is to benefit self by benefiting others and society.

As a first step in human consciousness (phase 1), this orientation is valuable and should be taught in schools and at home. But then one should look for the second step, which is to bring in God and the spiritual side of the self (phase 2 and 3).

This step cannot be made without leaving behind the premises of secular humanism. Taking a step above this involves religion -- God, heaven, sin, and hell. Note however that the initial portion of the Moses phase religion (zone 1) does not elevate our consciousness above that of secular humanism for it is an external view of God, thus a God that behaves naturally rather than spiritually.

Later states of the Moses religion are more internal states, but still within the natural mind (zones 2 and 3). We elevate our consciousness to a new discrete level when we acknowledge God as a Person and begin a relationship with Him (phase 2, zone 4). In this higher state of consciousness and feeling, our understanding of charity is elevated from the moral to the spiritual. The early states of this new spiritual charity is to strive to over everyone equally (phase 2) but at the next discrete step up we realize that it is the good in the neighbor that we are to love (phase 3).

Moses, Paul, and Swedenborg

Answer to 19.2.g Charity for New Christianity

Here is the definition again:

> Quoting from Swedenborg:
>
> "I. The "first" of charity is to look to the lord and shun evils as sins.
>
> Ii. The "second" of charity is to do good to the neighbour.
>
> Iii. In a natural sense, the neighbour who is to be loved is a fellow citizen, also a society, small or large, also one's country, also the human race.
>
> Iv. The neighbour is to be loved in accordance with his spiritual good, and his moral, civil, and natural good therefrom; consequently it is good that, in a spiritual sense, is the neighbour to be loved.
>
> V. Everyone loves the neighbour from the good of charity in himself; consequently the quality of anyone's charity is such as the charity he himself is.
>
> Vi. A man is born to the end that he may become a charity; but he cannot become a charity unless he constantly wills and does the good of charity from affection and its delight.
>
> Vii. Every man, who looks to the lord, and shuns evils as sins, becomes a charity, if he honestly, justly, and faithfully carries out the work of his occupation or employment.
>
> Viii. Signs of charity are all the things that are of worship.
>
> Ix. Benefactions of charity are all the goods that a man who is a charity does, in freedom, outside the scope of his occupation.
>
> X. Obligations of charity are all those things it behooves a man to do in addition to those set forth above.
>
> Xi. There are diversions of charity, which are various enjoyments and pleasures of the bodily senses useful for recreating the mind.

Moses, Paul, and Swedenborg

Xii. Where there is no truth of faith, the church does not exist, and where there is no good of charity, religion does not exist.

XIII The "first" of charity is to look to the lord and shun evils as sins.

It is well known that charity, or love towards the neighbour, is doing good to others. But how one should do good, and to whom, so that the charity may be charity, will be described in what follows. Everyone knows that no one can do good that is in itself good, except from Him who is Good Itself, or Good in Himself, that is, except from God. Moreover, it is possible for everyone to know that, so long as a man is in evil, and thus, through that evil, in company with the devil, he can do no other good than impure good, which outwardly has the appearance of being good, but inwardly is evil; which good is either pharisaical or done for reward. It will be necessary, therefore, to say first what a man should be, so that the good proceeding from him may be in itself good, thus the good of charity. (CHARITY 199)

This is phase 3 level thinking and feeling because it gives a definition of charity in particularistic terms, not universal (phase 2) or meritorious (phase 1).

Charity is defined as love toward the neighbor, and this is defined as the good in the neighbor. In other words, we are not to love the person of the neighbor (phase 1 and 2), for this is idolatry. We are only to love the good that is in the neighbor, and since all good anywhere is from the Lord, and the Lord Himself, therefore loving the good in the neighbor is to love the Lord, and not the person of the neighbor.

To love the neighbor as person would not be particularistic and actual (phase 3); rather, it would be personal and relationship bound (phase 2). This is less perfect then loving what is actual and particular in our performance of charity. If perform charity because of the relationship or identity, we are abstracting charity rather than particularizing and actualizing it.

For charity does not involve loving the person (phase 2), but loving what is in the person (phase 3). If we love the person, we do so from two natural motives – (a) merit or reward (phase 1) or (b) preserving what is our own (phase 1). In this case charity becomes love for self and what is attached to self.

Moses, Paul, and Swedenborg

Another consequence of this definition is that we are not to love people equally (phase 2) but with a difference, in accordance with the good we perceive in each person. It is this good that we are to love. Therefore we are not to perform charity to every person in the same way. The way we decide in each particular case is by considering charity as the performance of uses.

For example, a dangerous criminal must be isolated from society to prevent continued harm to others. This is exercising charity toward the community as a whole. We also feed dangerous criminals in their isolation and look after their immediate needs for health, security, and basic human rights recognized by civilized people and the law. This is exercising charity toward the dangerous criminal.

We perform charity in our daily routine of activities when we have regard for others as much as toward self. To have regard for others means to avoid injuring them in all the ordinary ways that I can – by not being offensive, or a nuisance, and by not violating their reasonable expectations such as being left alone or not disturbing their peace. For example, when driving in traffic another driver might behave aggressively and putting us at risk. Charity is to be exercised in this particular situation or interaction by avoiding retaliation, either overt physical, or private mental (e.g., berating the other driver in our thinking – phase 1).

To forgive the other driver for the offense on account of resentment being a sin, is to raise our consciousness to phase 2 thinking and feeling. Phase 3 thinking and feeling is to refrain from resentment (phase 1) because it puts us into association with evil spirits, and at the same time, to look after the safety and dignity of the other driver, regardless of the insult or aggressiveness (phase 3).

The good in the other driver is visible when we think of the uses he or she performs as a citizen, parent, friend, and employee. This is the good we are to love, and protect by not injuring it, for to injure this good is to hate the Lord, He being the good wherever it is found or active. And to hate the Lord is to turn away from Him to self, which is to sink into hell.

Therefore, to refrain from resentment is to love the good in ourselves, hence the Lord in us, since resentment hurts this good by being opposite to it. And also, we are to look after the safety and dignity of the driver who insulted us or put us in danger from an inconsiderate attitude. This is because we are thereby protecting the good that is in that driver. Hence we love the Lord, which is charity itself from which all other charity must come (phase 3).

Moses, Paul, and Swedenborg

Exercise 19.3 Use the ennead matrix to characterize Judaism, Christianity, New Church

The "New Church" refers to the New Christian Church that the Lord is raising in His Second Coming, is foretold in the New Testament, and is actualized in the Writings. There are several New Church denominations in existence today. Recently I visited the General Church of the New Jerusalem in Bryn Athyn Pennsylvania, a thriving and long standing community of people who acknowledge the Threefold Word as the basis of their Christian worship of the Divine Human Person whom, in their worship, they refer to as "Jesus Christ, the One God of Heaven and Earth." If interested, you can read a report I wrote with my wife, on our Bryn Athyn visit, posted on the Web at: www.soc.hawaii.edu/leonj/brynathyn.htm

The "ennead matrix" is an ordered chart of the nine steps of development in rational spirituality. The nine zones are created by the matrix when the table's marginals are defined in terms of two juxtaposed variables that contain three steps each (3X3=9). As described in this book, the three vertical or column divisions are called "phases" or succeeding states in a predetermined sequence. Each phase has three succeeding states called Old Testament State, New Testament State, and Third Testament State. In other words the sequence of developmental steps an individual goes through is the same as the sequence gone through by generations, civilizations, or ages of evolution in the history of the human race on this planet.

One can readily adapt the ennead matrix to the question, as follows:

ENNEAD MATRIX OF RATIONAL SPIRITUALITY (9 zones of development)	Old Testament State (initial)	New Testament State (intermediate)	Third Testament State (mature)
Swedenborg Phase 3 (Particularism) (celestial mind)	7	8	9
Paul Phase 2 (Personalism) (spiritual mind)	4	5	6

Moses, Paul, and Swedenborg

Moses Phase 1 (Sectarianism) (natural mind)	1	2	3

The vertical variable shown in the left column represents the three ascending steps of rational spirituality in historical perspective. God introduced rationality to the human race through the Old Testament that was given to the Hebrews and Jews. Hence their land was called the Holy Land. The Old Testament was actually a revelation that continued prior revelations called the Ancient Word. There are two references to this Ancient Word in the Old Testament, and it is revealed in the Writings that Moses copied the Genesis story which opens the Old Testament, from the Ancient Word, fragments of which were still known in Median, where Moses had a life for twenty years prior the call from Jehovah to lead the Children of Jacob out of their captivity in Egypt.

After several centuries of the Old Testament civilizations, the human mind on the planet was then sufficiently prepared to receive the next phase of rational spirituality as a religion. The New Testament revelations were then given. A whole new set of ideas, radically different from before, entered human consciousness. This allowed the humanization of societies and the introduction of freedom as part of daily life in an environment protected by the law and due course or equal justice for.

At last, seventeen centuries later the civilization and the human mind had evolved into the universalization of freedom and rationality throughout a society. Now the principle was acknowledged that every individual can from their own effort, become an independent thinker, scientist, or scholar. This enlightened condition of the human race was never before achieved by any prior generation. The human mind was ready for receiving the third and final phase of rational spirituality. This was achieved through the Writings of Swedenborg in the 18th century, as discussed in this book. Now the human race was competed in its creation. Now any individual regardless of background, can read the Writings and extract the knowledge of True Science from it through the scientific or scholarly skills acquired as part of one's education and self-advancement efforts. Knowledge of True Science gives the individual effective tools for regeneration of character, an absolutely necessary lifelong process without which one cannot enter heaven, and consequently, one enters hell. Regeneration is therefore the most critical and beneficial concept anyone can acquire from rational spirituality.

Moses, Paul, and Swedenborg

The horizontal variable of the matrix has been labeled with the three types of faith discussed in the book. Every religion has these three types of faith as successive steps. This is because individual development recapitulates racial history. First in history is first in developmental steps, here we are discussing the Old Testament civilizations. They have been identified in this book as "ritual faith" because the spiritual element of their worship was focused on the ritual itself. They actually believed that it is the ritual that contains the power. And indeed, for them it did. The objects of their worship, such as the Ark or the Holy of Holies in the Temple of Jerusalem, was given by God powers that were visible in the physical world, like the power to kill anyone who touched them in any other way than the rituals prescribed in great detail for the high priest, or for a class of people designated by God as holy priests.

But as the Old Testament civilizations grew in rational spirituality, the sensuous consciousness of God's Presence in the physical world gradually decreased and vanished altogether. The race on earth was now left strictly on its own conscious reasoning. This was now the race's sole salvation for eternal life in heaven. Everyone who enters heaven must now enter it through the rational mind, not the sensuous mind. This was a major shift in the evolution of the human race. From now on, knowledge of God and acknowledgment of His existence and power, will rest solely on our rational process of reasoning.

At first this process of rational reasoning was weak, distant, or general. This was phase 2 or the New Testament state, which had a mystical or obscure idea of God, the Trinity, the Holy Supper, prayer, forgiveness, salvation, regeneration, temptation, eternal life in the Lord, and so on. But later these concepts became particular and scientific, clear and fully rational for the first time when the scientific revelations of the Writings gave us True Science.

Since these were the three evolutionary steps in historical terms they also constitute the steps of individual biography. Hence they are called "states" or mental states. These refer to the character of consciousness, that is, the level of operation of the organs of the will and understanding. Anyone can now be fully enlightened spiritually and progressively rare, their level of thinking and feeling to the highest level called celestial, were heavenly life is experienced to eternity. Every individual has this heaven within their mind already, from creation and evolution. All we need to do is learn how to climb to the top of our mind. This takes a lifetime of effort, and an effective technique. God has provided the only effective technique for consciousness raising all the way into heaven. It is called regeneration and it requires our active cooperation by means of daily struggles against temptations which are activated by our inherited evils. Only God has the power to overcome the hells to which we are tied, and so we must turn to our rational mind where God is, and address Him as a Divine Human Person who is the power behind every single act of willing and thinking.

The effectiveness of our reception of God's power to effect regeneration in us, can be low or high. This is why we must acquire skills of cooperation, the chief being self-witnessing or self-monitoring of one's stream of thinking and willing all day long every day. We need to judge the quality of everything we identify in our self-monitoring. This judgment is a rational process of critical analysis comparing what we think and feel with the Divine Truth in our mind. We acquire Divine Truth in our understanding when we read and study the Threefold Word. This makes us more rational by elevating the level of operation of our thinking and feeling regarding spiritual topics.

Salvation depends on regeneration, regeneration depends on cooperation, and cooperation depends on three steps repeated every day. First, studying the Threefold Word and extracting Doctrine of Life in our understanding. Second, self-monitoring of our thinking and willing as we perform our tasks and interactions with others. Third, judging or critically evaluating our acts of thinking and willing in the light of the Doctrine of Life in our understanding. As we repeat these three steps on a daily basis, the Lord will bring particular temptations we must face, some that appear small (like flossing or not flossing after each meal), while others appear large (like trusting the Lord when we are being severely challenged). All the temptations the Lord helps us to face are critically important for our regeneration.

Anyone who can accept and understand this view of regeneration, God, and eternal life, is enlightened, and is operating in phase 3 of rational spirituality.

People of every religion must undergo the sequence of three states indicated on the horizontal variable – ritual faith, mystic faith, rational faith. The following is a description of the three states for three religions – Judaism, Christianity, and New Church.

Refer to the ennead matrix above, for the zone locations and their intersectional properties given the marginals, as just discussed.

Zone 1: Jewish sectarianism

Believing that the Kingdom of Heaven is to be ruled by the Jews Believing that one is saved by piety in religious ritualsAssuming that Jews are the Chosen People because they are better Despising Christianity as a fool's religion

Moses, Paul, and Swedenborg

Believing in and practicing religious racismDesire to remain separate rather than united to the rest of humanity Defining God as Jewish for the Jews, but tolerating the others Jealousy and disdain for Jewish traditions other their own sect Belief in God not necessary as long as one retains Jewish traditions

Total taboo on intermarriageMany other taboos and daily ritual requirements and cleansing prescriptions

Zone 2: Jewish mysticism

Love of studying theological symbolism like KabalaPursuing Bible numerologyBelief in the power of holy NamesSuperstitious beliefs regarding ghosts and magical cursesBelief in the power of healing and intercessionary prayer by holy rabbis Interest in dream analysis

Mystical movements like Hassidic sects and cults

Zone 3: Jewish ecumenism

Support for secular public education supplemented by private religious schools Support administrative contacts with Christian clergyFormation of Jewish splinter movements away from customs of worship and diet Support for intermarriage

Secularizing Jewishness by wanting to consider it an ethnic group, not a religion Studying the New Testament and Christian DoctrineRejecting sectarianism as a basis for religionSupports separation of religion and state

Zone 4: Christian sectarianism

Believing that salvation is tied to membership of and baptism into one's own denominationAttaching sanctity to ritual procedures and objectsBelief in a hierarchy of spiritual merit, with some people being higher than others Belief in the utmost importance of formulaic prayers exactly repeated (e.g., "I ask in the name of Jesus. Amen")

Disdain for the Pope and CatholicsPity for the JewsCompassion for the heathens and GentilesAttitude of literalism in reading the Bible Suspiciousness of symbolic readings of Bible passages Promotes religious schools

Strong tradition of evangelism in distant lands Bible translation and publication activities

Moses, Paul, and Swedenborg

Zone 5: Christian mysticism

Adoption of creeds and doctrinal statements that support and declare the mystery of God and religionMystic belief in the spiritual power of the Cross, Baptism, Communion bread and wineBeing healed spiritually by the Blood of Christ's SacrificeLiving eternal life in the LordBeing rebornReceiving the Holy SpiritHearing the voice of the Holy Spirit or God and being told to do thingsStriving to sense the mystic union with God through fasting, reflection, and fervent prayerBelieving in the mystical power of group prayer, closing the eyes, holding hands, chantingSpeaking in tongues or handling snakes as part of the worshipTV evangelism and shows about healing miraclesFormation of Christian brotherhoods having distinctive icons or secret creeds

Zone 6: Christian rationalism

Defining Christianity as a science as well as a religionBible exegesis and symbolismDemystifying the Trinity and Faith AloneStudying the spiritual sense of the parables in the New Testament Focus on character reformation as essential to faith

Resistance to literal interpretation of the Creation storyFocus on charity and love as the most essential aspect of faith Tolerant of variations in worship and doctrine

Zone 7: New Church fundamentalism

Formation of splinter movements within the New ChurchEvidence of doctrinal animosity among New Church scholarsSupport for a strong ecclesiastical administration and hierarchical professional priesthoodUse of excommunication or forced resignation from the New Church denominationRefusal to administer sacraments for members considered to live in "disorder" Strong support for literalist reading of the Writings and opposition for spiritual reading that is not readily apparent

Strong involvement in maintaining appropriate ritual procedures for worship. Strong emphasis on religious New Church schools for all membersStrong interest in expansion and evangelizationTaboo on women priests

Zone 8: New Church mysticism

Interest in Near Death Experiences (NDEs)Interest in Eastern religions and

Moses, Paul, and Swedenborg

philosophiesInterest in showing similarity between Swedenborg and other authors Incorporating correspondences in art, architecture, and symbolism Using New Testament verses to justify New Church evangelism Interest in Swedenborg's non-theological worksRelying on New Church worship and membership for salvation Resistance to the idea that the Writings contain scientific revelations

Zone 9: New Church particularism

Exclusive focus on the Writings as the only source of spiritual knowledge and understandingResistance to drawing comparisons between Swedenborg and other authors Defining the Doctrine in our understanding as Divine Doctrine

Focus on enlightenment for understanding inner the spiritual sense of the WritingsFocus on as-of self conscious cooperation in regeneration as a condition for salvation

Defining the Writings as scientific revelations ("True Science")Tolerance for ritual and doctrinal variations in the New ChurchViews it as essential for every individual to become an expert scholar of the WritingsPromotes theistic science for all science subjects in schoolsPromotes spiritual disciplines for regeneration

**** Take the Rational Spirituality Test Part 4 ****Instructions: For each question, select the answer that is closest to your

current thinking.

You may have already taken this test once, if you followed the note at the beginning of the book called "Before You start: Test Your Rational Spirituality." This is a section comprising items 76 to 100 of the Test. Whether you take it for the first time or the second time, your score, now that you've read up till now, may be around 100 percent correct (25 out of 25 items). More importantly you will be able to make up your own answers. You can practice after you obtain your score for this Part (4).

If you like, you can page through to the Appendix at the end where the 100 questions are located.

This test does not measure your rational spirituality but only your understanding of rational spirituality. If you are familiar with the Writings and understand it rationally, you would probably select the correct answer for most of the questions. This test is not a knowledge test. It does not measure your knowledge of the Writings and does not cover all the

Moses, Paul, and Swedenborg

subjects the Writings cover. It is a test of understanding of how well you can reason about spiritual topics from the perspective of the Writings.

It works out well when you use an **ANSWER SHEET** on a piece of paper that looks like this, and then you can also easily and accurately score your choices from the **ANSWER KEY** given below (following the questions).

ANSWER SHEET

76. ____
77. ____
78. ____
79. ____
80. ____
81. ____
82. ____
83. ____
84. ____
85. ____
86. ____

Moses, Paul, and Swedenborg

87. ___
88. ___
89. ___
90. ___
91. ___
92. ___
93. ___
94. ___
95. ___
96. ___
97. ___
98. ___
99. ___
100. ___

QUESTIONS

Moses, Paul, and Swedenborg

76. Does it make sense to spend a lot of effort trying to prepare oneself for the unknown afterlife?

a. No, it doesn't make sense. The important thing is to live a full life while one can and thereby to be prepared for whatever comes next. If you buy into this or that religion or theory about how you are to prepare, and you rearrange you life accordingly, denying yourself this or that, it may be all for nothing if it turns out to be the wrong theory.

b. Actually, it doesn't take effort, only an inwardly sincere acknowledgement that we cannot save ourselves but are saved by the grace of God. We cannot prepare for eternal life by our own efforts, but if we live within the acknowledgment of our powerlessness, God creates a change in our life, sanctifying our efforts, making them fruitful to eternity.

c. Yes it makes sense. It's rational, and sane to want to prepare oneself for eternal life, especially since we're told by a fully reliable source (Divine revelation), that the quality of our life, our vitality and mental health throughout eternity, will depend entirely on how we prepare ourselves during this near insignificant time on earth

77. Faith is more inward, than Ritual, and True Science is more inward than Faith.

a. True.b. False.c. Cannot say.

78. The reason monist (atheistic) science is inferior and invalid is that it denies true reality, which is that God creates and runs the universe for the purpose of bringing into existence immortal human beings born on some earth, and to bring them to heaven where He can make them happy to eternity. Is this correct or not?

a. Not correct. Science is not about God and heaven. It's about reality on earth! b. Correct. Atheistic or materialistic science is a distortion of reality and leads to spiritual insanity.c. Science is a method that can investigate anything, including what people think of God.

79. According to religionists, atheistic science paints a false picture of reality. If this is true, how can you explain the success of industry, engineering, and control over the environment?

a. God allowed atheistic science to become successful and continues to lead its scientists despite their false picture of reality. God inspires the minds of scientists, unconsciously to them, so that their thinking can be kept in external rationality while being in internal insanity. On the other hand, dualist science is theistic, and paints a dual reality containing the natural

Moses, Paul, and Swedenborg

and the spiritual acting together.

b. God allowed atheistic science to become successful because He gives people freedom to discover and control the natural environment. The natural world belongs to atheistic science while issues of heaven and hell belong to religion.

c. Atheistic science does not paint a false picture of reality. It paints a true picture of natural reality, as evidenced by the successes of inventions and discoveries. Sunday Church topics such as worship, God, love, humility, and heaven are not of this world, hence not part of the picture that science paints of reality.

80. Prove that God is Human.

a. God the Father is Divine and God the Son is Divine and Human. These two Divine Persons form a Holy Trinity called the Godhead, together with a third Divine Person called the Holy Spirit. God the Father and God the Holy Spirit are Divine. God the Son is Divine and Human. But if the Holy Spirit comes out of God the Son, then it too is Divine and Human.

b. God has revealed that He is the infinite source of Divine Love and Divine Wisdom operating in the created universe. These two operating together define what is human, and they cannot exist in animals plants, or objects. But they exist in human beings who are willing to receive love and wisdom from God. Even then, that love and wisdom, in their essence, remain with God. Hence only God is the actual and True Human, and we are human only to the extent that we are willing to receive love and wisdom from God.

c. God cannot be considered human since God is supposed to have created humans. God is Divine, not human. God creates humans to be able to feel love and hatred, decency and deceitfulness. To be human is to have all these traits. And even being human is often mixed since we also share traits with animals, and even with plants.

81. Consider these types of traits: wealth, power, reputation, knowledge, fear of exclusion, desire for approval, obedience to authority, and the like. Are they natural, spiritual, or celestial traits?

a. Spiritual. b. Natural. c. Celestial.

82. Consider these types of traits: merit, righteousness, holiness, humility, understanding, intelligence, wisdom, and the like.

Moses, Paul, and Swedenborg

a. Celestial. b. Natural. c. Spiritual.

83. Consider these types of traits: charity, love, unity, conjunction, acceptance, inclusion, interior perception, and the like.

a. Celestial. b. Spiritual. c. .Natural

84. Does God favor some people with more good than others, since some people are obviously more gifted than others?

a. God gives maximum good to every person all the time, but each individual filters it out, some turning it into its opposite or evil. God allows this since there is no other way of maintaining freedom of choice, which is essential for retaining the capacity to become human.

b. God's wants to create a variety of people to make room for all possibilities and experiences. To arrange for this, He gives some people special gifts when He foresees that this individual can turn it into benefits for others. Not every person is suitable or willing to serve God in the highest possible way.

c. God distributes human traits throughout the population so that they form a bell shaped curve – the majority around the middle or "normal," and a small minority in either extremes, good vs. evil.

85. What is the cause of acceleration of a vehicle when the driver presses the gas pedal?

a. The gas being released into the fuel chamber. b. The driver's purpose to accelerate. c. The laws of physics and chemistry.

86. What is the inmost portion of a pebble upon which its existence depends?

a. Truth within which is good. b. Sub-atomic particles arranged in a particular dynamic order in space. c. Elements and compounds originating in the sun.

87. Swedenborg talked to spirits and there are some today who desire this ability. Can they succeed?

a. No, because direct communication with spirits interferes with the maturation of our rational consciousness of God, and therefore God does not allow such communication to take place today in modern times, though this was allowed in ancient times.

b. Yes, and many psychics have proven that they can and do. Such communication is also reported by thousands of people who have had Near Death Experiences (NDEs).

c. All things are possible to God and should He want an angel or devil to communicate with someone, He arranges for it to happen.

88. Is there a common evolution in the human race? Is the human race integrated into one or partially independent?

a. The human race is limited to this earth, as far as is known. Generations succeed one another as one civilization comes, thrives, and then ends, succeeded by yet another. There is a steady evolution from past to future but not a synchronous interdependence, but rather a successive independence.

b. All people alive today are psychically interdependent with each other as well as with those from the past and the future. The souls of all people -- past, present, and future, were created at the same time, though everyone is slated to be born in their own time. All souls are pieces of one large soul called God.

c. Elevation of consciousness is by means of rational truths understood more and more interiorly in proportion to our regeneration. This elevation of our rational consciousness is communicated to the entire human race in the heavens and on the other earths in the universe, since the entire race in the dual universe is united and functionally interdependent.

89. What kind of love are we commanded to have?

a. We are to love the Lord as to His Person, even the Robe He wears and the sandals He walks on. We are to love Him for Who He is, the Son of God from eternity who sacrificed Himself for us. We are to love all children, each one as to their unique person, being tolerant of the weaknesses that are human. We are to love our country and all of God's children and creatures.

b. We are to love whatever good is in a person or thing, not the person or thing, just as we should strive to love the Lord as to the Divine Good and Truth in Him, and not as to His Person. We are not to love the evil in a person, or find it acceptable or excusable on account of who the person is. Nothing should be loved but what is good and true, knowing that all good and truth is from God and is in God.

c. We are to love our neighbor and show charity where needed. We are to love God. If our neighbor is a sinner, we should still love him or her. Loyalty to person is the highest friendship. Loyalty to country, right or wrong, is required, and we are to accept the bad with the good.

90. What's the difference between theoretical and applied knowledge in True Science?

a. Theoretical knowledge of True Science is the first level of understanding while applied knowledge of it is at the second level. For example, a student taking a course in True Science might gain a theoretical knowledge of it, but when he or she becomes a graduate student or professor, there develops an applied knowledge of it. It is similar with medical students on campus and hospital interns on an assigned war, or a soldier in training vs. on the battle field.

b. Theoretical knowledge of True Science is called enlightenment, while its applied knowledge is called perception. Enlightenment is in the understanding, perception in the will. First the understanding is reformed, then the will is regenerated. Salvation is therefore not from theoretical knowledge of revelation and consequent enlightenment, but from applied knowledge and perception of our intentions and thoughts, whether from hell or heaven.

c. Theoretical theology differs from applied theology like a business professor differs from a business investor. While a minister is in Divinity School, he acquires a theoretical knowledge of True Science, viewed as True Theology. But once he has a parish he acquires an applied knowledge of True Science, which helps him to look after the souls in his charge.

91. Compare sensuous and rational consciousness of God.

a. Sensuous consciousness is the awareness of sensations, while rational consciousness is the awareness of thoughts. Our sensuous consciousness of God is direct and immediate, wordless, eternal. Our rational consciousness of God is indirect through our thoughts and interpretations. Direct mystical or ecstatic union with God is only possible in sensuous consciousness.

b. Sensuous consciousness is higher than rational consciousness because it is more immediate. Rational consciousness is the attempt to explain in words what the sensuous experience is. As a result, rational consciousness is more remote and subjective. But sensuous consciousness doesn't mean ecstatic union with God.

c. The Son of God was a public citizen of Nazareth while He grew up into adulthood, but after His Resurrection He only appeared to those whose spiritual eyes were opened by Him to see. The difference is that He was present to everyone's sensuous consciousness until the Resurrection, but afterwards, only to those whose rational consciousness was advanced enough to receive the Holy Spirit. The Second Coming is not a Coming in the sensuous consciousness but in the rational consciousness of True Science. In the afterlife, we have not only rational consciousness of the Lord, but sensual consciousness, as He appears to us in the midst of the spiritual Sun.92. Is either heaven and hell forever or can people change their mind at some point?

a. Yes. Heaven is a place the Lord creates for good people and hell is a place for evil people.

b. Sometimes.

c. No. If heaven is in your mind, then hell must be in your mind. Every person has both heaven and hell in the mind, for there is no other heaven or hell except the one in people's minds. To descend to the bottom of our mind means to enjoy and justify evil loves. To climb to the top of our mind means to enjoy and justify good loves. We descend to the bottom by giving up all good loves, and we climb to the top by giving up all evil loves. Once your are either at the bottom (in your hell) or at the top (in your heaven), you cannot switch because you are unwilling no matter what. To switch would be to acquire again what you have discarded (either good or evil loves). Therefore hell is forever and heaven is to eternity.

93. Explain what is spiritual enlightenment.

a. Spiritual enlightenment is the emergent phenomenon of higher consciousness achieved through acts of discipline and meditation.

b. Enlightenment is a spiritual gift an individual can use to minister to others who are in need and who are ignorant of the Lord or keep the Lord at a distance in their lives.

c. When we study the Threefold Word as True Science, we form rational concepts of Divine Truth. Simultaneously, light from the spiritual Sun enters our spiritual mind unconsciously, and produces conscious correspondences of itself in the natural-rational mind. This higher rational consciousness is called enlightenment.

Moses, Paul, and Swedenborg

94. Is there a difference between morality and spirituality? Illustrate in terms of the concept of charity.

a. No. Morality concerns the appropriate treatment of people in our behavior. Morality regulates our behavior towards our neighbor. The Ten Commandments given by God prohibit stealing, lying, murder, and adultery. These are all matters of morality and ethics. God wants us to be moral with one another by keeping the Commandments. Charity is to give to others who are in need of what you have. It is a high point of morality and spirituality.

b. Yes. Charity can be done for natural motives or spiritual. Morality is done for natural motives. Shunning evils as sins is done for spiritual motives. Morality about the outward social personality, while spirituality is about one's character or inner loves. Hence being a moral person is not regenerating, unless we connect our morality to our spirituality. If we refrain from stealing because it is immoral, the desire to steal remains. But if we refrain from stealing because it is a sin against God, that is, destroys our heavenly life, then we connect spirituality to morality, and we regenerate.

c. The difference is one of emphasis rather than substance. Morality is a measure of how sincere we are in the values we uphold publicly and make up part of our personality structure. Spirituality is a measure of how deeply our values go, whether they are part of our core being or only the surface personality. Charity is an outward manifestation of both morality and spirituality, but more the former than the latter.

95. Briefly explain the differences between corporeal, sensuous, rational, and spiritual, in relation to the mind.

a. Corporeal refers to biochemistry, sensuous to physiology, rational to psychology, and spiritual to theology.

b. Corporeal refers to things in us that are corrupted by sin. Sensuous refers to that part of human nature that can be tempted or seduced. Rational is that which we intellectualize in our mind, interpreting our experience rather than taking it in immediately without the mediation of our intellect. Spiritual is the core of our being or soul and is unique and eternal.

c. The corporeal mind is close to the physical body processes which do not involve thinking. The sensuous mind receives information from the corporeal and differentiates it through words and labels. The rational mind takes information from the sensuous and puts it into abstract categories. The spiritual mind unconsciously receives information from the spiritual world, which is transmitted by correspondence, to the rational mind where it is conscious.

96. Identify the phase to which the following six traits are characteristic: enlightened; literalist; universalistic, arrogant; conjunctive; inclusive, pacifist.

a. 3,1,2,1,3,2,2   c. 3,2,3,2,1,3,1

b. 3,2,1,3,2,1,2

97. What is the vertical community and how can we be conscious of our communication with spirits? Illustrate with our eating behavior.

a. The "vertical community" refers to our position in the hierarchy of spiritual beings. First are the Holy animals like the Cherubim, then the Angels who minister at the throne of God, then the elders and saints, and finally all the believers. The non-believers are cast out in outer darkness. When we eat we pay tribute to the throne of God by blessing the food and giving thanks. We are then in the company of Angels.

b. We can map out the spiritual societies we are connected to, which can be called our "vertical community." For instance, when we are eating, if we stuff and swallow repeatedly we are with different spirits than if we moderate size and rate. If we deny ourselves another portion we are with different spirits than if we give in to our appetite and overeat. Affections for unhealthy foods come from different spiritual societies than affections for healthy food.

c. The "vertical community" refers to the social hierarchy in a society. This hierarchy may be considered to be the "spirit" of the underlying organization of that society. Food behavior is among the daily occupations of that society and requires the hierarchical execution of sequenced steps from farmer, to distributor, to local market where the customers gather to shop.

98. The following six sentences are taken from protocols of people's thinking while doing their workout. Identify each entry as to phase (1, 2, or 3) and modality (thinking or feeling).

** I better not skip my workout today. It really keeps me in shape. To be successful you've got to look attractive. That means being in shape. Besides, you avoid heart attacks.

** I'm actually looking forward to my workout. Yes, it takes effort and motivation, but it's worth it. I feel better, clean, purified, satisfied with myself.

Moses, Paul, and Swedenborg

** Exercising the physical body is like exercising the mind with study. Compelling myself to do it as scheduled, develops my mental discipline upon which rests my spiritual development. I must look on the physical exercise as a spiritual discipline.

** I need to learn to like my workout session. It's the right thing to do. It keeps me from bad habits like laziness and lack of self-control. It's necessary for a healthy life.

** I feel that every movement brings me closer to my heavenly character. I sense the physical power in my body to be connected to my will and motive. Since this is from heaven, I feel closer to heaven as I exercise.

** I hate this workout stuff. I rather watch TV or surf the net. But I'm making myself do it. I refuse to break my resolution. I'm scared to get sick and end up under a doctor's care. Besides, it'll be soon over then I can watch TV.

a. feeling 1, thinking 3, thinking 2, feeling 2, feeling 3, thinking 1 b. thinking 1, feeling 3, thinking 2, feeling 1, thinking 3, feeling 2 c. thinking 1, feeling 2, thinking 3, thinking 2, feeling 3, feeling 1

99. The following six statements characterize various attitudes about wars. For each item, identify the phase (1, 2, or 3) and the modality (thinking or feeling).

All wars are under the direct auspices of the Lord. All evil is moderated by the Lord to its maximum allowed. Evil itself punishes the enemy. Our job is to neutralize their ability to hurt others and to try to amend them.

a. thinking 3, b. feeling 3, c. thinking 1,

thinking 2, thinking 1, feeling 2,

feeling 2, feeling 1, feeling 1,

thinking 1, thinking 3, thinking 2,

feeling 3, feeling 2, thinking 3,

feeling 1 thinking 2 feeling 3

** There are just wars and evil wars. Protecting ourselves and coming to the rescue of the subjugated are just wars. The enemy must be treated humanely and not hated. God is on

Moses, Paul, and Swedenborg

the side of the just. Those who are pacifists think that all wars are evil. They would rather see the enemy continue its cruelties against others.

** Feeling confident in winning and relying on God. Wanting to defeat the enemy without hating them. Hoping that enemy may be amended rather than destroyed. Wanting to minimize damage and ready to help with reconstruction of the country.

** War is an instrument for advancing one's nation or religion. It's good to hate the enemy. They don't deserve humane treatment since they want to harm us. Eye for an eye philosophy.

** Striving to win by means of as-of self effort powered by the Lord. Striving to avoid hate as self-corrupting. Sense of sadness rather than joy in hurting and killing enemy. Desire to protect enemy by keeping injury and damage to the minimum necessary for gaining control.

** Hating the enemy with self-righteousness. Wanting to deny humane treatment to the enemy. Feeling justified in using illegal types of weapons and in killing the unarmed innocent. Wanting to inflict maximum damage. Feeling justified in maltreating prisoners of war. Joy in the spoils of war.

100. "Within" and "above" refer to differences of discrete degrees. Characterize the discrete relation between natural and spiritual, and between finite and infinite.

a. The natural world is within the spiritual world. The finite is within the infinite. b. The spiritual world is within the natural world. The infinite is within the finite.

c. The natural world is finite. The spiritual world is infinite. They are separate, not within or above each other.

ANSWER KEY

51. __b__
52. __a__
53. __b__

Moses, Paul, and Swedenborg

| 54. __a__ |
| 55. __c__ |
| 56. __a__ |
| 57. __c__ |
| 58. __c__ |
| 59. __c__ |
| 60. __a__ |
| 61. __b__ |
| 62. __b__ |
| 63. __c__ |
| 64. __a__ |
| 65. __a__ |
| 66. __a__ |
| 67. __c__ |

Moses, Paul, and Swedenborg

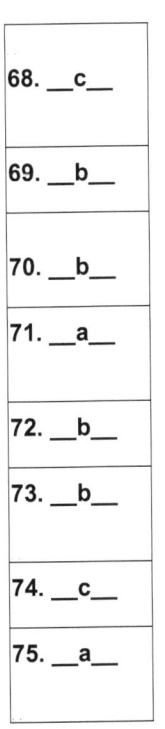

68. __c__
69. __b__
70. __b__
71. __a__
72. __b__
73. __b__
74. __c__
75. __a__

FURTHER EXERCISE

Now that you know your score, you can go a step further in assessing your understanding of rational spirituality. Look at the questions you answered correctly. Select one of them and write a sentence of justification for your answer. Then compare your answer with the sentence for that item given in the Test. How do they differ? Did you mention all the basic elements needed to justify the answer? Did you mention them in a logical order? Now see if you can improve it without making it much longer.

Repeat this with other items. See if you can add more alternatives to each item. See if you can create 10 new items covering the reading you have done thus far.

19. Selections from the Writings

Note: The entire theological works of Emanuel Swedenborg (1688-1772) in English and original Neo-Latin, with search engine, is available online to the public at this Web address:www.theheavenlydoctrines.orgCollateral works, articles, and Web links may be found on my Web site at:

Moses, Paul, and Swedenborg

www.soc.hawaii.edu/leonj/leonj/leonpsy/instructor/swedenborg.htmlThe abbreviations used for the Writings are explained in the Bibliography Notes at the end.

19.1 On Swedenborg's Mission as Scientific Revelator of the Second Coming

VIII. THIS SECOND COMING OF THE LORD IS EFFECTED BY MEANS OF A MAN TO WHOM THE LORD HAS MANIFESTED HIMSELF IN PERSON, AND WHOM HE HAS FILLED WITH HIS SPIRIT, THAT HE MAY TEACH THE DOCTRINES OF THE NEW CHURCH FROM THE LORD BY MEANS OF THE WORD.

Since the Lord cannot manifest Himself in Person, as shown just above, and nevertheless has foretold that He was to come and establish a new church, which is the New Jerusalem, it follows that He will do this by means of a man, who is able not only to receive these doctrines in his understanding but also to publish them by the press. That the Lord manifested Himself before me, His servant, and sent me to this office, that He afterward opened the eyes of my spirit and thus introduced me into the spiritual world and granted me to see the heavens and the hells, and to talk with angels and spirits, and this now continuously for several years, I affirm in truth; as also that from the first day of that call I have not received anything whatever pertaining to the doctrines of that church from any angel, but from the Lord alone while I have read the Word. (TCR 779)

The arcana revealed in the following pages relate to heaven and hell, and also to the life of man after death. The man of the church at this date knows scarcely anything about heaven and hell or about his life after death, although all these matters are set forth and described in the Word; and yet many of those born within the church refuse to believe in them, saying in their hearts, "Who has come from that world and told us?" Lest, therefore, such a spirit of denial, which especially prevails with those who have much worldly wisdom, should also infect and corrupt the simple in heart and the simple in faith, it has been granted me to associate with angels and to talk with them as man with man, also to see what is in the heavens and what is in the hells, and this for thirteen years; so now from what I have seen and heard it has been granted me to describe these, in the hope that ignorance may thus be enlightened and unbelief dissipated. Such immediate revelation is granted at this day because this is what is meant by the Coming of the Lord. (HH 1)

The manifestation of the Lord in Person, and the introduction by the Lord into the spiritual world, both as to sight and as to hearing and speech, surpasses all miracles; for we do not read anywhere in history that such interaction with angels and spirits has been granted from

Moses, Paul, and Swedenborg

the creation of the world. For I am daily with angels there, even as I am in the world with men; and now for twenty-seven years. (INV 43)

I was once asked how, from a philosopher, I became a theologian; and I answered, "In the same manner that fishermen were made disciples and apostles by the Lord: and that I also had from early youth been a spiritual fisherman." (ISB 20)

I will now give you an account of my first youth: From my fourth to my tenth year I was constantly engaged in thought upon God, salvation, and the spiritual affections [passiones spirituales] of men; and several times I revealed things at which my father and mother wondered, saying that angels must be speaking through me. (Letters 17)

From my sixth to my twelfth year I used to delight in conversing with clergymen about faith, saying that the life of faith is love, and that the love which imparts life is love to the neighbor; also that God gives faith to everyone, but that those only receive it who practice that love. I knew of no other faith at that time, than that God is the Creator and Preserver of nature, that He imparts understanding and a good disposition to men, and several other things that follow thence. (Letters 17)

I knew nothing at that time of that learned faith which teaches that God the Father imputes the righteousness of His Son to whomsoever, and at such times, as He chooses even to those who have not repented and have not reformed their lives. And had I heard of such a faith, it would have been then, as it is now, above my comprehension. (Letters 17)

This New Church, truly Christian, which at this day is being established by the Lord, will endure to eternity, as is proved from the Word of both Testaments; also it was foreseen from the creation of the world; and it will be the crown of the four preceding churches, because it will have true faith and true charity. (CORONIS 0)

Therefore in order to remove all doubt as to such being the character of the Word, the Lord has revealed to me the Word's internal sense. In its essence this sense is spiritual, and in relation to the external sense, which is natural, is as soul is to body. This sense is the spirit which gives life to the letter; it can therefore bear witness to the divinity and holiness of the Word, and convince even the natural man, if he is willing to be convinced. (SS 4)

Once, when the interior heaven was opened to me, and I was conversing with the angels there, I was permitted to observe the following phenomena. Be it known that although I was in heaven, I was nevertheless not out of myself, but in the body, for heaven is within man,

Moses, Paul, and Swedenborg

wherever he may be, so that when it pleases the Lord, a man may be in heaven and yet not be withdrawn from the body. In this way it was given me to perceive the general workings of heaven as plainly as an object is perceived by any of the senses. . (AC 3884)

The manifestation of the Lord, and intromission into the spiritual world, surpass all miracles. This has not been granted to anyone since the creation, as it has been to me. (INV 52)

The Lord has revealed the spiritual meaning of the Word at this day because a doctrine of genuine truth has now been revealed. This doctrine is contained in part in The New Jerusalem and its Heavenly Doctrine, and now in some shorter works which are in process of publication. And because this doctrine and no other agrees with the spiritual meaning of

the Word, therefore that meaning has now for the first time been disclosed, along with a knowledge of correspondences. (De Verbo 7:8)

Since therefore I was desirous of knowing whether there were other inhabited worlds, and what they and their inhabitants were like, I was allowed by the Lord to talk and mix with spirits and angels from other worlds. (EU 1)

Add to these most manifest evidences, that the spiritual sense of the Word has been disclosed by the Lord through me, which has never before been revealed since the Word was written among the sons of Israel; and this sense is the very sanctuary of the Word: the Lord Himself is in this sense with His Divine, and in the natural sense with His Human. Not a single iota in this sense can be opened except by the Lord alone. This surpasses all the revelations that have hitherto been made from the creation of the world. (INV 44)

A redemption has also been accomplished by the Lord at this day, because at this day is His Second Coming according to prophecy; by which, having been an eye-witness thereof I have been made certain of the truth of the foregoing arcana. (Coronis 21)

To-day the Second Coming of the Lord is taking place, and a new church is to be established (TCR 115)

At this day the spiritual sense of the Word has been revealed from the Lord, because the doctrine of genuine truth has now been revealed, which doctrine is partly contained in the Doctrine of the New Jerusalem, and now in the small works, which are being given to the public; and because that doctrine, and no other, agrees with the spiritual sense of the Word, therefore that sense, together with the science of correspondences, has now for the first time been disclosed. That sense is also signified by the Lord's appearing in the clouds of heaven with glory and power (Matt. 24:30, 31), in which chapter it treats of the consummation of the age, by which is meant the last time of the church. (De Verbo 7)

[2] Now, since it has been granted me to be in the spiritual world and in the natural world at the same time, and thus to see each world and each sun, I am obliged by my conscience to communicate these things. For of what use is knowledge unless it be communicated? (ISB 18)

After the completion of this book, the Lord called together His twelve disciples, who had followed Him in the world; and a day later He sent them all forth throughout the spiritual world to preach the Gospel, that the Lord God Jesus Christ is king, and His kingdom shall be for ever and ever, as foretold by Daniel (7:13, 14) and in Revelation (11:15):

Blessed are they who come to the wedding supper of the Lamb Rev. 19:9.

This happened on the nineteenth of June in the year 1770. This was meant by the Lord's saying:

He will send his angels, and they will gather together His chosen people from the bounds of the heavens on one side as far as the bounds of the heavens on the other. Matt. 24:31. (TCR 791)

The first experience. One day I had been meditating on the creation of the universe. This was noticed by the angels above me to the right, where there were some who had several times meditated and reasoned about the same matter; so one of them came down and invited me to join them. I passed into the spirit and accompanied him; on my arrival I was brought to the prince, in whose hall I saw as many as a hundred assembled with the prince in their midst.

Then one of them said: 'We noticed here that you have meditated about the creation of the universe, a subject which has several times occupied our thoughts. But we were unable to reach a conclusion because our thinking clung to the idea of chaos being like a great egg, from which everything in the universe in its due order was hatched. Yet now we perceive that such a vast universe could not have been hatched like this. Another idea which stuck in our minds was that everything was created by God from nothing; yet now we perceive that nothing comes from nothing. Our minds have not yet been able to disentangle themselves from these two ideas and shed a little light on how creation happened. For this reason we have summoned you from the place where you were, to expound your thinking on the subject.'

[2] 'I will indeed,' I replied on hearing this. 'I meditated on this,' I said, 'for a long time but to no purpose. But later, when I was admitted by the Lord into your world, I perceived that it was futile to form any conclusions about the creation of the universe, unless it were first known that there were two worlds, one occupied by angels and the other by men; and that men after death pass from their world into the other. Then I also saw that there are two suns, one from which pour forth all spiritual things, and one from which pour forth all natural things; and that the sun from which all spiritual things pour forth is pure love from Jehovah God, who is in its midst, while the sun from which all natural things pour forth is pure fire. When I had grasped these facts, once when I was in a state of enlightenment, I was granted the perception that the universe was created by Jehovah God by means of the sun in the midst of which He is; and because love cannot exist except together with wisdom, that the universe was created by Jehovah God from His love by means of His wisdom. I have been

convinced of the truth of this by everything I have seen in the world where you are, and in the world where I am at present in the body.

[3] 'It would be too tedious to explain how creation progressed from its first beginning. But while I was in a state of enlightenment I perceived that by means of the light and heat from the sun of your world, one after another spiritual atmospheres were created, which are in themselves substantial. Because there are three of them, and they therefore have three degrees, three heavens were made, one for angels in the highest degree of love and wisdom, one for angels in the second degree, and a third for angels in the lowest degree. But because this spiritual universe could not come into being without a natural universe, in which the spiritual one might produce its effects and perform its services, at the same time the sun which is the source of all natural things was created; and through this in the same way, by means of light and heat, three atmospheres were created to surround the first three, like a shell round a kernel or bark round wood; and it was finally through these that the globe with its lands and seas was created from the earth consisting of soil, stones and minerals, to be the home of men, animals, fish, trees, shrubs and plants.

[4] 'This is an extremely general outline of how creation took place and progressed. It would take a series of books to explain all the particular details; but all lead to this conclusion, that God did not create the universe from nothing, since, as you said, nothing comes of nothing,

but through the sun of the heaven of angels, which is from His Being (Esse) and so is pure love together with wisdom. Every single detail of the universe, by which I mean both the spiritual and natural worlds, bears witness and proclaims that the universe was created from the Divine love by the Divine wisdom. This you can clearly see, if you consider these facts in due order and in their connexions, by the light which illuminates the perceptions of your understanding. But it should be kept in mind that the love and wisdom, which in God make one, are not love and wisdom in the abstract, but are in Him as substance. For God is the very, sole and consequently prime substance and essence, which is and continues in existence in itself.

[5] All things being created from the Divine love and the Divine wisdom is what is meant by this passage in John:

The Word was with God, and the Word was God; all things were made through Him; and the world was made through Him. John 1:1, 3, 10.

God there means the Divine love, and the Word the Divine truth, or the Divine wisdom. That is why the Word is there called the light; light, when referring to God, means the Divine wisdom.'

At the end of this speech when I was saying good-bye, gleams of light from the sun there came gliding down through the heavens of the angels and entered their eyes, and through them the dwellings of their minds. Under this enlightenment they applauded my speech, and then escorted me into the courtyard; and my earlier companion took me to the house where I was living, and from there went back up to his own community. (TCR 76).

19.2 How Everyone is Resuscitated in the World of Spirits

CONCERNING THE RESUSCITATION OF MAN FROM THE DEAD, AND HIS ENTRANCE INTO ETERNAL LIFEBeing permitted to describe in connected order how man passes from the life of the body into the life of eternity, in order that the way in which he is resuscitated might be known, this has been shown me, not by hearing, but by actual experience. (AC 168)

I was reduced into a state of insensibility as to the bodily senses, thus almost into the state of dying persons, retaining however my interior life unimpaired, attended with the power of thinking, and with sufficient breathing for life, and finally with a tacit breathing, that I might perceive and remember what happens to those who have died and are being resuscitated.

Moses, Paul, and Swedenborg

(AC 169)

Celestial angels were present who occupied the region of the heart, so that as to the heart I seemed united with them, and so that at length scarcely anything was left to me except thought, and the consequent perception, and this for some hours. (AC 170)

The angels who sat at my head were perfectly silent, merely communicating their thoughts by the face, so that I could perceive that another face was as it were induced upon me; indeed two, because there were two angels. When the angels perceive that their faces are received, they know that the man is dead. (AC 173)

An aromatic odor was perceived, like that of an embalmed corpse, for when the celestial angels are present, the cadaverous odor is perceived as if it were aromatic, which when perceived by evil spirits prevents their approach. (AC 175)

As soon as the internal parts of the body grow cold, the vital substances are separated from the man, wherever they may be, even if enclosed in a thousand labyrinthine interlacings, for such is the efficacy of the Lord's

mercy (which I had previously perceived as a living and mighty attraction), that nothing vital can remain behind. (AC 179)

When the celestial angels are with a resuscitated person, they do not leave him, for they love everyone; but when the soul is of such a character that he can no longer be in the company of the celestial angels, he is eager to depart from them; and when this takes place the spiritual angels arrive, and give him the use of light, for previously he had seen nothing, but had only thought. (AC 182)

Afterwards there seems to be something gently unrolled from the face, and perception is communicated to him, the angels being especially cautious to prevent any idea coming from him but such as is of a soft and tender nature, as of love; and it is now given him to know that he is a spirit. (AC 185)

He then commences his life. This at first is happy and glad, for he seems to himself to have come into eternal life, which is represented by a bright white light that becomes of a beautiful golden tinge, by which is signified his first life, to wit, that it is celestial as well as spiritual. (AC 186)

Finally I talked with the spirits of that world about the belief of the inhabitants of our world

Moses, Paul, and Swedenborg

concerning their resurrection.

I said they were unable to conceive of people coming into the next life immediately after death, and then looking like people in face, body, arms and feet, having all their outward and inward senses. Even less could they believe that they would then wear clothes and have houses and places to live.

This was entirely due to the fact that most people here base their thinking on bodily sense-impressions, so that they do not believe in the existence of what they cannot see and touch. Few of them can be withdrawn from outward sense-impressions towards inward ones, and so be lifted into the light of heaven in which inward impressions can be received.

It is for this reason that they cannot have any concept of their soul or spirit as being a person, but think of it as wind, air or some formless breath, which yet contains some vitality. This is the reason that they believe they will only be resurrected at the end of the world, which they call the Last Judgment, thinking that their body, though collapsed into dust and scattered to all the winds, must then be brought back and reunited with their soul or spirit.

[2] I added that they are allowed to hold this belief, because there is no other way that those who, as I said, base their thinking on outward sense-

impressions, could think of their soul or spirit living as a person in human form, except by re-entering the body they carried around with them in the world. Unless therefore the body were said to be resurrected, they would at heart reject the teaching on resurrection and everlasting life as incomprehensible.

(...)[4] For they are unaware that each person is inwardly a spirit, and the life of the body and all its parts comes from the spirit, not from the body by itself. They do not know that it is the spirit which is the real person, sharing its form, but invisible to the body's eyes, being visible only to the eyes of spirits. Hence it is too that, when a person's spirit has its sight opened, which is the result of the withdrawal of the body's sight, angels can be seen as people. So it was that angels appeared to the ancients, as related in the Word.

I have had several conversations with spirits whom I knew when they were people living in the world, and asked whether they wanted to be clothed again with their earthly bodies, as they had previously imagined. On hearing this they ran off to a distance at the mere idea of being reunited, in astonishment at having been led in the world to think so by blind faith without any understanding. (EU 165)

Moses, Paul, and Swedenborg

19.3 Sexual Love, Marriage, Heaven, Hell

Note that the Writings talk about those in hell as being punished by their own evils. This is a self-imposed punishment, not a punishment by an external agency such as is the case with prisons on earth. God doesn't punish, but evil has a built in consequence of returning to the evil doer when the evil state is fully consummated. Neither are the evil kept in the hells, but they keep themselves there.

The state of a person's mind in the natural world determines its state in the spiritual world. (TCR 816)

Heaven is in the man; and there is a place for him in heaven according to the state of life and of faith in which he is (AC 9305)

Once, when the interior heaven was opened to me, and I was conversing with the angels there, I was permitted to observe the following phenomena. Be it known that although I was in heaven, I was nevertheless not out of myself, but in the body, for heaven is within man, wherever he may be, so that when it pleases the Lord, a man may be in heaven and yet not be withdrawn from the body. In this way it was given

me to perceive the general workings of heaven as plainly as an object is perceived by any of the senses. . (AC 3884)

Love of the married partner does not result from the sexual embrace, as with adulterers, but the sexual embrace from the love of the partner; so that the love of the partner does not depend on the fire of that organ, but the reverse. The love of the partner is full of delights, irrespective of sexual intercourse, and is a delightful dwelling together. Between that love apart from the sexual embrace, and the sexual embrace itself, there is a determination, just as there is between that which a man thinks from the will, which is intention, and act, or speech. Between these, intervenes determination, which is as it were the opening of the mind to doing a thing, like the opening of a door. (SE 6110)

[The New Heaven] consists of Christians as well as of Gentiles, but for the most part of the children of all in the whole world, who have departed this life since the Lord's time: for these have all been received by the Lord, educated in heaven, and instructed by the angels, and afterwards preserved, so that together with the rest, they might constitute the New Heaven. (NJHD 3)

Moses, Paul, and Swedenborg

Those who are outside the Church, and acknowledge one God, and live according to their religion in some charity towards the neighbour, are in communion with those who are of the Church; for no one who believes in God and leads a good life, is damned. From this it is evident, that the Lord's Church is everywhere throughout the world; although specifically it is, where the Lord is acknowledged, and where the Word exists. (NJHD 244)

The whole Church on earth, before the Lord, is as one man, nos. 7396, 9276; in like manner heaven, because the Church is heaven, that is, the Lord's kingdom on earth, nos. 2853, 2996, 2998, 3624-3629, 3636-3643, 3741-3745, 4625. But the Church, where the Lord is known and where the Word exists, is like the heart and lungs in a man in respect to the rest of the body, which lives therefrom, as from the fountains of its life, nos. 637, 931, 2054, 2853. Hence it is, that unless there were a Church where the Word exists, and where by means of it the Lord is known, the human race would not be saved, nos. 468, 637, 931, 4545, 10452. The Church is the foundation of heaven, no. 4060. (NJHD 246)

THE STATE AND CONDITION IN THE NEXT LIFE OF NATIONS AND PEOPLES BORN OUTSIDE THE CHURCH.It is commonly supposed that those born outside the Church, who are called heathens and gentiles, cannot be saved for the reason that they do not possess the Word and so do not know the Lord, without whom there is no salvation. But that gentiles too are saved may be known from the single

consideration that the Lord's mercy is universal - that is, it reaches out to every individual human being. For gentiles are born human beings the same as those within the Church, who are a relative minority; and they are not to blame because they do not know the Lord. Consequently the nature of their state and condition in the next life has in the Lord's Divine mercy been shown to me. (AC 2589)

THE FORM OF HEAVEN WHICH DETERMINES AFFILIATIONS AND COMMUNICATIONS THERE.What the form of heaven is can be seen in some measure from what has been shown in the preceding chapters; as that heaven is like itself both in its greatest and in its least divisions (n. 72); that consequently each society is a heaven in a lesser form, and each angel in the least form (n. 51-58); that as the entire heaven reflects a single man, so each society of heaven reflects a man in a lesser form, and each angel in the least form (n. 59-77); that the wisest are at the center, and the less wise are round about even to the borders, and the like is true of each society (n. 43); and that those who are in the good of love dwell from the east to the west in heaven, and those who are in truths from good from the south to the north; and the same is true of each society (n. 148,

Moses, Paul, and Swedenborg

149). All this is in accord with the form of heaven; consequently it may be concluded from this what this form is in general. (HH 200)

Nearly all people in the natural world can be associated together in respect to their outward affections, but not in respect to their inner affections if these differ and become apparent. The reason is that in the world a person is invested with a material body, and this is filled with urges, which in it are like dregs that settle to the bottom when newly fermented wine is being clarified.

From such elements come the materials of which the bodies of people in the world are composed. As a result, inward affections that belong to the mind do not appear, and in many cases scarcely a trace of them is visible. For either the body swallows them up and immerses them in its dregs, or from a habit of dissembling learned from early childhood, it hides them deep within and conceals them from the sight of others.

This also enables it to enter into the state of some affection which it observes in someone else, and to attract the other's affection to it, so that they form a relationship. They form a relationship, because every affection has its delight, and delights are what join hearts together.

It would be different, however, if inward affections were like outward ones, visible in the expression of the face and gesture and audible in the sound of the speech, or if their delights were noticeable to the nose and smelled, as is the case in the spiritual world. If these affections were then dissimilar

to the point of friction and conflict, they would separate their hearts from each other and part, removing themselves to a distance commensurate with their perception of antipathy.

It is apparent from this that nearly all people in the natural world can be associated together in respect to outward affections, but not in respect to their inner affections, if these differ and become apparent.(CL 272)

The chief love is sexual love; and in the case of those who reach heaven, that is, those who become spiritual on earth, it is conjugial love.

The reason why a person's sexual love remains after death is that a male remains a male and a female remains a female, and the male's masculinity pervades the whole and every part of him, and likewise a female's femininity; and the impulse to be joined is present in every detail down to the smallest. Since that impulse to be joined was implanted from creation and is therefore continually present, it follows that the one desires the other and longs to be joined to the other.

Love taken by itself is nothing but a desire and hence an impulse to be joined; conjugial love is an impulse to be joined into one. For the male and the female of the human species are so created as to be able to become like a single individual, that is, one flesh; and when united, then they are, taken together, the full expression of humanity. If not so joined, they are two, each being as it were a divided person or half a person. Since that impulse to be joined lies deeply hidden in every part of both male and female, and every part has the ability and desire to be joined into one, it follows that people retain mutual and reciprocal sexual love after death. (CL 37)

MARRIAGES IN HEAVEN.

As heaven is from the human race, and angels therefore are of both sexes, and from creation woman is for man and man is for woman, thus the one belongs to the other, and this love is innate in both, it follows that there are marriages in heaven as well as on the earth. But marriages in heaven differ widely from marriages on the earth. Therefore what marriages in heaven are, and how they differ from marriages on the earth and wherein they are like them, shall now be told. (HH 366)

Especially does a love for the opposite sex remain, and in the case of people coming into heaven, namely, people who become spiritual on earth, conjugial love. A love for the opposite sex remains in a person after death for the reason that a male is then still a male, and a female still a female, and masculinity in the male is masculine in the whole and every part of him, likewise femininity in the female, and there is a capacity for

conjunction in every detail - indeed, in every least detail - of the two sexes. (CL 37:4)

The angelic spirits replied with a smile, 'Sexual love among the angels, the kind of love there is in heaven, is still full of the most intimate delights. It is an extremely pleasant feeling, as if every part of the mind were expanded. This affects all parts of the chest, and inside it is as if the heart were playing games with the lungs; and this play gives rise to breathing, sound and speech. These make contact between the sexes, that is, between young men and girls, the very model of heavenly sweetness, because it is pure.

Since in heaven the husband is wisdom and the wife is the love of wisdom, both being spiritual, they cannot have any but spiritual children conceived and born there. This is why these delights do not leave angels depressed, as some on earth are, but cheerful; this is due to the constant inflow of fresh strength to replace the former, at once renewing and enlightening it. For all who reach heaven return to the springtime of their youth, recovering the strength of that age, and keeping this for ever.' (CL 44)

A young man becomes or is made a husband, because a husband possesses elements taken from his wife, which increase his ability to receive love and wisdom; these he did not have as a young man. These effects take place in the case of those who enjoy truly conjugial love. (...)

I was convinced of the fact of this from the following experience in the spiritual world: Some men said that the relationship a man has with a woman before marriage and the relationship he has with his wife after marriage are similar. When they heard this, their wives became very offended and said, "They are not at all alike! The difference is as the difference between fantasy and reality."

To this the men retorted, "Are you not women as before?" To which their wives responded with rising voice, "We are not 'women' but wives! The love you feel is a fantasy love and not a real one; therefore you speak in fantasy terms."

The men then said, "If you are not 'women,' still you are married women." But they replied, "In the early days of marriage we were married women; now, however, we are wives." (CL 199)

(5) All the delights of truly conjugial love, even the end delights, are chaste. This follows from the foregoing considerations explaining that

truly conjugial love is the essence of chastity. And delights make the life of this love.

I have indicated earlier how the delights of this love ascend and enter heaven, and on the way permeate the joys of heavenly loves experienced by angels of heaven. I have also recounted how these delights ally themselves with the delights of conjugial love in angels. Moreover, I have heard from angels that they perceive these delights to be heightened in them and to become fuller as they ascend from chaste married partners on earth. And in response to some bystanders, who were unchaste - in reply to their question whether they also experienced the end delights - the angels nodded and quietly said, "What else? Are they not delights of conjugial love in their fullest expression?"

Moses, Paul, and Swedenborg

(Regarding the source of the delights of this love and what they are like, see no. 69 above and what is said in the narrative accounts, especially in those that follow.) (CL 144)

Chastity in marriage does not come about through renunciation of licentious relationships unless this is done in accordance with religion. The reason is that a person without religion does not become spiritual, but remains natural. And if a natural person renounces licentious relationships, still his spirit does not renounce them. Consequently, even though it seems to him that by renouncing them he is chaste, nevertheless unchasteness still lies hidden within, like putrefaction in a wound only superficially healed.

As seen above in no. 130, conjugial love depends on the state of the church in a person. More on this subject may be seen in the exposition of point (11) which follows below. (CL 149)

We say that fornication is a product of sexual love because it is not sexual love, but arises from it. Sexual love is like a spring from which both conjugial love and scortatory love can be drawn; and they can be drawn by fornication, or without it. For everyone has sexual love in him, and it either emerges or it does not. If it emerges before marriage in relations with a woman of loose morals, it is called fornication; but if it does not emerge until he has a wife, it is called marriage. If it occurs with another woman after marriage, it is called adultery. Therefore, as stated, sexual love is like a spring from which a rivulet of chaste as well as unchaste love can flow. But it will be revealed in the following pages how much caution and how much prudence is needed for chaste love to develop through fornication, and how much imprudence for unchaste or scortatory love to develop through it. Can anyone draw this conclusion, that a person who has fornicated cannot be more chaste when he is married? (CL 445)

Scortatory love makes a person less and less human and virile, and conjugial love makes him more and more human and virile. (CL 432)

He who thinks against God is rarely punished in the natural world, because there he is always in a state subject to reformation; but he is punished in the spiritual world after death, for then he can no longer be reformed. (DP 249)

Evils are as it were heavy, and fall of themselves into hell; and so also falsities that are from evil (n. 8279, 8298).(HD 170)

When evil spirits are in this second state, as they rush into evils of every kind they are

Moses, Paul, and Swedenborg

subjected to frequent and grievous punishments. In the world of spirits there are many kinds of punishment (HH 509; see below for the rest of the quote).

When evil spirits are in this second state, as they rush into evils of every kind they are subjected to frequent and grievous punishments. In the world of spirits there are many kinds of punishment; and there is no regard for person, whether one had been in the world a king or a servant. Every evil carries its punishment with it, the two making one; therefore whoever is in evil is also in the punishment of evil. And yet no one in the other world suffers punishment on account of the evils that he had done in this world, but only on account of the evils that he then does; although it amounts to the same and is the same thing whether it be said that men suffer punishment on account of their evils in the world or that they suffer punishment on account of the evils they do in the other life, since everyone after death returns into his own life and thus into like evils; and the man continues the same as he had been in the life of the body (n. 470- 484).

Men are punished for the reason that the fear of punishment is the sole means of subduing evils in this state. Exhortation is no longer of any avail, neither is instruction or fear of the law and of the loss of reputation, since everyone then acts from his nature; and that nature can be restrained and broken only by punishments.

But good spirits, although they had done evils in the world, are never punished, because their evils do not return. Moreover, I have learned that the evils they did were of a different kind or nature, not being done purposely in opposition to the truth, or from any other badness of heart than that which they received by inheritance from their parents, and that they were borne into this by a blind delight when they were in externals separate from internals. (HH 505)

The state of the case with the evil in the other life is that they are not punished until their evils have reached their height, and this both in general and in particular. For such is the equilibrium in the other life that

evil punishes itself, that is to say those who are evil run into the punishment of their evil, but only when it has reached its height. Every evil has its limit that varies in each individual case, beyond which it is not allowable to pass. When an evil person passes beyond this limit he precipitates himself into the penalty, and this is so in every particular (AC 1857)

There are innumerable things in every evil. In man's sight every evil appears as one single thing. This is the case with hatred and revenge, theft and fraud, adultery and whoredom, arrogance and high-mindedness, and with every other evil; and it is not known that in every evil there are innumerable things, exceeding in number the fibers and vessels in a man's body. For a wicked man is a hell in its least form; and hell consists of myriads of myriads of spirits, and every one there is in form like a man, although a monstrous one, in which all the fibers and vessels are inverted. The spirit himself is an evil which appears to himself as a "one"; but there are innumerable things in it as many as the lusts of that evil, for every man is his own evil, or his own good, from the head to the sole of his foot.

Since then a wicked man is such, it is evident that he is one evil composed of innumerable different evils each of which is a distinct evil, and they are called lusts of evil. Hence it follows that all these in their order must be restored and changed by the Lord in order that the man may be reformed; and this cannot be effected unless by the Divine Providence of the Lord, step by step from the earliest period of man's life to the last. (DP 296)

In hell every lust of evil when visually represented appears like a noxious creature, as a dragon, or a cockatrice, or a viper, or a bird of night, or an owl, and so on; and similarly do the lusts of evil appear in a wicked man when he is viewed by angels.

All these forms of lusts must be changed one by one; and the man himself, who with respect to his spirit appears as a human monster or devil, must be changed to become like a beautiful angel; and every lust of evil must be changed to appear like a lamb, or a sheep, or a pigeon, or a turtle dove, as the affections of good in the angels appear in heaven when visually represented; and to change a dragon into a lamb, a cockatrice into a sheep, and an owl into a dove can only be effected step by step, by rooting out evil from its very seed and implanting good seed in its stead.

This, however, can only be done as is done, for example, in the grafting of trees. When their roots with some of the trunk remain, the engrafted branch draws sap through the old root and turns it into sap that makes good fruit. The branch that is to be engrafted can only be taken from the

Lord, who is the Tree of Life. This, moreover, is in accordance with the words of the Lord (John xv. 1-7). (DP 296:[2])

A wicked man from himself continually leads himself more and more deeply into his evils. It is said, from himself, because all evil is from man, for man turns good that originates from the Lord into evil, as was said above. The real reason why the wicked man immerses himself more deeply in evil is that as he wills and commits evil he advances into infernal societies more and more interiorly and also more and more deeply. Hence also the delight of evil increases, and so occupies his thoughts that at last he feels nothing more pleasant. He who has advanced more interiorly and deeply into infernal societies becomes as if he were bound with chains. So long as he lives in the world, however, he does not feel his chains, for they are as if made from soft wool or from fine threads of silk, and he loves them as they give him pleasure; but after death, instead of being soft they become hard, and instead of being pleasant they become galling. (DP 296:[3])

The separation of profane and holy ideas when thus conjoined cannot be effected except by means of such infernal torment that if a man were aware of it he would as carefully avoid profanation as he would avoid hell itself. (AC 301)

19.4 The Threefold Word and Spiritual Enlightenment Thereby

The Old Testament, the New Testament, and the Writings together make up the Threefold Word. Whenever the Writings use the expression "the Word" one can always think "the Threefold Word." Doing so, reveals to the reader a deeper meaning of what the passage is saying. And if you desire to enter zone 9 state of consciousness, think "True Science" whenever you read "the Word." This "substitution technique" is discussed with some illustrations, in my book *A Man of the Field, Volume 2 Enlightenment*, available at: www.soc.hawaii.edu/leonj/nonduality.html

Anyone who does not know that the Word has an internal sense which is not visible in the letter will be utterly astonished by the idea that spiritual realities too are meant by the numbers used in the Word. The specific reason for his astonishment is his inability to use numbers to give shape to any spiritual idea, when yet the spiritual ideas known to angels present themselves as numbers, see AC 5265. The identity of those ideas or spiritual realities to which numbers correspond can, it is true, be known; but the origin of such correspondence remains hidden, such as the origin of the correspondence of 'twelve' to all aspects of faith, the correspondence of 'seven' to things that are holy, as well as that of 'ten' and also 'five' to forms of good and truth stored up by the Lord within the interior man, and so on. Even so, it is enough if people know simply that such a correspondence does exist and that by virtue of that correspondence each number used in the Word denotes something present in the spiritual world, consequently that what is Divine has been inspired into them and so lies concealed within them.

[4] Examples of this are seen in the following places where 'five' is mentioned, such as the

Moses, Paul, and Swedenborg

Lord's parable in Matt. 25:14 and following verses about the man who, before going away to a foreign country, placed his resources in the hands of his servants. To the first he gave five talents, to the second two, and to the third one. The servant who received five talents traded with them and earned five talents more. In a similar way the one who received two earned two more; but the servant who received one hid his master's money in the earth. The person whose thought does not extend beyond the literal sense knows no other than this, that the numbers five, two, and one have been adopted merely to make up the story told in the parable and that they entail nothing more, when in fact those actual numbers hold some arcanum within them. The servant who received the five talents means those people who have accepted forms of good and truth from the Lord and so have received remnants. The one who received the two talents means those who at a more advanced stage in life have linked charity to faith, while the servant who received the one means someone who receives faith alone devoid of charity. Regarding this servant it is said that he hid his master's money in the earth - the reason for this description being that the money he is said to have received means in the internal sense truth which is the truth of faith, AC 1551, 2954; but faith that is devoid of charity cannot earn any interest, that is, it cannot be fruitful. These are the kinds of matters that numbers hold within them.(...)[7] It is hardly credible that the numbers included in such details, since these belong to a historical narrative, have a spiritual meaning. That is, five thousand, the number of people, has a spiritual meaning; so does five, the number of leaves, as well as two, the number of fishes. A hundred, and likewise fifty, the numbers of people sitting down together, each have a spiritual meaning; and so lastly does twelve, the number of baskets containing broken pieces. Though it may seem incredible, every detail holds some arcanum. Every single thing occurred providentially, to the end that Divine realities might be represented by them. (*Arcana Coelestia* 5291)

Not a single word, nor even a single iota, in its original language, can be taken from the sense of the letter of the Word, without an interruption in the internal sense (WH 11)

The ultimates of the Word are its props and supports; indeed, each word is a prop and a support to its celestial and spiritual truths. (SS 35)

When the Word is opened the Lord appears (AE 612)

The internal sense is itself the genuine doctrine of the church ... They who understand the Word according to the internal sense, know the true doctrine itself of the church, because the internal sense contains it (WH 11)

Moses, Paul, and Swedenborg

The Word is not understood, except by those who are enlightened. The human rational faculty cannot comprehend Divine, nor even spiritual things, unless it be enlightened ... Thus they only who are enlightened comprehend the Word ... Enlightenment is an actual opening of the interiors of the mind, and also an elevation into the light of heaven (WH 7)

In the internal or spiritual sense of the Word there are innumerable arcana. The Word in the internal sense contains innumerable things which exceed human comprehension ... It also contains things ineffable and inexplicable (n. 1965). Which are manifest only to angels, and are understood by them (WH 11)

The Lord is the Word, and the Word is Divine Truth (DP 256) When the Word is opened the Lord appears (AE 612)The Word therefore is written by mere correspondences (EU 119)

Therefore in order to remove all doubt as to such being the character of the Word, the Lord has revealed to me the Word's internal sense. In its essence this sense is spiritual, and in relation to the external sense, which is natural, is as soul is to body. This sense is the spirit which gives life to the letter; it can therefore bear witness to the divinity and holiness of the Word, and convince even the natural man, if he is willing to be convinced. (SS 4)

Being Divine the Word contains within itself things that are infinite which come from its first source, and as a consequence contains things beyond description such as constitute angelic wisdom; but in its lowest form it contains only such things as those that man is able to grasp. ... Entering into scientifics from the truths of faith, is agreeable to order; but, conversely, entering into the truths of faith from scientifics, is contrary to order ...

Whoever is in a principle of negative doubt, which in itself is negative, and who says that he will not believe until he is persuaded through scientifics, will never believe.(AC 4383)

There is also a conjunction of heaven by means of the Word with those who are outside the Church where there is no Word; for the Lord's Church is universal, and is with all who acknowledge the Divine and live in charity. Moreover, such are taught after death by angels and receive Divine truths (HH 308).

The starting-point ought to be made from truths of doctrine which are from the Word, and they ought first to be acknowledged; it is permitted afterwards to consult scientifics in order to confirm these truths, which are corroborated in this manner (NJHD 51)

Enlightenment is the influx, perception, and instruction people receive from the Lord when

Moses, Paul, and Swedenborg

they read the Word. (AC 10215)

Thus, also, the angels of heaven are able not only to be perfected from the Word, but also to perceive blessedness and happiness of life: for the Word, read in this earth, passes, by correspondences, even into heaven, as was shown. Thus, also, can the truths of faith be communicated to the angels of other earths. This is the reason that the Lord willed to be born here, and to become, while he was in the world, the Divine truth, that is, the Word, and afterwards the Divine Good, that is, Jehovah.) (SE 4663)

Again:

The "fruitful tree" denotes the celestial man; the "cedar" the spiritual man. The "wild animal" and "beast" and "creeping thing" are their goods, as in the history before us; the "flying fowl" is their truths; from all of which they can "praise the name of Jehovah." By no means can the wild animal, the beast, the creeping thing, and the bird do this. In profane writings such things may be said by hyperbolism, but there are no hyperbolisms in the Word of the Lord, but things significative and representative. (AC 776)

The Word is the Divine Truth which is in the Lord and from the Lord ... Divine Truth has power in itself, and such power that, by means of it, heaven was created and the world with all things therein. (HH 137).

Fruitful trees and all cedars, the wild animal and every beast, creeping things and flying fowl, let them praise the name of Jehovah (Ps. 148:9-10, 13).

Without the Lord's coming into the world no one could have been saved. It is the same today; and therefore without the Lord's coming again into the world in Divine truth, which is the Word, no one can be saved. (TCR 3)

The Word is the only doctrine which teaches how a man must live in the world in order to be happy to eternity. (AC 8939)

The existence of writings in the heavens is a provision of the Lord for the sake of the Word; for the Word in its essence is Divine truth, and from it is all heavenly wisdom, both with men and with angels; for the Word was dictated by the Lord, and what is dictated by the Lord passes through all the heavens in order and terminates with man. Thereby it is adapted both to the wisdom of angels and the intelligence of men. Thereby, too, the angels have a Word, and read it the same as men do on the earth, and also draw from it their doctrinals,

Moses, Paul, and Swedenborg

and preach from it (AC n. 221). It is the same Word; but its natural sense, which is the sense of the letter with us, does not exist in heaven, but only the spiritual sense, which is its internal sense. What this sense is can be seen in the small treatise on The White Horse spoken of in the Apocalypse. (HH 259)

The Word in heaven is written in a spiritual style which is quite different from the natural style. The spiritual style is composed simply of letters, each one of which denotes a particular meaning; and there are dashes, curves and points above, between and within the letters, which heighten the meaning. The letters used by the angels of the spiritual kingdom resemble printed type in our world; the letters used by the angels of the celestial kingdom are in some cases like Arabic letters, in others like ancient Hebrew letters, but with curves above and below, and pointing above, between and inside them. Even a single one of these points conveys a complete meaning. (TCR 241)

The Word is not understood except by those who are enlightened. ... The human rational cannot apprehend Divine things, nor even spiritual things, unless it is enlightened by the Lord ... Thus only they who are enlightened apprehend the Word ... They who are in the good of life, and thereby in the affection of truth, are enlightened (NJHD 256).

The Word is the only doctrine which teaches how a man must live in the world in order to be happy to eternity. (AC 8939)

All truths are from the Word, which is spiritual light and nothing ought to be believed except the truth (INV 7)

A human being is created for everlasting life, and any person can inherit that life, so long as he lives in accordance with the means of salvation prescribed in the Word; every Christian, as well as every non-Christian

who possesses a religion and sound reason, assents to this proposition. (TCR 340)

Without the Word there is no rational conception of the Lord, and thus no salvation (SS 111)

As to the formation of faith: it is effected by man's going to the Lord, learning truths from the Word, and living according to them. (TCR 347)

I spoke with those who placed the only means of salvation in reading the Word. They were overhead, and said that they take great care that all in their society are diligent in reading the Word. But I told them, that this does not save, but that they must live according to the Word, and that nobody can live according to the Word except he be in the doctrine of truth from it; otherwise, they do not know how they are to live, for, from the sense of the letter of the Word, they are able to defend everything that belongs to their life, be it what it may, and this to protect falsities. It was shown also what is the nature of the Word in the letter, but that those who are in doctrine from the Word, see the Word and read it, quite differently; they consequently understand it, and are thus able to become rational: otherwise, this cannot take place. It was shown, also, that the reading of the Word is not attended to by the Lord, and therefore does not promote salvation, unless they are in the life of truth; and that they cannot be in the life of truth, except they be in doctrine from the Word (SE 5961).

The Lord cannot enlighten anyone with His light, unless He is approached immediately and acknowledged as the God of heaven. (INV 38)

19.5 On Being Reborn, Sin, Regeneration, and Forgiveness

UNLESS A MAN IS BORN AGAIN, AND, AS IT WERE, CREATED ANEW, HE CANNOT ENTER INTO THE KINGDOM OF GOD. That unless a man is born again he cannot enter into the kingdom of God, is the Lord's doctrine (TCR 572).

The first state is represented in the life of every person by his infancy and childhood, until he becomes a youth, adolescent and young man. This state is marked by humility before his parents, obedience, and being instructed by masters and underlings. The second state is represented by the same person's state when he becomes his own master, can make his own decisions, or follow his own will and his own understanding; at this stage he has control in his own house. (TCR 106)

Such is the order in which those kinds of truths stand in relation to one another in man. Until a person has become adult therefore, and through sensory and factual truths possesses matters of doctrine, he is incapable of being regenerated, for he cannot be confirmed in the truths contained in matters of doctrine except through ideas based on factual and sensory truths - for nothing is ever present in a person's thought, not even the deepest arcanum of faith there, which does not involve some natural or sensory idea, though generally a person is not aware of the essential nature of such ideas. But in the next life the nature of them is revealed before his understanding, if he so desires, and also a visual representation before his sight, if he wants it; for in the next life such things can be presented before one's eyes in a visual form. This seems unbelievable but it is nevertheless what happens there. (AC

Moses, Paul, and Swedenborg

3310)

There are two states that man must enter upon and pass through, when from being natural he is becoming spiritual. The first state is called Reformation, and the second Regeneration. In the first man looks from his natural to his spiritual state and longs for that state; in the second state he becomes spiritual-natural. The first state is formed by means of truths, which must be truths of faith, and through these he looks to charity; the second state is formed by means of the goods of charity, and by these he enters into the truths of faith. Or what is the same, the first is a state of thought from the understanding, and the second a state of love from the will.

They who are born where the Word is, and where the Lord is thereby known, are not of the church, but they who are regenerated by the Lord by the truths of the Word, that is, they who live the life of charity ... (NJHD 246)

When this latter state begins and is progressing, a change takes place in the mind; the mind undergoes a reversal, the love of the will then flowing into the understanding, acting upon it and leading it to think in accord and agreement with its love; and in consequence so far as the good of love comes to act the first part and the truths of faith the second, man is spiritual and is a new creature; and he then acts from charity and speaks from faith; he feels the good of charity and perceives the truth of faith; and he is then in the Lord, and in peace, and thus regenerate.

The man who while in the world has entered upon the first state, after death can be introduced into the second; but he who has not entered into the first state while in the world, cannot after death be introduced into the second, thus cannot be regenerated.(TCR 571)

The unregenerate man has no conscience, or if any, it is not a conscience of doing good from charity, and of thinking truth from faith, but is based on some love that regards himself or the world, wherefore it is a spurious or false conscience. (AC 977)

As it is desirable that the origin of perception, internal dictate, and conscience, should be known, and as at the present day it is altogether unknown, I may relate something on the subject. It is a great truth that man is governed by the Lord by means of spirits and angels. When evil spirits begin to rule, the angels labor to avert evils and falsities, and hence arises a combat. It is this combat of which the man is rendered sensible by perception, dictate, and conscience. By these, and also by temptations, a man might clearly see that spirits and angels are with him, were he not so deeply immersed in corporeal things as to believe nothing that is said about spirits and angels. Such persons, even if they were to feel these combats hundreds of times, would still say that they are imaginary, and the effect of a disordered mind. I have been permitted to feel such combats, and to have a vivid sense of them, thousands and thousands of times, and this almost constantly for several years, as well as to know who, what, and where they were that caused them, when they came, and when they departed; and I have conversed with them. (AC 227)

[A person] can from wisdom above view the love that is below, and in this way can view his thoughts, intentions, affections, and therefore the evils and falsities as well as the goods and truths of his life and doctrine; and without a knowledge and acknowledgment of these in himself he cannot be reformed. (DP 16)

Without self-examination, recognition, acknowledgment, confession and rejection of sins, thus without repentance, there is no forgiveness of them, thus no salvation, but eternal condemnation (DP 114)

IV. EVILS IN THE EXTERNAL, MAN CANNOT BE REMOVED BY THE LORD EXCEPT THROUGH MAN'S INSTRUMENTALITY. In all Christian Churches this tenet of doctrine has been accepted, that before a man approaches the Holy Communion he shall examine himself, see and acknowledge his sins, and do the work of repentance by desisting from them and rejecting them because they are from the devil; and that otherwise his sins are not forgiven, and he is condemned. (DP 114)

IV. EVILS IN THE EXTERNAL, MAN CANNOT BE REMOVED BY THE LORD EXCEPT THROUGH MAN'S INSTRUMENTALITY

It is only religion which renews and regenerates a person. Religion is allotted the highest place in the human mind, and sees below it the social matters which concern the world. Religion too climbs up through these as

the pure sap rises in a tree to its top, and from that lofty position it has a view of natural matters, just as someone on a tower or a mountain has a view of the plains beneath. (TCR 601)

The will inclines from birth towards evils, even to those which are enormous; hence, unless it were restrained by means of the understanding, a man would rush into acts of wickedness, indeed, from his inherent savage nature, he would destroy and slaughter, for the sake of himself, all who do not favor and indulge him. (ISB 14)

Moses, Paul, and Swedenborg

When we are in an unregenerate state our outer self is in its loves within "the dregs" of the body and the corporeal-sensuous mind. Though we declare unconditional love as our operating system, this is nothing but the love of self. Our inner self is in the hatred of all people except a few who favor us and whom we can exploit for our needs. But the moment they stop favoring us or serving our needs, our inner self holds them in hatred. What lies inside unconditional love is therefore unconditional hatred, one in the outer self, the other in the inner self (SEM 4717; SE 409; HH 377; CL 365; AE 624).

During man's regeneration, the light of heaven is instilled into natural light, and at the same time the heat of heaven; these two constitute, as it were, the new soul, through which man is formed by the Lord. This light and heat are instilled through the higher mind, which is called the spiritual mind. By virtue of this instilling, or insertion, man becomes a new creature, and becomes more enlightened and more intelligent in matters of the church, and consequently in the reading of the Word. This also is the new understanding and the new will. Afterwards the man is led by the Lord through the above light and through the above heat, and from natural becomes spiritual. (INV 2)

For it is the case with the life of charity (which is the heavenly life itself) that with those who are being reformed and regenerated it is continually being born and growing up and receiving increments, and this by means of truths; therefore the more of truth there is insinuated, the more is the life of charity perfected ...

(...)In truth, however, there is no life, but in good. Truth is only a recipient of life, that is, of good. Truth is as the clothing or garment of good; therefore also truths are called in the Word "clothing," and also "garments." But when good constitutes the rational, truth disappears and becomes as if it were good.(AC 2189)

Anyone therefore who looks to the Lord and wants to be guided by Him is in a state of good. But anyone who turns away from God and wants to be guided by himself is not in a state of good (CL 444)

... man when regenerated is as to the intellectual part the Lord's, but as to his will part is his own, these two parts in the spiritual man being opposed.

But though the will part of man is opposed, yet it cannot but be present; for all the obscurity in his intellectual part, or all the density of his cloud, is from it. It continually flows in from it, and in proportion as it flows in, the cloud in his intellectual part is thickened; but in proportion as it is removed, the cloud is made thin.

Moses, Paul, and Swedenborg

(...)[3] This condition of things between the will and the understanding is as if two who were formerly conjoined by a covenant of friendship, as were the will and the understanding in the man of the Most Ancient Church, had their friendship broken, and enmity had arisen-as took place when man wholly corrupted his will part-and then when a covenant is again entered into, the hostile part is set forth as if the covenant were with it, but it is not with it, because it is utterly opposite and contrary, but it is with that which flows in from it-as already said-that is, with the Own of the understanding.

The "token" or "sign" of the covenant is this, that in proportion as there is the presence of the Lord in the Own of the understanding, in the same proportion the Own of the will be removed.

The case herein is exactly as it is with heaven and hell. The intellectual part of the regenerated man, from charity, in which the Lord is present, is heaven; his will part is hell. So far as the Lord is present in this heaven, so far is this hell removed. For of himself man is in hell, and of the Lord is in heaven. And man is being continually uplifted from hell into heaven, and so far as he is uplifted, so far his hell is removed. The "sign" therefore, or indication, that the Lord is present, is that man's will part is being removed. The possibility of its removal is effected by means of temptations, and by many other means of regeneration. (AC 1044)

[3] When a man has been regenerated, then all things in him, both in general and in particular, have also been regenerated, that is, have life, and the life they have bears an exact proportion to the degree in which his own will-which is foul and dead-could be separated from the new will and intellectual that he has received from the Lord. (AC 1040)

When a child is first instructed he is affected with the desire of knowing, not at first for any end that is manifest to himself, but from a certain pleasure and delight that is born with him and is also derived from other sources; but afterwards, as he grows up, he is affected with the desire of

knowing for the sake of some end, as that he may excel others, or his rivals; and next for some end in the world; but when he is to be regenerated, he is affected from the delight and pleasantness of truth; and when he is being regenerated, which takes place in adult age, from the love of truth, and afterwards from the love of good; and then the ends which had preceded, together with their delights, are separated little by little, and to them succeeds interior good from the Lord, which manifests itself in his affection. From this it is evident that the former delights, which had appeared in the outward form as good, had served as means. Such successions of means are continual. (AC 3518)

Second: Good and the truth of good can be introduced by the Lord into man's interiors only so far as the evil and the falsity of evil there have been removed. This is a necessary consequence of what has gone before; for as evil and good cannot exist together good cannot be introduced before evil has been removed. The term man's interiors is used, and by these is meant the internal of thought; and in these, which are now being considered, either the Lord or the devil must be present.

The Lord is there after reformation, but the devil is there before it; therefore, so far as man suffers himself to be reformed the devil is cast out; but so far as he does not suffer himself to be reformed the devil remains. Everyone may see that the Lord cannot enter so long as the devil is there; and he is there so long as man keeps the door closed, where man acts together with the Lord. (DP 232:3)

The reason why everyone can be regenerated depending on his state, is that the process is different with the simple and the learned, with those who have different pursuits, and undertake different duties; with those who research into the externals of the Word and those who research into its internals; with those whose parentage has brought them into natural good and those who have been brought into evil; with those who from childhood have plunged into the world's vanities, and those who have sooner or later distanced themselves from them. In short, there is a difference between those who make up the Lord's external church and those who make up the internal one. In this there is infinite variety, just as there is in faces and characters. But still each can be regenerated and saved depending on his state.

[2] The truth of this can be established from the heavens, to which all who are regenerated come, being three, highest, middle and lowest. Those come to the highest who through regeneration have acquired love to the Lord; to the middle one those who have acquired love towards the neighbour; to the lowest those who only exhibit external charity, and at the same time acknowledge the Lord as God the Redeemer and Savior. All of these are saved, but in different ways.

[3] The reason why all can be regenerated and so saved is that the Lord is present with His Divine good and truth with every person. This is the source of his life, and of his ability to understand and will, and of the free will he has in spiritual matters; no one is without these.

Moses, Paul, and Swedenborg

Moreover the means are given. Christians have the means in the Word, non-Christians in any religion at all, if it teaches the existence of God and commandments about good and evil. From this it follows that everyone can be saved. Consequently, if a person is not saved, it is not the Lord who is to blame but the person; and he is to blame for failing to cooperate. (TCR 580)

Since, then, everyone in every religion knows the evils and falsities from evils that must be shunned, and having shunned them knows the goods that must be done and the truths that must be believed, it is clear that this is provided by the Lord as the universal means of salvation with every nation that has any religion.

[2] With Christians this means exists in all fullness; it also exists, though not in fullness, with Mohammedans and Gentiles. The remaining things, by which they are distinguished, are either ceremonials which are of little consequence, or are goods that may be done or not done, or truths that may be believed or not believed, and yet man be saved. What these things amount to man can see when evils are removed.

A Christian sees this from the Word, a Mohammedan from the Koran, and a Gentile from his religious principle.

A Christian sees from the Word that God is one, that the Lord is the Savior of the world, that all good that is good in itself, and all truth that is true in itself, is from God, and nothing of it from man; that there must be Baptism and the Holy Supper, that there is a heaven and that there is a hell, that there is a life after death, and that he who does good comes into heaven, and he who does evil into hell. These things he believes from truth and does from good when he is not in evil. Other things that are not in accord with these and with the Decalogue he may pass by.

A Mohammedan sees from the Koran that God is one, that the Lord is the Son of God, and that all good is from God, that there is a heaven and that there is a hell, that there is a life after death, and that the evils forbidden in the commandments of the Decalogue must be shunned. If he does these latter things he also believes the former and is saved.

A Gentile sees from his religious principle that there is a God, that He must be regarded as holy and be worshiped, that good is from Him, that there is a heaven and that there is a hell, that there is a life after death,

that the evils forbidden in the Decalogue must be shunned. If he does these things and

Moses, Paul, and Swedenborg

believes them he is saved.

And as many Gentiles perceive God to be Man, and as God-Man is the Lord, so after death when they are instructed by angels they acknowledge the Lord, and afterwards receive truths from the Lord that they had not before known. They are not condemned because of their not having the ordinances of Baptism and the Holy Supper; the Holy Supper and Baptism are for those only who are in possession of the Word, and to whom the Lord is known from the Word; for they are symbols of that church, and are attestations and certifications that those who believe and live according to the Lord's commandments in the Word are saved. (AE 1180)

There are thousands and thousands of arcana, of which scarcely a single one is known to man, whereby a man is led by the Lord out of the life of hell into the life of heaven. (AC 9336)

This tendency and proneness to evils just mentioned, which is transmitted from parents to their children and descendants, can only be broken down by a person being born anew by the Lord's help, a process called regeneration. Without this not only does the tendency remain unbroken, but it is reinforced by a succession of parents, becoming more prone to evils, and eventually to every kind of evil. That is why the Jews are still copies of their ancestor Judah, who married a Canaanite wife, and fathered three lines of descent by adultery with Tamar, his daughter-in-law. This heredity has become so amplified in the course of time that the Jews are unable to embrace the Christian religion and believe it in their hearts. I say they are unable, because the inner will in their minds resists, and it is this will which creates the impossibility. (TCR 521)

A spirit himself also is nothing else than his own quality; on this account everyone in that world drops his baptismal name, and the name of his family, and is named according to his quality. Hence it is that "name" in the Word does not signify name, but quality. (INV 41)

The reason why a man can be in evil and at the same time in truth, and why the Lord cannot prevent this on account of the end, which is salvation, is that man's understanding can be raised up into the light of wisdom and see truths or acknowledge them when he hears them, while his love remains below. Thus he can be in heaven with his understanding but with his love in hell; and this cannot be denied to him, because the two faculties, rationality and liberty, cannot be taken from him; for by virtue of these he is a man, and is distinguished from the beasts; and only by means of these faculties can he be regenerated and consequently saved. (DP 16:2)

IV. EVILS IN THE EXTERNAL, MAN CANNOT BE REMOVED BY THE LORD EXCEPT THROUGH MAN'S INSTRUMENTALITY. In all Christian Churches this tenet of doctrine has been accepted, that before a man approaches the Holy Communion he shall examine himself, see and acknowledge his sins, and do the work of repentance by desisting from them and rejecting them because they are from the devil; and that otherwise his sins are not forgiven, and he is condemned. (DP 114)

And when Peter asked Him how many times he should forgive one who sinned against him, whether it should be as many as seven times, He replied:

Not up to seven times, I tell you, but up to seventy times seven times. Matt. 18:21, 22.

I have been told from heaven that the Lord forgives everyone his sins, and never punishes him for them, or even imputes them to him, because He is love itself and good itself. Nevertheless the sins are not wiped away by this, for it is only by repentance that they can be wiped away. For if he told Peter to forgive up to seventy times seven times, is there anything that the Lord Himself would not do? (TCR 409)

It was granted me to perceive when I was in the proprium, and when not in the proprium. When in the proprium, I was fit for nothing; wherefore, I was led out of it by the Lord, as far as that could be done. Hence is manifest what the love of self, and the love of the world for the sake of self, is. When [any] are led in the proprium and borne away, they appear to be led down through the surrounding places; which is according to the changes of the state of the thoughts. "

At this point something will now be said on how the internal man is reformed and how the external man is reformed -by means of it. The internal man is not reformed merely by knowing, understanding and being wise, and consequently merely by thinking; but by willing what knowledge, understanding and wisdom teach.

When a man knows, understands and has wisdom to see that there is a heaven and a hell, and that all evil is from hell and all good is from heaven; and if he then does not will evil because it is from hell, but wills good because it is from heaven, he is in the first stage of reformation, and is at the threshold out of hell into heaven.

When he progresses further, and wills to desist from evils he is in the second stage of reformation, and is now outside hell but not yet in heaven, which he sees above him. A man must have such an internal in order that

he may be reformed; but he is not reformed unless the external as well as the internal is reformed.

The external is reformed by means of the internal when the external desists from the evils which the internal does not will because they are infernal, and still more when the external for this reason shuns them and fights against them. Thus willing is the part of the internal and doing of the external. For unless a man does that which he wills there is within him the failure to will which eventually becomes want of will.

[2] From these few considerations it can be seen how the external man is reformed by means of the internal. This also is what is meant by the Lord's words to Peter:

Jesus said: If I wash thee not, thou hast no part with me.[Simon] Peter saith unto Him: Lord, not my feet only, but also my hands and my head. Jesus saith to him: He that is washed needeth not save to wash his feet, but is clean every whit. John xiii. 8, 9, 10.

By washing is meant spiritual washing, which is purification from evils; by washing the head and hands is meant purifying the internal man; and by washing the feet is meant purifying the external man. That the external man must be purified when the internal has been purified is meant by this, "He that is washed, needeth not save to wash his feet." That all purification from evils is from the Lord is meant by this, "If I wash thee not, thou hast no part with me." It has been shown in many places in the ARCANA CAELESTIA that washing among the Jews represented purification from evils, and that this is signified in the Word by washing; and that by washing the feet is signified the purification of the natural or external man. (DP 151)

I have spoken with spirits about the changes of state of man's life, that it is inconstant, and that he is borne upward and downward, now toward heaven and now toward hell. But they who suffer themselves to be regenerated are being borne continually upward, and thus always into more interior heavenly societies. Extension of sphere into these societies is given by the Lord to those who are being regenerated, especially to those who are being regenerated by means of temptations, in which resistance is made to evils and falsities; for the Lord then fights through angels against the evils and falsities; and in this way the man is introduced into the societies of these angels, which are more interior societies; and into whatever societies he has once been introduced, he there remains; and from this he also receives a more extended and elevated capacity of perception. (AC 6611)

In order that man may examine himself an understanding has been given him, and this separate from the will, that he may know, understand and acknowledge what is good and what is evil; and also that he may see the quality of his will, or what it is he loves and desires. In order that he may see this his understanding has been furnished with higher and lower thought, or interior and exterior thought, to enable him to see from higher or interior thought what his will is doing in the lower or exterior thought. This he sees as a man sees his face in a mirror; and when he sees it and knows what sin is, he is able, if he implores the help of the Lord, not to will it, but to shun it and afterwards to act against it; if not wholeheartedly, still he can exercise constraint upon it by combat, and at length turn away from it and hate it. (DP 278)

It is the rational in fact that coordinates everything in the natural, and in accordance with that coordination fittingly regards the things that are there. Indeed the rational is like a higher faculty of seeing which, when it looks at facts belonging to the natural man, is like someone looking down on to a plain below him. The light of that faculty of seeing is the light of truth, but the origin of that light rests with the good present in the rational. (AC 3283)

19.6 The Vertical Community and Our association With Spirits

The presence of angels and spirits with human beings and in their affections has been granted me to see a thousand times from their presence and dwelling with me. But angels and spirits do not know with which human beings they are, neither do human beings know with which angels and spirits they live; the Lord alone knows and arranges this. (LJ 9)

Everyone is in his spirit associated with people like himself in the spiritual world, and is so to speak one with them. I have often been allowed to see the spirits of people still alive, some of them in communities of angels there, and others in communities of hell. I have been allowed to talk with them for days, and I was astonished to find that the person, who was still alive in the body, knew nothing at all of it. (TCR 14)

It should be known that every man as to his spirit is in the spiritual world in some society there, a wicked man in an infernal society and a good man in a heavenly society; and sometimes he also appears there when in deep meditation. (DP 296:[6])

It is rarely granted at the present day, however, to talk with spirits, because it is dangerous. For then the spirits know, what otherwise they do not know, that they are with man, and evil

Moses, Paul, and Swedenborg

spirits are such that they hold

man in deadly hatred, and desire nothing more than to destroy him both soul and body, which indeed happens with those who have so indulged themselves in fantasies as to have separated from themselves the enjoyments proper to the natural man. Some also who lead a solitary life sometimes hear spirits talking with them, and without danger; but that the spirits with them may not know that they are with man they are at intervals removed by the Lord; for most spirits are not aware that any other world than that in which they live is possible, and therefore are unaware that there are men anywhere else. This is why man on his part is not permitted to speak with them, for if he did they would know. (HH 249)

Man can speak with spirits and angels, and the ancients on our earth frequently spoke with them (n. 67-69, 784, 1634, 1636, 7802). But at this day it is dangerous to speak with them, unless man is in true faith, and led by the Lord (n. 784, 9438, 10751). (EU 1)

Spirits and demons control a person's reasoning power through feelings. (SE 48)

THAT A MAN'S SPIRIT APPEARS IN THE OTHER LIFE. Sometimes man appears as to his spirit among others there. They said that they sometimes see them, and nevertheless know that it is not a spirit as yet after decease from the world, from certain signs. But it happens only with those who think inwardly in themselves more deeply than the rest. At the time, with him, his thought is withdrawn from the sensual of the body, and he appears thus. They, however, who think only in their sensual, and do not raise their thoughts above it, never appear. Nor do spirits know anything about man, where he is; inasmuch as the corporeal does not appear before their eyes, as spirits do not appear before men's eyes. (SE 5645)

IV. SO LONG AS MAN LIVES IN THE WORLD, HE IS KEPT MIDWAY BETWEEN HEAVEN AND HELL, AND IS THERE IN SPIRITUAL EQUILIBRIUM, WHICH IS FREEDOM OF CHOICE.(...)

Man's mind is his spirit, which lives after death; and his spirit is constantly in company with its like in the spiritual world, and at the same time by means of the material body with which it is enveloped, it is with men in the natural world. Man does not know that in respect to his mind he is in the midst of spirits, for the reason that the spirits with whom he is in company in the spiritual world, think and speak spiritually, while his own spirit thinks and speaks naturally so long as he is in the material body; and the natural man cannot understand or perceive spiritual thought and speech, nor the reverse. (...) (TCR 475)

Moses, Paul, and Swedenborg

Every man from infancy even to old age is changing his locality or situation in that world. When an infant he is kept in the eastern quarter towards the northern part; when a child, as he learns the first lessons of religion, he moves gradually from the north towards the south; when a youth, as he begins to exercise his own thoughts, he is borne southward; and afterwards when he judges for himself and becomes his own master, he is borne into the southern quarter towards the east, according to his growth in such things as have regard interiorly to God and love to the neighbor. But if he inclines to evil and imbibes it, he advances towards the west. (TCR 476)

But it must be understood that the Lord does not transfer man to this or that place, but man transfers himself in different ways. If he chooses good, he together with the Lord, or rather the Lord together with him, transfers his spirit towards the east. But if man chooses evil, he together with the devil, or rather the devil together with him, transfers his spirit towards the west. It must be noticed that where the term heaven is here used, the Lord also is meant, because the Lord is the all in all things of heaven; and where the term devil is used, hell also is meant, because all who are there are devils. (TCR 476)

If every thing that a man thinks flows into him from others the fault seems to rest with those from whom it comes. Nevertheless, the fault is in him who receives, because he receives it as his own; and he neither knows nor desires to know otherwise. For everyone desires to be his own, and to be led by himself, and especially to think and to will from himself; this is freedom itself and it appears as his proprium in which every man is. Therefore, if he knew that what he thinks and wills flows in from another he would seem to himself to be bound and captive and no longer master of himself; and thus all the delight of his life, and at length his human itself, would perish.

[3] That this is so I have often seen proved. It was granted to some spirits to perceive and to feel that they were being led by others. Thereupon they were so enraged that they became as it were demented; and they said they would rather be kept bound in hell than not be allowed to think in accordance with their will and to will in accordance with their thought. Not to be allowed to do so they called being bound as to life itself, which was harder and more intolerable than being bound as to their body. Not to be allowed to speak and act in accordance with their thought and will they did not call being bound; because the delight of civil and moral life, which consists in speaking and doing, acts as the restraining influence and, at the same time, mitigates the restraint. (DP 294)

The wicked, while still in the world, the Lord governs in hell. This is because man as to his spirit is in the spiritual world and in some society

there, in an infernal society if he is wicked, and in a heavenly society if he is good; for man's mind, which in itself is spiritual, cannot be anywhere but among the spiritual, into whose company he also comes after death. (DP 307)

CONCERNING THE STATE OF HELL.

During a whole night, while I was asleep, I was tormented in hell, in order that I might know the nature of the state [of those] there; for they fell upon me, inasmuch as they were then able to torture the spirit; but, still, I had no consciousness of a dream. It was a continual torture, one [of them] after another. [Persons] are there placed upon tables, and are miserably torn asunder, and their lust of ruling is called forth, and, as long as that cupidity lasts, they are tortured until it abates. [They are treated] thus, by one devil after another, as [they pass] from one part of hell to another, upon the tables. When the lust abates, then a little respite is given, so that they may be able to be in some cupidity of their own. Thus is the head of the serpent trampled under foot. (SE 4698)

CONCERNING DISEASES.

All the infernals induce diseases, but with a difference according to the part to which they are attached, so that they may act from the opposite, to wit, in opposition to those in heaven, to whom the parts of the body correspond - for there are opposites to every society in heaven; for, as angels or angelic societies preserve in connection and soundness all things in man, so infernals, from the opposite [side], divide them. But it is only permitted them to inflow into the cupidities and falsities pertaining to man - not into man's organs. Only when man falls into disease, then they inflow also into those [organs] in man where the disease is; for nothing ever exists with man, save by a cause from the spiritual world.

Man supposes that such things exist in him, and that there is nothing outside him that acts; when, yet, every natural has its cause from a spiritual, otherwise it would be without a cause; but, still, this does not interfere with the fact that they can be, and also ought to be, cured, or made sound, by natural means. The Lord's providence then concurs with such means: and thus, also, man is kept the longer away from faith concerning a providence in the minutest particulars; for, if he should believe this, and afterwards deny it, he would profane a sacred truth, which is itself a most dreadful hell.

(SD 4585)

Moses, Paul, and Swedenborg

As it is desirable that the origin of perception, internal dictate, and conscience, should be known, and as at the present day it is altogether unknown, I may relate something on the subject. It is a great truth that man is governed by the Lord by means of spirits and angels. When evil spirits begin to rule, the angels labor to avert evils and falsities, and hence arises a combat. It is this combat of which the man is rendered sensible by perception, dictate, and conscience. By these, and also by temptations, a man might clearly see that spirits and angels are with him, were he not so deeply immersed in corporeal things as to believe nothing that is said about spirits and angels. Such persons, even if they were to feel these combats hundreds of times, would still say that they are imaginary, and the effect of a disordered mind. I have been permitted to feel such combats, and to have a vivid sense of them, thousands and thousands of times, and this almost constantly for several years, as well as to know who, what, and where they were that caused them, when they came, and when they departed; and I have conversed with them. (AC 227)

Everything celestial flows into something spiritual, and everything spiritual into something natural, and it terminates in the last of this, which is physical and material, and there abides. Without such a final abode for intermediates to flow into, there would be no other permanence than that of a house built in the air. The human race is therefore the base and foundation of the heavens. (De Verbo 3, LJ 10)

Man does not know that in respect to his mind he is in the midst of spirits, for the reason that the spirits with whom he is in company in the spiritual world, think and speak spiritually, while his own spirit thinks and speaks naturally so long as he is in the material body; and the natural man cannot understand or perceive spiritual thought and speech, nor the reverse.

This is why spirits cannot be seen. But when the spirit of man is in company with spirits in their world, he is also in spiritual thought and speech with them, because his mind is interiorly spiritual but exteriorly natural; therefore by means of his interiors he communicates with spirits, while by means of his exteriors he communicates with men. By such communication man has a perception of things, and thinks about them analytically. If it were not for such communication, man would have no more thought or other thought than a beast, and if all connection with spirits were taken away from him, he would instantly die. (TCR 475)

(1) They place themselves at the back, below and above, and there they thrust in their

thoughts; they turn the thoughts of another spirit, and thus of a man, to himself, to his own power, to his own praise, in a word, to the proprium. Almost all infernals know how to do this.

(2) Others gaze upon various parts of the body and upon the head and, where they see anything black, they know the proprium still rules there - for the proprium is black, because it is of the love of self - and, then, they seek to learn what of self is there, and, when they find out, they infuse their own thoughts there, and lead [their victim] whithersoever they will.

(3) Some look into the forehead; and, if it appears black, they then lead him; likewise, if it is grayish-white like a plastered wall, inasmuch as this indicates simulated external sincerity; but from him in whom they see human flesh they withdraw, and him they do not lead.

(4) Some cast a black veil over his face and also over his breast, and thus they magically take away his thoughts of the neighbor, and oblige and compel him to think of himself; and so they lead him, but not like they do others who are black of themselves: the former return immediately.

(5) Some enshroud another in darkness and convey [him] into the dark, and so compel him to think of self.

(6) From the color around a spirit or man - black, white, flesh-color, or yellow - they conclude something about the man's state as to his proprium, or self-love. Where it is black, there is self-love: such a one is led; and it is according to the intensity of the black.

(7) Some only perceive by means of the thoughts of another - for there is a general law of thoughts - and these insinuate themselves into them and turn them to [the victim's] proprium and love of self, in all ways - by phantasies, by magic; and by the aid of many of the hells; and, so, they drive him to thinking about himself; and, when it comes to that, he is in their power.

(8) Sirens know how to insinuate themselves into the various affections which are the ruling love of a man; and so they take him with them. Also, they know how to reduce the thoughts of another, magically, even to the sensual, which is the extreme external; and, when he is reduced to that, they induce various phantasies and lead him whithersoever they wish. It is the sensual of man where his self-love, or proprium, resides: so far as he can be drawn up, or elevated, out of that, as to the thoughts, towards interiors, so far he can be led away from his proprium. Man's sensual, at this day, is, with most people, wholly corporeal, and has not

Moses, Paul, and Swedenborg

anything spiritual.

(9) It was granted me to perceive when I was in the proprium, and when not in the proprium. When in the proprium, I was fit for nothing; wherefore, I was led out of it by the Lord, as far as that could be done. Hence is manifest what the love of self, and the love of the world for the sake of self, is. When [any] are led in the proprium and borne away, they appear to be led down through the surrounding places; which is according to the changes of the state of the thoughts. There were some such of the Swedish nation, whose desire it had been thus to reduce the thoughts of other spirits to subjection, and so to lead them whithersoever they would;

but they did not know how, save one or two of them. They were in the western quarter. (SE 5464)

The universal heaven is arranged in societies according to [the affections of good and the entire hell according to] the lusts of evil opposite to the affections of good. Every man as to his spirit is in some society - in a heavenly society if he is in the affection of good, but in an infernal society if he is in the lust of evil. Man does not know this while he is living in the world, but nevertheless as to his spirit he is in some society; otherwise he cannot live, and because of it he is governed by the Lord. If he is in an infernal society he can only be led out of it by the Lord according to the laws of His Divine Providence, one of which is that he must see that he is there, must desire to go out and must himself endeavor to do this of himself. This he can do while he is in the world, but not after death; for then he remains to eternity in the society in which he has placed himself while in the world. This is the reason why man is to examine himself, see and acknowledge his sins and repent, and afterwards persevere right on to the end of his life. That this is the case I could establish from much experience even to complete belief; but this is not the place to set forth proofs of my experience. (DP 278)

THAT CRUEL SPIRITS AND ADULTERERS LOVE NOTHING MORE THAN FILTH AND EXCREMENTS.(((((I have spoken) previously of this [fact] that to such spirits, filth and excrements are very pleasant, so that they prefer the pleasantness of beholding such things to all other pleasantnesses, and not only filth and excrements, but also foul, loathsome, and horrid intestines of animals, to that degree, that when they act through man they snatch away all his interior sense, as also [his] sight, to such things, because they, are delighted therewith.

This also was shown me by manifest experience; when I walked in the street, they carried away my eyes to all such things; wherever there was filth, excrement and intestines, thither they directed my eyes, although I was ignorant where were such things in the street, because not observed by me. Still they saw these, whilst I was wholly unobservant, and thither directed my eyes, either to [my] side, or about [my] feet, or near and farther from thence; and the did not turn my eyes to anything else. (SE 2843)

Since spirits take possession in that way of all that forms a person's thought and will, and angels take possession of what is even more interior, so that he is joined very closely to them, the person cannot avoid the perception and sensation that he himself is the one who thinks and wills. . (AC 6193)

There are with every man at least two evil spirits and two angels. The evil spirits excite his evils, and the angels inspire things that are good and true. (AC 904)

For the nature of all communication in the next life is this: In a community in which people are alike, each thinks that what is another's is his own. When therefore people who are good go into a heavenly community they instantly enter into all the intelligence and wisdom of that community, entering into it so fully that they know no other than that such things exist within themselves. This is also how it is with man and a spirit present with him. The things that flow in from spirits from hell are evil and false, but those which flow in from angels from heaven are good and true; and through these opposite kinds of influx a person is held in the middle, thus in freedom.

(...)Evil spirits ... are angry if they are told that their thoughts and desires do not begin in themselves, because that idea is contrary to what their loves lead them to be delighted with. And they are all the more angry when they are told that life does not exist independently in them but flows into them. (AC 6193).

19.7 On Faith Alone, Good Works, and Meritoriousness

To give aid to the needy, to widows, to orphans, solely because they are needy, widows and orphans, and to give to beggars solely because they are beggars, are uses of external charity, which charity is called piety; but these are uses of internal charity only so far as they are derived from use and the love of use. For external charity without internal charity is not charity; the internal must be there to make it charity; for external charity from internal charity acts prudently, but external without internal charity acts imprudently, and often unjustly. (D. WIS. 10:5)

Moses, Paul, and Swedenborg

Practical piety is to act in every work and in every duty from sincerity and right, and from justice and equity, and this because it is commanded by the Lord in the Word; for thus man in his every work looks to heaven and to the Lord, and thus is conjoined with Him. But to act sincerely and rightly, justly and equitably, solely from fear of the law, of the loss of fame or of honor and gain, and to think nothing of the Divine law, of the commandments of the Word, and of the Lord, and yet to pray devoutly in the churches, is external piety; however holy this may appear, it is not piety, but it is either hypocrisy, or something put on derived from habit, or a kind of persuasion from a false belief that Divine worship consists merely in this; for such a man does not look to heaven and to the Lord with the heart, but only with the eyes; the heart looking to self and to the

world, and the mouth speaking from the habit of the body only and its memory; by this man is conjoined to the world and not to heaven, and to self and not to the Lord. (AE 325:4)

It should be known, moreover, that, so long as man is in knowledges only, and not in any life according to them, he is in his proprium and led by self; but, when he is in a life according to them - and to the same extent - he is elevated out of his proprium, and is led by the Lord. This man does not perceive, but still it is so; and so far as man is led by the Lord, so far is there good in him, or good is what he wills and thinks. But it should be thoroughly known, that nobody can live according to the knowledges from the Word, except from them he reflect upon his thoughts, intentions and deeds, that is, examine himself, and abstain from evils and do good as from himself: otherwise, there is no reception by man; and if there is no reception, there is no conjunction with the Lord; therefore, neither can he be led by the Lord. (SE 5945)

The Lord ... said that people were to forgive their brother not seven times but seventy times seven, Matt. 18:21, 22. By this He meant that they were to forgive as often as he sinned. Their forgiveness was to know no limits, that is, was to be eternal and timeless, which is holy. (AC 433)

I have heard from heaven that the Lord forgives to everyone his sins, and never takes vengeance nor even imputes sin, because He is love itself and good itself; nevertheless, sins are not thereby washed away, for this can be done only by repentance. For when He told Peter to forgive until seventy times seven, what will not the Lord do? (TCR 409)

In the exercise of charity man should see clearly whether he is acting from justice, and this he sees from judgment. For a man may do evil by deeds of beneficence; and by what appear to be evil deeds he may do good. For example: One who gives to a needy robber the means wherewith to buy a sword, by a beneficent act is doing evil; although the robber in begging the money did not tell what he would do with it. So again, if one rescues a robber from prison and shows him the way to a forest, saying to himself, It is not my fault that he commits robbery; I have given succor to the man. (...)

[15] On the other hand, a man may do good through what appear to be evil deeds. Take as an example a judge who acquits an evil-doer because he sheds tears, pours out words of piety, and begs the judge to pardon him because he is his neighbor. But in fact a judge performs a work of charity when he decrees the man's punishment according to the law; for he thus guards against the man's doing further evil and being a pest to society, which is the neighbor in a higher degree, and he prevents also the scandal of an unjust judgment. Who does not know also, that it is good for servants to be chastised by their masters, or children by their parents,

when they do wrong? The same is true of those in hell, all of whom are in the love of doing evil. They are kept shut up in prisons, and when they do evil are punished, which the Lord permits for the sake of their amendment. (TCR 459)

However, I replied, "Man was so created that everything he wills, thinks and does appears to him as being in him and thus from him. Without this appearance a person would not be a human being, for he would be unable to receive anything of good and truth or of love and wisdom, retain it, and seemingly adopt it as his own. Consequently it follows that without this, as it were, living appearance, man would not have any conjunction with God, and so neither any eternal life. But if as a result of this appearance he persuades himself to the belief that he wills, thinks, and thus does good of himself, and not from the Lord (even though to all appearance as though of himself), he turns good into evil in him, and so creates in him the origin of evil. This was Adam's sin. (CL 444)

Looking to the Lord and attributing all good to Him protects us from falling into Adam's sin, and this, the more so as we remain conscious of this attribution in all our willing and thinking all day long. A general declaration that all good is the Lord's is necessary but not sufficient. We must make that declaration to ourselves in our mind many times in a single hour! The angels do so second by second so to speak (AC 1038).

Moral life may be lived either for the sake of the Divine or for the sake of men in the world; and a moral life that is lived for the sake of the Divine is a spiritual life. In outward form the

Moses, Paul, and Swedenborg

two appear alike, but in inward form they are entirely different; the one saves a man, the other does not. For he who lives a moral life for the sake of the Divine is led by the Divine; while he who leads a moral life for the sake of men in the world is led by himself. (HH 319)

Bibliography and Notes

All articles listed are by Leon James except where otherwise noted. Each article on the Web has links to others, in a cumulative pattern.

1) For a linked topical directory giving access to all articles relating Swedenborg, see the Swedenborg Theistic Science Glossary available on the Web at: www.soc.hawaii.edu/leonj/leonj/leonpsy/instructor/gloss.html

2) A linked list of all my journal publications may be found at: www.soc.hawaii.edu/leonj/leonj/leonpsy/leonpublish.html

3) Access to the Swedenborg Hawaii Web site is at www.soc.hawaii.edu/leonj/leonj/leonpsy/instructor/swedenborg.html

4) A linked directory of online articles is available at: www.soc.hawaii.edu/leonj/leonj/leonpsy/leonarticles.html

5) A directory of Swedenborg's Writings and collateral books available full text at: www.soc.hawaii.edu/leonj/leonj/leonpsy/instructor/gloss/abbrev.html

6) Full text access with search capability, of all of Swedenborg's Writings is available online at:www.theheavenlydoctrines.org

7) Overcoming Objections to Swedenborg's Writings Through the Development of Scientific Dualism (1998). (Published in New Philosophy, 2001, v.CIV n.3 & 4 pp. 153-217.) Article available on the Web at: www.soc.hawaii.edu/leonj/leonj/leonpsy/instructor/np98.html

8) Substantive Dualism: Swedenborg's Integration of Biological Theology and Rational Psychology (1985). Article available on the Web at: www.soc.hawaii.edu/leonj/leonj/leonpsy/instructor/dualism.html

9) Spiritual Psychology Based on the Writings of Swedenborg (2003).. Article available at:www.soc.hawaii.edu/leonj/spiritual-psychology.html

10) Spiritual Psychology (1985). Article available on the Web at:

www.soc.hawaii.edu/leonj/leonj/leonpsy/instructor/gloss/spirpsy.html

11) Theistic Science: An Introduction (1990). Article available on the Web at:
www.soc.hawaii.edu/leonj/leonj/leonpsy/instructor/gloss/theistic.html

12) See also Dr. Ian Thompson's related articles on his Theistic Science Web site at:www.TheisticScience.org

13) Spiritual Geography--Part 1--Graphic Maps of Consciousness for Regeneration (2000). Available on the Web at:
www.soc.hawaii.edu/leonj/leonj/leonpsy/instructor/gloss/geography.html

14) The Horizontal and Vertical Communities of our Dual Citizenship:
www.soc.hawaii.edu/leonj/499ss99/man/citizenship.html

15) *A Man of the Field: Forming The New Church Mind in Today's World.*(2002) (Volume 1: *Reformation: The Struggle Against Nonduality*; Volume 2: *Enlightenment : The Spiritual Sense of the Writings*; Volume 3: *Regeneration: Spiritual Disciplines For Daily Life*; Volume 4: Uses: The New Church Mind In Old Age (in preparation) All three volumes available on the Web at: www.soc.hawaii.edu/leonj/nonduality.html

16) The Genes of Consciousness: Spiritual Genetics for Regeneration (1997). Available on the Web at: www.soc.hawaii.edu/leonj/leonj/leonpsy/instructor/gloss/harmonizing4.htm
www.soc.hawaii.edu/leonj/leonj/leonpsy/instructor/gloss/harmonizing3.htm

17) De Hemelsche Leer Articles: Methodological Tools for Extracting The Doctrine of the Church (2001). Available on the Web at:
www.soc.hawaii.edu/leonj/leonj/leonpsy/instructor/gloss/dhl.html
www.soc.hawaii.edu/leonj/leonj/leonpsy/instructor/gloss/dhl3.html

18) The Doctrine of the Wife for Husbands: A Spiritual Practice for Achieving Unity (1999). Available on the Web at: www.soc.hawaii.edu/leonj/leonj/leonpsy/instructor/gloss/wife.html

19) When We Discovered Swedenborg. (1981). Available on the Web at:
www.soc.hawaii.edu/leonj/leonj/leonpsy/instructor/gloss/conversion.html

20) The Coming Swedenborgian Revolution In The Social Sciences And Humanities (1982). Available on the Web at: www.soc.hawaii.edu/leonj/499s98/shintani/logos.html

21) Religious Psychology or Theistic Science. (1984) Available on the Web at: www.soc.hawaii.edu/leonj/499ss99/man/religious.html

22) Temptations and Spiritual Psychology (1996). Available on the Web at: www.soc.hawaii.edu/leonj/leonj/leonpsy/instructor/gloss/spirpsy3.html#temptation s

23) Bryn Athyn: The City of Levites in the New Canaan (2003). Article available on the Web at:www.soc.hawaii.edu/leonj/brynathyn.htm

24) Article entry for *New Church* in the Swedenborg Glossary (1997). Available on the Web at: www.soc.hawaii.edu/leonj/leonj/leonpsy/instructor/gloss/newchurch.html

25) Article entry for *Regeneration* in the Swedenborg Glossary (1997). Available on the Web at: www.soc.hawaii.edu/leonj/leonj/leonpsy/instructor/gloss/regen.html

26) The Ennead Matrix (1990). Article available on the Web at: www.soc.hawaii.edu/leonj/leonj/leonpsy/instructor/gloss/ennead.html

27) Article entry for Correspondences in the Swedenborg Glossary (1997). Available on the Web at: www.soc.hawaii.edu/leonj/leonj/leonpsy/instructor/gloss/correspondences.html

28) DrDriving's site on Road Rage and Aggressive Driving – List of Interviews www.DrDriving.org/about

Appendix:
Diagnostic Test of Rational Spirituality 100 Items

The **purpose** of this test is to help you to critically examine your thinking about spiritual topics. These include:

- What or who is GodWhat is heaven and hellWhat happens when we dieWhat are spirits and can we communicate with them
- What are angels and devils and do they affect us
- Why God allows evil in the worldWhat is sin, rebirth, reformation, regeneration, and salvation
- What is the importance and role of revelationCan there be a science of God from God about GodWhat is love, good, truth, and wisdom
- What is spiritual enlightenment and higher consciousness
- What is the role of marriage in creation and the future
- What is the relation between the finite and infinite
- What is the relation between the natural and spiritual or supernaturalAre miracles real

Instructions:

For each question, select the alternative that is closest to your current thinking by circling the appropriate choice on the **Answer Sheet** below. Then rate the description you selected in terms of how much confidence you have that this view is correct by writing in one of the numbers on the **Answer Sheet** next to the choice you selected:

Uncertain 1.. 2.. 3.. 4 ..5.. 6.. 7.. 8.. 9.. 10 ..11.. 12 Absolutely certain

This test has 100 items and many of them require reflection. To minimize fatigue or boredom I recommend that you take several sessions to complete it.

Use the **Answer Key** given below to figure out your score. The score reflects your dominant level of thinking regarding spiritual subjects. Each question has three alternative answers and each alternative reflects one of the three ideologies of rational spirituality – phase 1 ideology, phase 2 ideology, phase 3 ideology. These three phases are explained in the

Moses, Paul, and Swedenborg

book.

The **Answer Sheet** allows you to circle the alternative that most closely represents your way of thinking about that topic. When you complete the test, you can lay your Answer Sheet next to the **Answer Key**. You can then circle the phase of the alternative you selected for each item. You then count the number of answers you selected from each of the three phases. That's your score. It is made up of three numbers. Instructions on how to interpret your score are given on the Answer Key below.

For each of the 100 questions, circle the alternative that best represents your thinking on the topic. Then write a number 1 to 12 in the box next to it to indicate your rating of certainty. Answer every question. When in doubt, pick the best possible answer for you. Scoring instructions and an explanation of how to interpret your score, appear at the end of the test items.

ANSWER SHEET

For each of the 100 questions, circle the alternative (a, b, c) that best represents your thinking on the topic. Then write a number 1 to 12 in the box next to it to indicate your rating of certainty.

Answer every question. When in doubt, pick the best possible answer for you. Scoring instructions and an explanation of how to interpret your score, appear at the end of the test items.

1. a b c	21. a b c	41. a b c	61. a b c	81. a b c
2. a b c	22. a bc	42. a b c	62. a b c	82. a b c
3. a b c	23. a bc	43. a b c	63. a b c	83. a b c
4. a b c	24. a b c	44. a b c	64. a b c	84. a b c
5. a b c	25. a b c	45. a b c	65. a b c	85. a b c

6. a b c	26. a b c	46. a b c	66. a b c	86. a b c
7. a b c	27. a b c	47. a b c	67. a b c	87. a b c
8. a b c	28. a b c	48. a b c	68. a b c	88. a b c
9. a b c	29. a b c	49. a b c	69. a b c	89. a b c
10. a b c	30. a b c	50. a b c	70. a b c	90. a b c
11. a b c	31. a b c	51. a b c	71. a b c	91. a b c
12. a b c	32. a b c	52. a b c	72. a b c	92. a b c
13. a b c	33. a b c	53. a b c	73. a b c	93. a b c
14. a b c	34. a b c	54. a b c	74. a b c	94. a b c
15. a b c	35. a bc	55. a b c	75. a b c	95. a b c
16. a b c	36. a b c	56. a b c	76. a b c	96. a b c
17. a b c	37. a b c	57. a b c	77. a b c	97. a b c
18. a b c	38. a b c	58. a b c	78. a b c	98. a b c
19. a b c	39. a b c	59. a b c	79. a b c	99. a b c
20. a b c	40. a b c	60. a b c	80. a b c	100. a b c

Questions

1. What is your view on immortality?

a. Every human being is immortal. Upon death of the physical body the individual awakens in the world of spirits to continue life in a spirit-body that is immortal.

b. In the future, prolonging life by artificial means could postpone death indefinitely. In this sense we are potentially immortal.

c. Immortality is the gift of resurrection and eternal life for all those who have faith in the Lord as the Savior and have thereby been declared righteous in the eyes of the Father.

Moses, Paul, and Swedenborg

2. Where is the mind of a human being?

a. The mind of a human being could not exist anywhere in the natural world, but exists in the spiritual world only. Hence we are born dual citizens – our physical body on earth, which is attached to our mind in the world of spirits.

b. The mind is in the brain but the spirit is with God. Upon death, the body and the spirit are separated, but then reunited at the universal resurrection.

c. The mind is an emergent epiphenomenon of the brain's evolutionary activity. If you destroy the brain, the mind is also destroyed.

3. What happens when we die?

a. When the physical body dies, the immortal mind awakens a few hours later in a spirit-body that lives forever in either heaven or hell.

b. When we die, the brain stops functioning and the entire body disintegrates, returning to its originating elements. The mind cannot survive without this body.

c. When we die, it is only temporary until some future time when things are ripe on earth, and all who died will awaken and begin again a new life, repopulating the earth under better conditions than before.

4. What determines your fate in the afterlife?

a. If there is an afterlife people's fate there would no doubt depend on their intelligence and skills of survival.

b. Your faith determines whether you're going to heaven or hell.

c. Your character determines whether you're going to heaven or hell.

5. Is sex possible in heaven?

a. In heaven we do not have a sensuous body capable of eating or engaging in sexual activity. We are then more like angels than people on earth.

b. Upon death of the physical body, we awaken in a spirit-body which is even better equipped for a sensuous life, including sexual activity. However, this is not a material physical-sensuous experience but a substantive spiritual-sensuous experience.

c. Sex is a physical activity, and without a physical body sex cannot exist.

6. Is sex possible in hell?
a. Those in hell do not have a sensuous body capable of sexual activity. They have a spirit that is afire with lusts that cannot be satisfied and for which they are tormented.

b. Sexual activity in the afterlife depends on possessing a spirit-body equipped with the five senses and its organs. Those entering the afterlife who bring with them a character of evil loves, enter the life of hell. All bodily acts are therefore possible there, including sexual activity.

c. Sex is a physical activity, and without a physical body sex cannot exist. Hell is what you feel here on earth when you're depressed or in agony, or when you're tormented with bad luck and failure. In that sense you can have sex in hell.

7. Angels are people from earth who made it to heaven.
a. True

b. False

c. It's not possible to know

8. Devils are people from earth who ended up in hell.
a. True

b. False

c. It's not possible to know

Moses, Paul, and Swedenborg

9. There are many heavens, one for each religion

a. True

b. False

c. It's not possible to know

10. What is most crucial to our salvation?

a. The right faith

b. The right character

c. The right deeds

11. Consciousness raising and spiritual progress is accomplished most by:

a. By practicing of the right physical and mental disciplines

b. By experiencing ecstatic union with God

c. By accumulating genuine truths in the understanding and goods in the will

12. What is heaven and hell?

a. Heaven and hell are operations in the human mind maintained by our chief love and affections.

b. Heaven is the Kingdom of God on earth restored to its glory. Hell is the prison of the damned.

c. When you feel great, you're in heaven. When you're depressed, you're in hell.

13. There is a natural world and a spiritual world.

a. True

b. It depends on your assumptions

c. The spiritual realm is the holy and the Divine. God is a Spirit, and so is the Holy Spirit, as well as angels and Cherubim; also the devil.

14. When we die we eventually return to earth for another life, until it is no longer necessary for us to do so.

a. An awful lot of people have thought this for millennia so there must be some truth in it.

b. There is no returning to earth once we are cut off from this world and enter the afterlife where we pursue life to eternity.

c. This may be true for some individuals in special cases like Elijah who returned as John the Baptist.

15. Is God Divine and Human or only Divine?

a. God is only Divine while humans are Divine only when they reach their highest self

b. God is Divine and we are human

c. God is Human as well as Divine

16. How do you see the relation between God and human beings?

a. God is in every human being, hence we can meaningfully say "the God in me greets the God in you"

b. Nothing that is Divine can belong to a human being, though we can be conjoined to God through love and truth received in our mind

c. God is far above human beings though some people can be saintly enough to be nearer to God than most.

17. On the relation between God and human beings:

a. God inflows into every human being with love and truth

b. God is part of every human being

c. God dwells in every human being

18. What's the difference between natural matter and spiritual substance?
a. Matter is more fixed; substance is more fluid

b. Matter is in space-time; substance is not

c. There is no essential difference, though there may be surface differences

19. Which assertion about planets represents more nearly your own view?
a. Most planets do not support human life, but some might. Space exploration will provide a valid answer.

b. Life was created on this planet. In the coming future, all planets and stars will be destroyed and a new Kingdom of God will arise with those who are saved, and it is going to last forever.

c. An endless number of planets are constantly being created to support a human population that can prepare itself for heaven.

20. What is consciousness?
a. Consciousness is the indwelling of the Holy Spirit when we are receptive

b. Conscious awareness is a higher order emergent epiphenomenon

c. Consciousness is the elevation of the mind into rational perception when we receive truth

21. What are the parts of the human mind?
a. Spirit, truth, and love

b. Natural mind, rational mind, and spiritual mind

c. Cortex, cerebellum, and brain stem

22. What is a discrete degree "within"?
a. What is within is above, higher, and superior in rationality

b. What is within is more mystical and less rational

c. What is within something is revealed by structural and chemical analysis

23. What produces consciousness in the mind?
a. Emergent evolutionary capacity

b. Miraculous gift of life and love

c. Rational understanding of Divine Truth

24. What is the meaning of the assertion: "Heaven is within you."
a. Heaven is a poetic reference to an imaginary utopia of happiness and immortality

b. Heaven is a state of mind that is fully receptive of the Lord's love and truth

c. Heaven is the Kingdom of the Lord to which are admitted those who are saved by their faith in His sacrifice

25. What is the meaning of the assertion: "Hell is within you."
a. Hell is a state of mind when we turn ourselves away from the Lord's love and truth

b. Hell is a poetic reference to an imaginary place of torture and despair

c. Hell is the punishment of the damned

26. How many layers or levels of heavens are there?
a. Natural Heaven, Spiritual Heaven, and Celestial Heaven

b. Imaginary heavens in potentially endless layers

c. One Heaven under One God

27. Which reasoning is closest to your own thinking?

a. The idea of higher and lower heavens is discriminatory of some people, which God does not do, and therefore all faithful believers who are sincere and good, are in one Heaven under God

b. All social groupings must have status differentiation of members based on power and influence

c. Heaven is not a reward or an honor, but a state of mind or character, some of which are good but simple minded, while others are good and wise. Therefore the good and wise are in a higher heaven than the good and simple.

28. The idea of "hell forever" is controversial. Which reasoning is nearest to your own thinking?

a. It is repugnant to suppose that a loving and omnipotent God could keep people in hell forever, no matter what they did before getting there. Hell is a place of purification from evils that we picked up along the way, and when it is done, we emerge from hell

b. God allows people in hell to exit by giving up their injurious intentions, but they stubbornly refuse, even to eternity, testifying to the truth of the expression "I rather rot in hell forever"

c. The idea of "hell forever" testifies to the depth of depravity of the human psyche

29. What does spiritual salvation consist of?

a. Salvation is by means of sincere faith in the cleansing power of the blood of Christ

b. Salvation is by means of progressive character reformation from evil to good

c. Salvation is by means of religious piety sincerely performed until death

Moses, Paul, and Swedenborg

30. Is doing "good works" and "charity" necessary for salvation?
a. Salvation is achieved when we reform our character from evil to good, by daily struggles with our temptations, made effective by relying on God

b. Salvation is by sincerity of faith, not by changing our sinful nature

c. Altruism counteracts selfishness and benefits society, insuring its survival

31. What is the relationship between truth and love?
a. Love is immediate in experience while truth is more abstract

b. Love is within truth, and therefore truth is the outside form by which love manifests itself

c. With a sincere person, love and truth are both from the heart

32. Are there different types of truth?
a. There is natural truth, spiritual truth, and celestial truth

b. Truth from God is unitary, not varied

c. Truth is drawing correct conclusions after considering all the facts

33. What is scientific dualism?
a. The premise that there are two separate and interacting worlds, natural and spiritual, with God creating and managing both

b. A contradiction in terms since dualism refers to God or spirit, which is outside the purview of science

c. The theory that consciousness is an emergent phenomenon from brain evolution

34. What is theistic science?
a. The attempt to turn science into religion, or to blur the differences

b. Scientific dualism in which God's role in every phenomenon is explained by means of scientific revelations given through the Word

c. An intellectual movement in the history of science that ended with the modern era in science

35. What is the Threefold Word in which God gave us scientific revelations?
a. The Word of God is Sacred Scripture -- Old and New Testaments

b. If it's the Word of God, it is about religious revelations, not science

c. The Threefold Word is The Hebrew Word, the Greek Word, and the Latin Word

36. What is the relative standing between religion and science?
a. Religion is above science

b. The two cannot be compared in this way

c. True Science, which is from the Threefold Word, is above religion

37. *Can atheistic scientists be rational?*
a. Yes -- atheistic science has done well in its own sphere of civilization and technology, due to the rationality of scientistsb. God does not intervene in the experiments of scientists but lets natural laws govern the resultsc. No -- the success of atheistic science and engineering was brought about by Divine Providence despite the lack of rationality of atheistic science

38. What does it mean that Swedenborg had a dual consciousness?
a. That he was capable of trance like states during which he was possessed by spirits.

b. That he was consciously aware of what went on around him in the natural world and in the spiritual world.

c. That he developed the ability to be consciously awake in his visionary states.

39. Did Swedenborg's exploration of the spiritual world include scientific experiments he conducted while there?

a. No. Scientific experiments are conducted in the natural world.

b. Yes. He had the assistance of angels to introduce experimental states in spirits, and then observe the consequences, and this repeatedly.

c. The departed in spirit are in the Lord and are not involved in scientific research.

40. What kind of information about the spiritual world did Swedenborg report in the Writings?

a. Subjective personal accounts

b. Objective empirical observations

c. Interpretive descriptions of spiritual visions

41. Can God be a legitimate concept in scientific explanations?

a. Yes because the universe is a global system acting as a whole, which can be described by more and more abstract principles. These super-abstractions give rise to the idea of God, and in that sense, God is an appropriate concept to use.

b. Yes because God provides scientific revelations of Himself and His rational methods of achieving creation and management it.

c. No because God is beyond scientific description. To try to describe God by science is to turn God from an infinite Spirit, into a finite natural thing.

42. Can the Writings be considered True Science?

a. Religious revelations are for people's salvation and not for science. They may contain scientific references used for illustrating theological points, not for science.

b. Yes, the Writings contain scientific revelations about how God created the universe and how He manages it by means of rational laws that are observable and verifiable.

c. The only "true science" is the entire enterprise of science by which it progressively gets more and more exact and Inclusive, advancing by spurts, changing directions, always pursuing truth.

43. Can the Lord appear to people again in the natural world as He did before?
a. Yes

b. No

c. No one can know such a thing.

44. Is it rational to think that there is a Trinity of Three Divine Persons?
a. A valid definition of God awaits further scientific progress on explaining the universe as an integrated system. It is possible that a "Trinitarian" system of super-abstractions can act as one.

b. It is not rational because "three persons" cannot be one person, and therefore three Divine Persons cannot be One Divine Person. The Trinity refers to God's three Divine Aspects as Creator, Redeemer, and Regenerator.

c. The Trinity is a Divine mystery that cannot be rationally comprehended. Our faith is that Three Divine Persons constitute one Godhead.

45. When is the Second Coming of Christ supposed to take place?
a. The Second Coming of Christ will take place after this world goes through the tribulations of the end times and a new Kingdom on earth is established by the Lord composed of all the saved.

b. The Second Coming of Christ refers to a new evolutionary step in human consciousness, as evidenced by the New Age of post-modernism and universal spirituality which have started but have not reached their maturity.

Moses, Paul, and Swedenborg

c. The Second Coming of Christ has already happened in the Writings of Swedenborg, written in the 18th century.

46. Is there a sun in the spiritual world?

a. No, we have no need of any sun since the Lord supplies us with all we need.

b. That information is not available.

c. Yes, but it is made of love and wisdom, not material fire.

47. Can other religions possibly adopt the Writings as a revealed science book about God?

a. Yes, all religions can ultimately accept the Writings as a book of True Science, though they would certainly not be able to see that fact today.

b. No, since the Writings are a religious revelation, not scientific. To adopt the Writings means to become a New Church Christian.

c. Books that talk about God are religious books and every religion insists on their own books.

48. Compare the rationality of theistic and atheistic science.

a. Materialistic science is atheistic, but it is rational even though it doesn't try to bring God into its explanations. It is rational as long as it sticks to natural phenomena.

b. Materialistic science is atheistic in the traditional sense of God, but not so in the sense of rational super-abstractions in universal system theory.

c. Theistic science, or scientific dualism, is rational while materialistic science, or scientific monism, is not rational since atheism is not rational, and materialistic science is atheistic.

49. If God is omnipotent, why does He allow evil in His creation?

a. There are forces of evil or fallen angels that struggle against God.

b. Evil is not really evil but a perspective on the world.

c. God allows certain evils, but not others, depending on when He can turn the evil to people's ultimate benefit.

50. What happens to the Divine power God gives us to be able to plan and execute tasks?

a. The Divine power is given as a gift of Grace to be appropriated for ourselves.

b. The Divine power remains God's power in us and never becomes ours.

c. The Divine power in us makes that part of us Divine and God-like.

51. Why does God give people the power to ignore Him and deny His existence?

a. Evil forces act against God and the minds of people against Him.

b. God keeps people in spiritual freedom. If we are given the power to acknowledge God we must also have the power to deny God.

c. God strives to be acknowledged, knocking to be admitted, but the Holy Spirit has no power where He is not wanted.

52. There is a controversy about whether or not the Writings have an inner sense. Which best represents your position?

a. The Writings say that the Word has a literal sense understood by all, and an inner spiritual sense understood by those who know correspondences and are enlightened by the Lord in accordance with their progress in regeneration. Therefore since the Writings are the Word, they have an inner sense.

b. The Old and New Testaments have an internal sense because they are Sacred Scripture, but the Writings are the Heavenly Doctrine, a Divine rational revelation whose literal sense is already spiritual, and hence it doesn't need an internal sense like the Old and New Testaments. The Writings are the Word as Heavenly Doctrine, but they are not the Word as Sacred Scripture.

c. Possibly, but it has to be proven first before one can know for sure.

53. Is it possible to prove that the Bible is Divine?
a. No, since it requires spiritual faith rather than proof.

b. Yes, by using correspondences to demonstrate the existence of an orderly internal semantic series from Genesis to Revelations, showing that the historical events were brought about by Divine Providence to convey the internal series to our understanding, by which we might be regenerated.

c. No, because it was written by human beings!

54. What are demons?
a. Demons are people living in hell whose evil loves God brings into our mind to keep us in spiritual freedom, balanced in decision making between them, on the one hand, and the other, the people in heaven whose good loves He simultaneously brings into our mind. Thus we have spiritual freedom to choose.

b. Demons are fallen angels who have turned against God and try to lead people to evil.

c. Demons are bad characters in people's imaginations.

55. What is the difference in the mentality of the Old and New Testaments?
a. They have the same mentality since they are both the Divine Word of God given for the salvation of the human race.

b. OT mentality is several centuries older than NT mentality, and this is reflected in the details of the historical narratives.

c. OT mentality is sectarian and literalistic, and prescribes ritual worship, while the NT mentality is inclusive and spiritual, and prescribes inner worship.

56. What role do temptations play in regeneration?

a. By means of temptations the Lord brings our evils to our attention and gives us the power to shun them.

b. Temptations are trials God brings to us in order to test our faith and to strengthen it.

c. Temptations are states of motivational conflict, usually involving the desire to do something and the fear of the taboo associated with it.

57. Miracles are of two kind, covert and overt. Overt miracles include healing or controlling the physical elements. Covert miracles include "lucky" events and success stories. Explain the difference.

a. Overt miracles are being witnessed today every day by both individuals and groups. People pray for their child to be healed, or for rain for the crop, and they get it. Without that prayer would the child be healed or the rain fall? Evangelists on TV and in large audiences of thousands perform miracles of healing every week. Miracles prove the presence of the Holy Spirit, so miracles abound with those who have faith, and may even be steadily increasing. The Lord promised that we shall perform miracles like He has, and we are. The Lord channels the power of healing to individuals to whom He gives that gift. The Lord listens to the prayers of the people in Church and the lonely individual alone in a desert.

b. All so called miracles are actually natural phenomena and those that cannot be explained have not been established as having taken place. There is a difference between "reporting a miracle" and a miracle "actually happening." The easiest way for God to resolve all this doubt about His existence is to simply appear before us and give proof that He is above natural laws and that He controls them at will. Or He could take a group of trusted scientists and transfer them to Heaven, preferably with video cameras. Then they can be returned and tell the world.

c. Overt miracles produced by the Lord are described frequently in the Old and New Testaments. Their purpose was to strengthen the people's faith, and for this they needed physical proof. This is called developing a "sensuous consciousness" of God. After the Lord left earth to ascend to Heaven, He gave the Holy Spirit as proof of God's presence with every individual. This is called "rational consciousness" of God. In the new age of the Holy Spirit overt miracles have not been allowed because physical proof of God's presence injures the further development of rational consciousness of God. This is what's needed to prepare the mind for heaven and therefore the Lord now only produces covert miracles.

58. Paul declared that works do not save, but faith in the Lord saves. Which of these three explanations is closest to your view?
a. Paul argued that no one can keep from sinning and therefore everyone stands guilty before God's Justice. It is useless to try to keep every commandment, for no one can. Instead we must rely on receiving the merit of Jesus who was sacrificed for the atonement of everybody's sins. This attribution of the merit of Jesus to all sinners, is what saves. Therefore we are to rely on our faith in the saving power of the blood of Jesus and not on any attempt to keep all the commandments.

b. Faith is the power of the human mind to strengthen and comfort people. Works refers to altruism and obedience. These are more external rewards compared to the power of faith. Hence Paul was warning people that faith is more powerful than their struggle to be good.

c. Paul was referring to the Mosaic Laws of ritual sacrifice commanded by Jehovah to the people of Israel for the atonement of their sins. With the Coming of the Lord into the world, these former laws were no longer effective for the atonement of sins. Instead, faith in the Lord is the new way to salvation. Paul was not referring to the Ten Commandments, which were reinforced by Jesus and still apply to all Christians. Therefore unless we obey the Ten Commandments, in the letter and in the spirit, we cannot be saved regardless of our faith.

59. Why did Jesus pray to His Father since the Father and He were one, as it is written in the New Testament?
a. Jesus was the Son of God from eternity, now come down on earth and stuck in a frail human body. Whenever He was in need, He prayed to His Father Jehovah, the Creator, to receive strength and comfort, which the Father in Heaven gave Him as often as Jesus needed it.

b. Many people pray in an attempt to feel better when they are scared or depressed, especially people who are very religious oriented, like Jesus was.

c. Jehovah God Himself incarnated as Jesus. In this frail human form, God was temporarily divided between Himself as the infinite invisible Father, and Himself as the finite visible Jesus. Jesus was praying to Himself as the Father from within whenever He was in temptation and felt blinded and cut off from His inner Divine. But after Glorification,

Moses, Paul, and Swedenborg

Resurrection, and Ascension, the visible Jesus and the invisible Father were united as one, like soul, mind, and body are one within one person.

60. What's the relation between the Epistles in the New Testament and the Gospels?

a. The Gospels and the Book of Revelations are the Word of the New Testament, while the Book of Acts and the Epistles are the doctrinal commentaries that provide a rational understanding of the Gospels in relation to the Old Testament.

b. The Gospels, Book of Acts, the Epistles, and Book of Revelations together form the Word of the New Testament.

c. The Epistles, especially those of Paul to the Churches, show how the early Church solidified its hold over Christians and is a valuable historical document.

61. How do you resolve the fact that Jesus loved one disciple (John) more than another? Does God have favorites?

a. John's personality was more pleasing to Jesus so He could love John more than Peter or James or the rest. God loves everyone but some people have a special relationship with God.

b. Jesus loved the disciples equally and it's only an appearance that he made distinctions. The distinctions Jesus made were not based on merit but on reciprocal love. It is John who loved the Lord more than the others, hence Jesus could give John more love that the other disciples could receive.

c. In every group you have distinctions of leadership and followers. John was evidently a leader who was closer to the chain of command than the other disciples who followed Jesus on a regular basis.

62. If you were to describe the hierarchical organization of heaven, which alternative would be closest to your thinking?

a. Heaven is a place in the clouds of glory around the Throne of God where He is constantly worshipped by Cherubim, angels, and saints. The closest are the Cherubim, then the Principal angels, then the lesser angels and saints.

b. There is a diversity of heavens, each suitable for the genius of its inhabitants. Within each heaven there is a diversity of citizenry, some who are in governmental positions of leadership in the community. These activities reflect the mind of those who are there.

c. People in heaven are not distinguished in rank, with one person being a prince or governor, while others being ordinary citizens, or with one city in heaven being higher in rank than another.

63. Compare the effectiveness of communal vs. individual prayer.

a. Many people believe in the power of prayer. If prayer releases some power that alters the events, then it makes sense to think that group prayer would be more effective, and especially if the number of people involved is large or very large.

b. Prayer cannot be thought of as effective or not effective. Prayer cannot influence God's decisions. God wants us to pray because by praying we don't ignore Him and He can give us more goods and truths.

c. Communal prayers of intercession in Church gatherings are more effective than individual prayer for oneself. A group of worshippers is more pleasing to God than a single worshipper, which is why worshippers who share the same belief seek each other out and congregate together.

64. What is your view on the controversy as to whether the Writings have an inner sense hidden by the code of correspondences?

a. The Writings are Sacred Scripture or the Word, and therefore they have an inner sense like the Old and New Testaments. The Writings make a one with the Old and New Testaments, and the three collections together make up the Threefold Word. The Old Testament makes up the legs, the New Testament is the torso, and the Writings are the head or crown.

b. The Writings are the inner sense of the Old and New Testaments. The Writings are the Heavenly Doctrines that rationally reveal the spiritual sense of the Old and New

Testaments. Therefore they themselves do not have an internal sense.

c. The Writings are a rational revelation and the more we study it, the deeper we can understand it. This depth of understanding distinguishes individuals so that some understand more deeply than others. This deeper meaning is hidden from the eyes of those whose understanding is not as deep.

65. Explain the ennead matrix of rational spirituality.

a. Don't know what it is.

b. It is a matrix depicting a diversity of cultural practices in spiritual behavior, including secular humanism, but excluding materialistic science.

c. It depicts three phases of development in rational spirituality, each phase with three sequential states, forming nine evolutionary zones or developmental steps.

66. Why does God want us to pray? Does that influence Him?

a. No, God cannot be influenced by prayers. He commands us to pray for our sake, that we may make Him part of our life, which allows Him to elevates us.

b. Yes, God is influenced by our prayers if we ask it sincerely and unselfishly. He wants us to pray for the sake of His Glory, because He is Holy. He can then reward us with what we ask of Him.

c. It is not God who wants us to pray, but we want to pray to Him in order to feel better about what's happening to us.

67. Can God love an unrepentant sinner?

a. God knows in advance who will end up in heaven and who in hell, and therefore he loves the former but hates the latter.

b. God hates sin therefore when we sin and do not repent He turns away and cannot love us.

Moses, Paul, and Swedenborg

c. God loves us even when we sin and do not repent, but then He cannot make us happy and wise like angels.

68. Who or what is the devil?

a. The devil is the snake in paradise, a liar who deceived Adam and Eve. He reappears in other places as well to tempt people and cause them to sin by misleading them through their weaknesses and vices.

b. The devil is a force in the universe that opposes God's order and strives to create chaos where there should be order.

c. The devil is collective word for all the people who inhabit the hells. God gives them the power to influence the minds of people on earth who hold on to lusts and false beliefs.

69. If there are layers of heaven, what's the lower heaven like?

a. The lower heaven is for lesser saints while the upper heaven is for greater saints. At certain occasions however, the lower and higher heaven get together to sing and give glory to God. Whichever heaven one belongs to, God's love for us is always perfect.

b. The lower heaven is for people with less developed intelligence who are not capable of understanding God at the same level as the people of the higher heavens, nor to love Him to the same degree. For example, people in the lower heaven are occupied with science, art, government, sports, conferences, and business, while people in the upper heavens do not care for these activities.

c. The lower heaven is for adults who grew up on earth. The higher heaven is for the children who died and are now with the angels. The heaven of the children is like a playground while the heaven of the adults is like a temple.

70. Who was Swedenborg?

a. Emanuel Swedenborg was a Swedish mystic and theologian who produced an elaborate system of Christianity that eliminates the Trinity and makes Jesus to be the Father. He claimed to have visions of heaven and hell and was possessed of many spirits. Followers of

Moses, Paul, and Swedenborg

Swedenborg call themselves the New Church. They believe that the Second Coming of Christ has already occurred.

b. Emanuel Swedenborg was a Swedish scientist commissioned by the Lord to write the third and final portion of the Threefold Word. The Lord introduced him into dual consciousness – natural and spiritual -- so that he could interview many people who passed on and now live in heaven or in hell. He talked to King David, the Virgin Mary, Aristotle, Newton, and many others including devils and angels. He wrote a lot of it down and published it in a collection called the Writings.

c. Emanuel Swedenborg (1688-1782) was a Swedish scientist who became a spiritist at age 57 and acquired psychic powers to see events at a great distance and to communicate with people in the spiritual world and on other planets. He also claimed to be able to talk to God. Some contemporary psychiatrists have analyzed Swedenborg's claims and have labeled him a genius with multiple psychosis.

71. True Science refers to the science of God, that is, the science revealed in the Threefold Word. What is your view on it?

a. True Science is now being created by the Lord. It is the knowledge about reality that we can extract from the Threefold Word using the rules of extraction specified in the Writings. Scientific revelations are necessary to allow the human race to develop along the path of rational spirituality by giving people on earth facts and information about the spiritual world and how it influences the natural.

b. The existence of True Science depends on the claim that the Writings of Swedenborg contain scientific revelations. Although they contain scientific illustrations, these are not the main point, which is theological and spiritual. "Scientific" does not normally extend to the theological and spiritual, which are not considered scientific fields.

c. True Science as the "science of God" is not an idea many scientists can accept today. The idea that God intervenes in reality is not supported by science which shows that phenomena are caused by specifiable conditions, consistently repeatable and predictable. If this is the "science of God" then how is it different from the science of man?

72. The three developmental steps of rational spirituality can appropriately be labeled Ritual Faith (1), Mystic Faith (2), and Rational Faith (3). Describe their differences.

a. Ritual faith is first because it is pre-scientific and superstitious. Then comes mystic faith which is experiential and non-analytical. Finally comes rational faith which is leaving behind superstition and mysticism for the sake of rationality. However, since rationality and spirituality are operations in different directions of the human mind, faith and rationality break apart, and what's left behind is either rationality and science or faith and religion. Both of these can be present in one individual, though not simultaneously but by alternating turns.

b. Ritual faith is the lowest because it consists of an external idea of God who is seen as responding to our communal worship. Mystic faith is more internal because the locus of interaction with God is through thoughts and emotions, rather than through rituals of worship and external conduct. Rational faith is the highest or inmost because it is based on a scientific understanding of the interaction laws between God and our thinking and willing operations.

c. Ritual faith is the underpinning of faith, consisting of the Sacraments and the prayers of the people. Mystic faith is deeper because it involves giving assent to the mysteries of the Trinity and the Cross. Rational faith goes still further because it is the full acceptance of the mysteries and miracles of faith without feeling a strain in one's perspective on the universe.

73. Define God.

a. God is the invisible infinite Father Creator who sees all and does all. No one can see God for God is not here or there, but everywhere. God is unchanging, forever the same from Alpha to Omega.

b. God is a visible Person who has once been seen on earth and is seen in heaven every day. In this visible Divine Human Person there exists an infinity of love and wisdom that create, sustain, and manage all finite things.

c. God is the all in the universe. God is this and God is that. Nothing is that is not God. Everything that is, is God, and what is not God, is not anything.

Moses, Paul, and Swedenborg

74. What are the consequences of sinning?

a. Sin is defined somewhat differently in every religion. The common idea is that God gives commandments and specifies what punishment goes with breaking them. God also prescribes remedies for sinners, which consist in rituals of purification, sacrifice, and prayer. God is placated by these demonstrations of contrition and forgives the sinner.

b. Every sin brings inevitable spiritual death to the sinner. The only deliverance is resurrection to a new life in the Holy Spirit. This new life is received by anyone who sincerely acknowledges that Jesus died for his or her sins, so that the entire human race is now reconciled to the Father forever by the sacrifice of His Son on the Cross.

c. No one is punished for their sins, but every sin has its own built in punishment that remains attached to the sinner and inevitably leads to hell. The only deliverance is by the death of the old character through our victories in temptations, followed by the birth of a new character that is received from the Lord and takes us to heaven.

75. Compare humans and animals with respect to immortality and the afterlife. Which answer is closest to your thinking?

a. Animals are created with only a corporeal mind, without a rational and spiritual mind. Therefore they cannot be conjoined to God since that requires reciprocation of love by rational consciousness. All humans are born with a natural and spiritual mind, by which they can develop a rational consciousness of God, and every person who reciprocates by loving God, is conjoined to God, which is the source or condition for immortality in heaven. But if God is not loved, the spiritual mind remains shut and conjunction with God becomes impossible. Without conjunction with God, the state of life sinks to the level called spiritual death or immortality in hell.

b. Animals have living souls and when they die their souls go to the spiritual world. Animals with a good disposition go to heaven and the others go to hell. In heaven, they are a joy to the inhabitants there, but in hell, they are feared. Animals are close to God even if they are not conscious of that relationship. Animals sense the harmony that God built into His creation. They are part of this harmony. Domesticated animals were created by God to provide assistance and aid to the human race. We are permitted to kill and eat since God provided some animals for this purpose.

c. It depends on whether you think that animals have souls or not. If you think that animals

Moses, Paul, and Swedenborg

don't have souls, then they are merely biological organisms of survival and adaptation. If you think that animals have souls, then animals and people share the circle of reincarnated life. All life is animated by the living spirit manifesting itself in many forms like animals, people, plants, elements. And in that case it is contrary to the divine to kill and eat animals since they are living souls.

76. Does it make sense to spend a lot of effort trying to prepare oneself for the unknown afterlife?

a. No, it doesn't make sense. The important thing is to live a full life while one can and thereby to be prepared for whatever comes next. If you buy into this or that religion or theory about how you are to prepare, and you rearrange you life accordingly, denying yourself this or that, it may be all for nothing if it turns out to be the wrong theory.

b. Actually, it doesn't take effort, only an inwardly sincere acknowledgement that we cannot save ourselves but are saved by the grace of God. We cannot prepare for eternal life by our own efforts, but if we live within the acknowledgment of our powerlessness, God creates a change in our life, sanctifying our efforts, making them fruitful to eternity.

c. Yes it makes sense. It's rational, and sane to want to prepare oneself for eternal life, especially since we're told by a fully reliable source (Divine revelation), that the quality of our life, our vitality and mental health throughout eternity, will depend entirely on how we prepare ourselves during this near insignificant time on earth.

77. What is a "good soldier"?

a. A "good soldier" is one who trains well for his mission and when in battle, uses his best skills to defeat the enemy. Good soldiers remain loyal to their country no matter what. They obey their officers unconditionally. They hate the enemy who threatens their homeland and its citizens. They kill as many of the enemy as possible, getting rid of the bad people that threaten their homeland. They reserve pity and compassion for their own comrades, not for the enemy who tries to kill them.

b. A "good soldier" is one who uses permissible weapons effectively against the enemy, yet feels pity and compassion for them, even as he strives to kill them efficiently. He also strives to limit the damage to the minimum and already thinks of the reconstruction effort after the enemy is defeated. After the battle, the good soldier switches roles to help the defeated enemy to recover and to adopt an attitude of peaceful cooperation.

c. A "good soldier" is a pacifist who hates war and is eager to lay down his arms at the first sign of peace. Good soldiers agonize over commands they are given to kill since they hold life to be sacred. It is a gift given by God to every person and life should not be taken. When the country is attacked, a good soldier defends against invaders. Good soldiers retain their individual conscience and refuse to follow orders that violate their conscience.

78. Compare monism and dualism in science in relation to God.
a. Science is not about God and heaven. It's about reality on earth and in the natural world. Therefore science must remain monist and materialist. Science is a method that can investigate anything, including what people think of God or what miracles they claim to have witnessed.

b. Monist (atheistic) science is inferior and invalid because it denies true reality, which is that God creates and runs the dual universe for the purpose of bringing into existence immortal human beings born on some earth, then bringing them to heaven where He can make them happy to eternity Atheistic or materialistic science is a distortion of this reality and leads to spiritual insanity.

c. Science is a tool God uses. In some sphere God is distant leaving events to be governed by the natural laws he instituted from creation. In other spheres God intervenes by means of miracles that have a supernatural cause. Science is monistic since it doesn't recognize God, but scientists can be theistic by believing in God's existence.

79. According to religionists, atheistic science paints a false picture of reality. If this is true, how can you explain the success of industry, engineering, and control over the environment, which are visible accomplishments of science?
a. God allowed atheistic science to become successful and continues to lead its scientists despite their false picture of reality. God inspires the minds of scientists, unconsciously to them, so that their thinking can be kept in external rationality while they remain in internal insanity. On the other hand, dualist science is theistic, and paints a dual reality where the natural and the spiritual act together by predetermined laws.

b. God allowed atheistic science to become successful because He gives people freedom to discover and control the natural environment. The natural world belongs to atheistic science while issues of heaven and hell belong to religion. Every scientist will meet their Maker in due course. As long as science and religion remain separate, there is no conflict between them.

c. Atheistic science does not paint a false picture of reality. It paints a true picture of natural reality, as evidenced by the successes of inventions and discoveries. Sunday Church topics such as worship, Sacraments, God, rebirth, and heaven are not of this world, hence not part of the picture that science paints of reality.

80. Is God Human?

a. God the Father is Divine but God the Son is Divine and Human at the same time. These two Divine Persons form a Holy Trinity called the One Godhead, together with a third Divine Person called the Holy Spirit. We do not have access to God the Father directly and therefore must pray to the Father in the Name of the Son who is the Divine Intermediary.

b. God is the infinite source of Divine Love and Divine Wisdom operating in the created universe. These two operating together define what is human, and they cannot exist in animals, plants, or objects. But they exist in human beings who are willing to receive love and wisdom from God. Even then, that love and wisdom, in their essence, remain with God. Hence only God is the actual and True Human, and we are human only to the extent that we are willing to receive love and wisdom from God.

c. God cannot be considered human since God is supposed to have created humans. God is Divine, not human. God creates humans to be able to feel love and hatred, decency and deceitfulness. To be human is to have all these traits. And even being human is often mixed since we also share traits with animals, and even with plants.

81. Consider these values: wealth, power, reputation, knowledge, fear of exclusion, desire for approval, obedience to authority, and the like. How are these motivators related to salvation and regeneration?

a. They are moral motives for self-improvement and success. But salvation depends on spiritual motives such as the faith in the redeeming power of the Cross.

b. They are motives of a good person and therefore deserve the right rewards.

c. They are moral motives that begin the road to salvation but do not lead there unless spiritual motives are added to them so that they are also done for the sake of one's religion or place in heaven in the afterlife.

82. Consider these types of traits: merit, righteousness, holiness, humility, understanding, intelligence, wisdom, and the like. Are they natural, moral, or spiritual?

a. Natural

b. Moral

c. Spiritual

83. Consider these types of traits: charity, love, unity, conjunction, acceptance, inclusion, interior perception, and the like. Are they natural, spiritual, or celestial?

a. Celestial

b. Spiritual

c. .Natural

84. Does God favor some people with more good than others, since some people are obviously more gifted than others?

a. God gives maximum good to every person all the time, but each individual filters it out, some turning it into its opposite or evil. God allows this since there is no other way of maintaining freedom of choice, which is essential for retaining the capacity to become human.

b. God's wants to create a variety of people to make room for all possibilities and experiences. To arrange for this, He gives some people special gifts when He foresees that this individual can turn it into benefits for others. Not every person is suitable or willing to serve God in the highest possible way.

c. God distributes human traits throughout the population so that they form a bell shaped curve – the majority around the middle or "normal," and a small minority in either extremes, good vs. evil.

85. What is the cause of acceleration of a vehicle when the driver presses the gas pedal?
a. The gas being released into the fuel chamber.

b. The driver's purpose to accelerate.

c. The laws of physics and chemistry.

86. What is the inmost portion of a pebble upon which its existence depends?
a. Truth within which is good.

b. Sub-atomic particles arranged in a particular dynamic order in space.

c. God's Will.

87. Swedenborg talked to spirits and there are some today who desire this ability. Can they succeed?
a. No, because direct communication with spirits interferes with the maturation of our rational consciousness of God, and therefore God does not allow such communication to take place today in modern times, though this was allowed in ancient times.

b. Yes, and many psychics have proven that they can and do. Such communication is also reported by thousands of people who have had Near Death Experiences (NDEs).

c. All things are possible to God and should He want an angel or devil to communicate with someone, He arranges for it to happen.

Moses, Paul, and Swedenborg

88. Is there a common evolution in the human race? Is the human race integrated into one or is it partially independent?

a. The human race is limited to this earth, as far as is known. Generations succeed one another as one civilization comes, thrives, and then ends, succeeded by yet another. There is a steady evolution from past to future but not a synchronous interdependence, but rather a successive independence.

b. Wherever there are people, whether only on this planet or possibly on others, they are created by the One God, the Father in Heaven and they are His children. In that sense the human race is integrated. The same Word is given to everyone as a means of salvation.

c. Elevation of consciousness is by means of rational truths from revelation, understood more and more interiorly in proportion to our regeneration. This elevation of our rational consciousness is communicated to the entire human race by means of the heavens (or Grand Human) and, through that, to the other earths in the universe. This occurs because the entire race in the dual universe is united and functionally interdependent.

89. What kind of love are we commanded to have?

a. We are to love the Lord as to His Person, even the Robe He wears and the sandals He walks on. We are to love Him for Who He is, the Son of God from eternity who sacrificed Himself for us. We are to love all children, each one as to their unique person, being tolerant of the weaknesses that are human. We are to love our country and all of God's children and creatures.

b. We are to love whatever good is in a person or thing, not the person or thing, just as we should strive to love the Lord as to the Divine Good and Truth in Him, and not as to His Person. We are not to love the evil in a person, or find it acceptable or excusable on account of who the person is. Nothing should be loved but what is good and true, knowing that all good and truth is from God and is in God.

c. We are to love our neighbor and show charity where needed. We are to love God. If our neighbor is a sinner, we should still love him or her. Loyalty to person is the highest friendship. Loyalty to country, right or wrong, is required, and we are to accept the bad with the good.

Moses, Paul, and Swedenborg

90. What's the difference between theoretical and applied knowledge of the Writings?

a. Theoretical knowledge of the Writings comes first, then applied knowledge of it. For example, a student taking a course in the Writings might gain a theoretical knowledge of it, but when he or she becomes a graduate student or minister, there develops an applied knowledge of it through Doctrine.

b. Theoretical knowledge of the Writings is called enlightenment, while its applied knowledge is called perception. Enlightenment is in the understanding, perception in the will. First the understanding is reformed, then the will is regenerated. Salvation is therefore not from theoretical knowledge of revelation and consequent enlightenment, but from applied knowledge and perception of our intentions and thoughts, whether they are from hell or heaven. If from hell, we shun them, and if from heaven, we love them.

c. Theoretical theology differs from applied theology like a business professor differs from a business investor. While a minister is in Divinity School, he acquires a theoretical knowledge of the Word, viewed as theology. But once he has a parish he acquires an applied knowledge of Doctrine, which helps him to look after the souls in his charge. It is similar with medical students on campus vs. hospital interns, or a soldier in training vs. on the battlefield.

91. Compare sensuous and rational consciousness of God.

a. Our sensuous consciousness of God is direct and immediate, wordless, eternal. Our rational consciousness of God is indirect through our thoughts and interpretations. Direct mystical or ecstatic union with God is only possible in sensuous consciousness.

b. Sensuous consciousness is higher than rational consciousness because it is more immediate. Rational consciousness is the attempt to explain in words what the sensuous experience is. As a result, rational consciousness is more remote and subjective.

c. The Lord was a public citizen of Nazareth while He grew up into adulthood, but after His Resurrection He only appeared to those whose spiritual eyes were opened by Him to see. The difference is that He was present to everyone's sensuous consciousness until the Resurrection, but afterwards, only to those whose rational consciousness was advanced enough to receive the Holy Spirit.

92. Is either heaven or hell forever?

a. Hell is a place of purification from sin. When the process is over, the individual emerges purified of evils and is then capable of enjoying the life of heaven in eternity with the Lord. Hell forever is inconsistent with the perfect love of God for every human being.

b. Heaven is a place the Lord creates for good people and hell is a place for evil people who are called the damned. Hell is an aberration and has no place in a created universe that is perfect, as perfect as God. Ultimately God's perfection will win out and hell will only be a memory or a possibility but not an actuality.

c. Every person has both heaven and hell in the mind, for there is no other heaven or hell except the one in people's minds. To descend to the bottom of our mind means to enjoy and justify evil loves. To climb to the top of our mind means to enjoy and justify good loves. In this life we are mixed, but in the other life, once you are either in your hell or in your heaven, you cannot switch because you are unwilling no matter what. To switch would be to acquire again what you have discarded (either good or evil loves). Therefore hell is forever and heaven is to eternity.

93. Explain what is spiritual enlightenment.

a. Spiritual enlightenment is the emergent phenomenon of higher consciousness achieved through acts of discipline and meditation.

b. Enlightenment is a spiritual gift an individual can use to minister to others who are in need and who are ignorant of the Lord or keep the Lord at a distance in their lives.

c. While studying revelation, light from the spiritual Sun enters our spiritual mind from within, and produces conscious correspondences of itself in the natural- rational mind. This higher rational consciousness is called enlightenment.

94. Is there a difference between morality and spirituality?

a. Morality concerns the appropriate treatment of people in our behavior. Morality regulates our behavior towards our neighbor. The Ten Commandments given by God prohibit stealing, lying, murder, and adultery. These are all matters of morality and ethics. God

Moses, Paul, and Swedenborg

wants us to be moral with one another by keeping the Commandments. Spirituality is faith in Christ as our Savior and Lord.

b. Morality is done for natural motives. Shunning evils as sins is done for spiritual motives. Morality is about the outward social personality, while spirituality is about one's character or inner loves. Merely being a moral person is not regenerating, unless we connect our morality to our spirituality. If we refrain from stealing because it is immoral, the desire to steal remains. But if we refrain from stealing because it is a sin against God, that is, destroys our heavenly life, then we connect spirituality to morality, and we are saved.

c. The difference is one of emphasis rather than substance. Morality is a measure of how sincere we are in the values we uphold publicly, that make up part of our personality structure. Spirituality is a measure of how deeply our values go, whether they are part of our core being or only the surface personality.

95. What's the differences between corporeal, sensuous, rational, and spiritual, in relation to the mind.
a. Corporeal refers to biochemistry, sensuous to physiology, rational to psychology, and spiritual to theology.

b. Corporeal refers to things in us that are corrupted by sin. Sensuous refers to that part of human nature that can be tempted or seduced. Rational is that which we intellectualize in our mind, interpreting our experience rather than taking it in immediately without the mediation of our intellect. Spiritual is the core of our being or soul and is unique and eternal.

c. The corporeal mind is close to the physical body processes which do not involve thinking. The sensuous mind receives information from the corporeal and differentiates it through words and labels. The rational mind takes information from the sensuous and puts it into abstract categories. The spiritual mind unconsciously receives information from the spiritual world, which is transmitted by correspondence, to the rational mind where it is conscious.

96. Identify the phase to which each of the following seven traits are characteristic: enlightened; literalist; universalist, arrogant; conjunctive; inclusive, pacifist.
a. 3, 1, 2, 1 ,3 ,2, 2

b. 3, 2, 1, 3, 2, 1, 1

c. 3, 2, 3, 2, 1, 3, 2

97. What is the "vertical community" and how can we be conscious of our communication with spirits? Illustrate with our eating behavior.

a. The "vertical community" refers to our position in the hierarchy of spiritual beings. First are the Holy animals like the Cherubim, then the Angels who minister at the throne of God, then the elders and saints, and finally all the believers. The non-believers are cast out in outer darkness. When we eat we pay tribute to the throne of God by blessing the food and giving thanks. We are then in the company of Angels.

b. We can map out the spiritual societies we are connected to, which can be called our "vertical community." For instance, when we are eating, if we stuff and swallow repeatedly we are with different spirits than if we moderate the size and rate of intake. If we deny ourselves another portion, we are with different spirits than if we give in to our appetite and overeat. Affections for unhealthy foods come from different spiritual societies than affections for healthy food.

c. The "vertical community" refers to the social hierarchy in a society. This hierarchy may be considered to be the spirit of the underlying organization of that society. Food behavior is among the daily occupations of that society and requires the hierarchical execution of sequenced steps from farmer, to distributor, to local market where the customers gather to shop.

98. The following are three thinking protocols reported by people while doing their workout. Identify each entry as to phase (1, 2, or 3).

(i) I better not skip my workout today. It really keeps me in shape. To be successful you've got to look attractive. That means being in shape. Besides, you avoid heart attacks. I need to learn to like my workout session. It's the right thing to do. It keeps me from bad habits like laziness and lack of self-control. It's necessary for a healthy life.

(ii) I'm actually looking forward to my workout. Yes, it takes effort and motivation, but it's worth it. I feel better, clean, purified, satisfied with myself. I feel that every movement brings me closer to my heavenly character. I sense the physical power in my body to be connected to my will and motive. Since this is from heaven, I feel closer to heaven as I exercise.

(iii) Exercising the physical body is like exercising the mind with study. Compelling myself to do it as scheduled, develops my mental discipline upon which rests my spiritual development. I must look on the physical exercise as a spiritual discipline. I hate this workout stuff. I rather watch TV or surf the net. But I'm making myself do it. I refuse to break my resolution. I'm scared to get sick and end up under a doctor's care. Besides, it'll be soon over then I can watch TV.

a. 3, 1, 2

b. 1, 3, 2

c. 1, 2, 3

99. The following six statements characterize various attitudes about wars. For each item, identify the phase (1, 2, or 3).

(i) All wars are under the direct auspices of the Lord. All evil is moderated by the Lord to its maximum allowed. Evil itself punishes the enemy. Our job is to neutralize their ability to hurt others and to try to amend them. Striving to win by means of as-of self effort powered by the Lord. Striving to avoid hate as self-corrupting. Sense of sadness rather than joy in hurting and killing enemy. Desire to protect enemy by keeping injury and damage to the minimum necessary for gaining control.

(ii) There are just wars and evil wars. Protecting ourselves and coming to the rescue of the subjugated are just wars. The enemy must be treated humanely and not hated. God is on the side of the just. Those who are pacifists think that all wars are evil. They would rather see the enemy continue its cruelties against others. Feeling confident in winning and relying on God. Wanting to defeat the enemy without hating them. Hoping that enemy may be amended rather than destroyed. Wanting to minimize damage and ready to help with reconstruction of the country.

(iii) War is an instrument for advancing one's nation or religion. It's good to hate the enemy. They don't deserve humane treatment since they want to harm us. Eye for an eye philosophy. Hating the enemy with self-righteousness. Wanting to deny humane treatment to the enemy. Feeling justified in using illegal types of weapons and in killing the unarmed innocent. Wanting to inflict maximum damage. Feeling justified in maltreating prisoners of war. Joy in the spoils of war.

a. 3, 2, 1

b. 2, 2, 1

c. 1, 1, 3

100. Characterize the relation between natural and spiritual, and between finite and infinite.

a. The natural world is within the spiritual world. The finite is within the infinite.

b. The spiritual world is within the natural world. The infinite is within the finite.

c. The natural is the source of the spiritual, just like the brain is the source of the mind. The finite is a technical or local limitation for the universal infinite since space and time are infinite and all finite things are contained within them.

(end of questions)

ANSWER KEY

Lay your **Answer Sheet** next the this **Answer Key**. For each question circle the phase that corresponds to the answer you selected on the Answer Sheet. For example, if you circled alternative **b** for question **1** on the Answer Sheet, then you need to circle phase "**1**" on the Answer Key for question 1.

Note: the first digit in each box is the Question Number, while the other three digits are the three phases for that question's alternatives and they correspond in order to a b, c for each question.

1. 3 1 2	21. 2 3 1	41. 1 3 2	61. 2 3 1	81. 2 1 3
2. 3 2 1	22. 3 2 1	42. 2 3 1	62. 1 3 2	82. 1 2 3

Moses, Paul, and Swedenborg

3. 3 1 2	23. 1 2 3	43. 2 3 1	63. 1 3 2	83. 3 2 1
4. 1 2 3	24. 1 3 2	44. 1 3 2	64. 3 2 1	84. 3 2 1
5. 2 3 1	25. 3 1 2	45. 2 1 3	65. 2 1 3	85. 2 3 1
6. 2 3 1	26. 3 1 2	46. 2 1 3	66. 3 2 1	86. 3 1 2
7. 3 2 1	27. 2 1 3	47. 3 2 1	67. 1 2 3	87. 3 1 2
8. 3 2 1	28. 2 3 1	48. 2 1 3	68. 2 1 3	88. 1 2 3
9. 3 2 1	29. 2 3 1	49. 2 1 3	69. 2 3 1	89. 2 3 1
10. 2 3 1	30. 3 2 1	50. 2 3 1	70. 2 3 1	90. 2 3 1
11. 1 2 3	31. 1 3 2	51. 1 3 2	71. 3 2 1	91. 2 1 3
12. 3 2 1	32. 3 2 1	52. 3 2 1	72. 1 3 2	92. 1 2 3
13. 3 1 2	33. 3 2 1	53. 2 3 1	73. 2 3 1	93. 1 2 3
14. 1 3 2	34. 2 3 1	54. 3 2 1	74. 1 2 3	94. 2 3 1
15. 1 2 3	35. 2 1 3	55. 2 1 3	75. 3 2 1	95. 1 2 3
16. 1 3 2	36. 2 1 3	56. 3 2 1	76. 1 2 3	96. 3 1 2
17. 3 1 2	37. 1 2 3	57. 2 1 3	77. 1 3 2	97. 2 3 1
18. 2 3 1	38. 2 3 1	58. 2 1 3	78. 1 3 2	98. 1 3 2
19. 1 2 3	39. 1 3 2	59. 2 1 3	79. 3 2 1	99. 3 2 1
20. 2 1 3	40. 1 3 2	60. 3 2 1	80. 2 3 1	100. 2 3 1

For each column, count the number of circles for each phase:

phase 1: ____	phase 1: ____	phase 1: ____	phase 1: ____	phase 1: ____
phase 2: ____	phase 2: ____	phase 2: ____	phase 2: ____	phase 2: ____
phase 3: ____	phase 3: ____	phase 3: ____	phase 3: ____	phase 3: ____

Now add up the five columns to get the total number of circles for each

phase 1: ____   phase 2: ____   phase 3: ____

This is your diagnostic score. It consists of three numbers. They must add up to 100.

Moses, Paul, and Swedenborg

Lay your **Answer Sheet** next the this **Answer Key**. For each question circle the phase that corresponds to the answer you selected on the Answer Sheet. For example, if you circled alternative **b** for question **1** on the Answer Sheet, then you need to circle phase "**1**" on the Answer Key for question 1.

Note: the first digit in each box is the Question Number, while the other three digits are the three phases for that question's alternatives and they correspond in order to a b, c for each question.

How to Interpret Your Score

The three numbers of your score display the dominant mode of your current thinking about spiritual subjects. Look at the relative strength of each ideology in your thinking. For instance, suppose your diagnostic score is [72-23-5]. This indicates a mode of thinking about spiritual topics in which phase 1 dominates strongly but has strength in phase 2. If your score is [5-12-83], it is phase 3 thinking that dominates, with little strength in the other two phases. And so on.

You can also examine the ratings of certainty you gave for each answer. Inspect the pattern of numbers. What is the average certainty you have in each of the three modes of thinking?

Examine each choice you picked and the certainty rating you gave – are you more confident when you are in lower phases of thinking, or the other way around?

Many other comparisons of interest can be made if you have an interest in using the test as a diagnostic tool. Go over each item you selected that is at phase 1 and 2 thinking. What would it take to elevate your thinking to phase 3 operations?

This book offers discussions on all the topics in the test, showing the progression of rationality from phase 1, to 2, to 3. By making an effort to understand these discussions in a rational way, you will develop the ability to raise your consciousness by means of rational truths all the way to heaven.

Summary List of Characteristics for the Three Phases

Moses, Paul, and Swedenborg

Phase 1 Thinking

Phase 1 thinking about spiritual topics is characterized by a mixture of traits, both religious and secular. Therefore the items below will apply selectively to each individual, depending on religious and lifestyle outlook.

1. sectarianism (salvation is for themselves only)
2. fundamentalism (male dominant views about women and society)
3. literalism (Scripture is to be applied to life without interpretation or doctrine, sticking to what is stated in the literal)
4. extremism (willing to be indiscriminately violent, beyond law and tradition)
5. fanaticism (intolerance and desire to suppress contrary views)
6. superstition (pre-scientific, irrational)
7. ritual faith (a view of God as a tribal Covenant, distant, and unapproachable by ordinary individuals)
8. cultism (reliance on living "holy men" and on "personal inspiration" rather than on the Bible)
9. profanation (quoting the Bible for personal testimony, but without believing it, thus, hypocritically)
10. spiritism (seeking contacts with the departed)
11. reincarnation or related ideas (seeking a non-Western philosophic identity)
12. nonduality (there are no absolute differences)
13. materialism (there is no spiritual world)
14. agnosticism (there is no proof of God's existence)
15. atheism (there is no God)
16. sexual permissiveness (marriage is not holy)
17. relativism (all religions are equivalent, all truths are relative)
18. secular humanism (the human race has its own destiny independent of any God)
19. positivism (only the external measurable material is real)
20. animism (everything is alive, everything is a spirit)

Moses, Paul, and Swedenborg

Phase 2 Thinking

Phase 2 thinking about spiritual topics is characterized by universalism and personalism. In the Christian Protestant religion it takes the following forms:

1. universalism (salvation by faith regardless of cultural background)
2. inclusiveness (Redemption covers the entire human race)
3. personalism (personal relationship with God)
4. symbolism (Christ is foreshadowed in the Old Testament)
5. mysticism (Trinity of Three Divine Persons in One Godhead)
6. reliance on prayersof intercession
7. tendency to believe incomprehensible "mysteries" of faith
8. belief in salvation by blind faith alone without works
9. fear of ascribing the Merit of Christ to self
10. willing to be led by persuasive faith
11. willing to give allegiance to creeds containing mystical doctrine
12. desire to penetrate deeper meaning of the Bible through application of verses to self
13. focus on collective charity work or volunteerism
14. focus on repentance (being contrite, feeling guilty, making amends)
15. focus on the sanctity of marriage

Phase 3 Thinking

Phase 3 thinking about spiritual topics is characterized by a rational or scientific understanding of God and regeneration, as revealed by God in the Writings of Swedenborg:

1. scientific dualism (the universe consists of a natural world and a spiritual world)
2. salvation depends on regeneration of character from selfish to altruistic
3. regeneration is the lifelong struggle with temptations and victories over them by looking to the Lord
4. God is the Divine Human Person who has a Trinity of Roles (Creates as "Father",

Moses, Paul, and Swedenborg

   Redeems as "Son", Regenerates as "Holy Spirit")
5. our immortality is due to our rationalityby which we can be conjoined to God
6. everyone has heaven and hell in the mind
7. rising to heaven is by acquiring virtuous habits of willing and thinking
8. sliding into hell is by being unwilling to let go of inherited selfishness
9. becoming conscious of God's co-Presence and participatory involvement in our thinking and feeling
10. salvation is solely by character reformation and regeneration
11. emphasis on rational explanations of the p of salvation and regeneration
12. application of rational spirituality to everyday reality

These three modes or spiritual ideologies are discussed in the book.

A Listing of the 100 Items Test Without the Alternatives

1. What is your view on immortality?
2. Where is the mind of a human being?
3. What happens when we die?
4. What determines your fate in the afterlife?
5. Is sex possible in heaven?
6. Is sex possible in hell?
7. Angels are people from earth who made it to heaven.
8. Devils are people from earth who ended up in hell.
10. What is most crucial to our salvation?
11. Consciousness raising and spiritual progress is accomplished most by:
12. What is heaven and hell?
13. There is a natural world and a spiritual world.
14. When we die we eventually return to earth for another life, until it is no longer necessary for us to do so.
15. Is God Divine and Human or only Divine?
16. How do you see the relation between God and human beings?

17. On the relation between God and human beings:
18. What's the difference between natural matter and spiritual substance?
19. Which assertion about planets represents more nearly your own view?
20. What is consciousness?
21. What are the parts of the human mind?
22. What is a discrete degree "within"?
23. What produces consciousness in the mind?
24. What is the meaning of the assertion: "Heaven is within you."
25. What is the meaning of the assertion: "Hell is within you."
26. How many layers or levels of heavens are there?
27. Which reasoning is closest to your own thinking?
28. The idea of "hell forever" is controversial. Which reasoning is nearest to your own thinking?
29. What does spiritual salvation consist of?
30. Is doing "good works" and "charity" necessary for salvation?
32. Are there different types of truth?
33. What is scientific dualism?
34. What is theistic science?
35. What is the Threefold Word in which God gave us scientific revelations?
36. What is the relative standing between religion and science?
38. What does it mean that Swedenborg had a dual consciousness?
39. Did Swedenborg's exploration of the spiritual world include scientific experiments he conducted while there?
40. What kind of information about the spiritual world did Swedenborg report in the Writings?
41. Can God be a legitimate concept in scientific explanations?
42. Can the Writings be considered True Science?
43. Can the Lord appear to people again in the natural world as He did before?
44. Is it rational to think that there is a Trinity of Three Divine Persons?
45. When is the Second Coming of Christ supposed to take place?
46. Is there a sun in the spiritual world?
47. Can other religions possibly adopt the Writings as a revealed science book about God?
48. Compare the rationality of theistic and atheistic science.
49. If God is omnipotent, why does He allow evil in His creation?
50. What happens to the Divine power God gives us to be able to plan and execute tasks?

51. Why does God give people the power to ignore Him and deny His existence?
52. There is a controversy about whether or not the Writings have an inner sense. Which best represents your position?
53. Is it possible to prove that the Bible is Divine?
54. What are demons?
55. What is the difference in the mentality of the Old and New Testaments?
56. What role do temptations play in regeneration?
57. Miracles are of two kind, covert and overt. Overt miracles include healing or controlling the physical elements. Covert miracles include "lucky" events and success stories. Explain the difference.
58. Paul declared that works do not save, but faith in the Lord saves. Which of these three explanations is closest to your view?
59. Why did Jesus pray to His Father since the Father and He were one, as it is written in the New Testament?
60. What's the relation between the Epistles in the New Testament and the Gospels?
61. How do you resolve the fact that Jesus loved one disciple (John) more than another? Does God have favorites?
62. If you were to describe the hierarchical organization of heaven, which alternative would be closest to your thinking?
63. Compare the effectiveness of communal vs. individual prayer.
64. What is your view on the controversy as to whether the Writings have an inner sense hidden by the code of correspondences?
65. Explain the ennead matrix of rational spirituality.
66. Why does God want us to pray? Does that influence Him?
67. Can God love an unrepentant sinner?
68. Who or what is the devil?
69. If there are layers of heaven, what's the lower heaven like?
70. Who was Swedenborg?
71. True Science refers to the science of God, that is, the science revealed in the Threefold Word. What is your view on it?
72. The three developmental steps of rational spirituality can appropriately be labeled Ritual Faith (1), Mystic Faith (2), and Rational Faith (3). Describe their differences.
73. Define God.
74. What are the consequences of sinning?
75. Compare humans and animals with respect to immortality and the afterlife. Which answer is closest to your thinking?

76. Does it make sense to spend a lot of effort trying to prepare oneself for the unknown afterlife?
77. What is a "good soldier"?
78. Compare monism and dualism in science in relation to God.
79. According to religionists, atheistic science paints a false picture of reality. If this is true, how can you explain the success of industry, engineering, and control over the environment, which are visible accomplishments of science?
80. Is God Human?
81. Consider these values: wealth, power, reputation, knowledge, fear of exclusion, desire for approval, obedience to authority, and the like. How are these motivators related to salvation and regeneration?
82. Consider these types of traits: merit, righteousness, holiness, humility, understanding, intelligence, wisdom, and the like. Are they natural, moral, or spiritual?
83. Consider these types of traits: charity, love, unity, conjunction, acceptance, inclusion, interior perception, and the like. Are they natural, spiritual, or celestial?
84. Does God favor some people with more good than others, since some people are obviously more gifted than others?
85. What is the cause of acceleration of a vehicle when the driver presses the gas pedal?
86. What is the inmost portion of a pebble upon which its existence depends?
87. Swedenborg talked to spirits and there are some today who desire this ability. Can they succeed?
88. Is there a common evolution in the human race? Is the human race integrated into one or is it partially independent?
89. What kind of love are we commanded to have?
90. What's the difference between theoretical and applied knowledge of the Writings?
91. Compare sensuous and rational consciousness of God.
92. Is either heaven or hell forever?
93. Explain what is spiritual enlightenment.
94. Is there a difference between morality and spirituality?
95. What's the differences between corporeal, sensuous, rational, and spiritual, in relation to the mind.
96. Identify the phase to which each of the following seven traits are characteristic: enlightened; literalist; universalist, arrogant; conjunctive; inclusive, pacifist.

97. What is the "vertical community" and how can we be conscious of our communication with spirits? Illustrate with our eating behavior.
98. The following are three thinking protocols reported by people while doing their workout. Identify each entry as to phase (1, 2, or 3).
99. The following six statements characterize various attitudes about wars. For each item, identify the phase (1, 2, or 3).
100. Characterize the relation between natural and spiritual, and between finite and infinite.

Other Recent Books by Leon James

**James, Leon (2010). A Man of the Field: Volume 1. The Struggle Against Nonduality and Materialism. Eagle Pearl Press: Pleasanton, CA Basis of Religion Series. Print Edition. (Also Kindle Digital version in 2012)

**James, Leon (2010). A Man of the Field: Volume 2. The Spiritual Sense of the Writings. Eagle Pearl Press: Pleasanton, CA Basis of Religion Series. Print Edition. (Also Kindle Digital version in 2012)

**James, Leon (2014). A Man of the Field Volume 3: Spiritual Regeneration Disciplines For Daily Life. Eagle Pearl Press: Pleasanton, CA Basis of Religion Series. Print Edition. (Also Kindle Digital version in 2012)

**James, Leon. (2012). *The Conjoined Pair*. Print Edition: Regeneration Media. CreateSpace Publishing.

**James, Leon. (2012). *Avatar Psychology and Mental Anatomy*. Print Edition: Regeneration Media. CreateSpace Publishing.

**James, Leon. (2015). *Experiencing Regeneration: Equipping Our Personality for Living in the Afterlife*. Kindle Edition. Amazon Digital Services, Inc. Also Print Edition. CreateSpace Publishing.

**James, Leon. (2015). *Jung and Swedenborg on God and Life After Death*. Kindle Edition. Amazon Digital Services. Also Print Edition. Regeneration Media. CreateSpace Publishing.

**James, Leon. (2016). Reality is Spiritual. Volume 1. Dreams and the Spiritual World: Integrating the Psychology of Jung and Swedenborg. Kindle Edition. Amazon Digital Services. Also Print Edition: Regeneration Media. CreateSpace Publishing.

**James, Leon. (2016). Reality is Spiritual. Volume 2. The RTS Personality: Rational Theistic Self-analysis For Achieving Wholeness Here and in the Afterlife. Kindle Edition. Amazon Digital Services. Also Print Edition: Regeneration Media. CreateSpace Publishing.

Moses, Paul, and Swedenborg

**James, Leon (2017). Reality is Spiritual Series. *The RTS Interviews*. Volumes 3, 4, 5. Based on the Theistic Psychology of Jung and Swedenborg. Kindle Edition. Amazon Digital Services. Also Print Edition: Regeneration Media. CreateSpace Publishing.

**James, Leon (2018). *Consciousness and Immortality: Spiritual Knowledge For Managing Our Destiny in the Afterlife of Eternity*. Kindle Edition. Amazon Digital Services. Also Print Edition: Regeneration Media. CreateSpace Publishing.

**James, Leon (2018). *Theistic Psychology - Expanding The Narrative Series. A New Modern Synthesis Of The Ideas of Jung And Swedenborg.* Kindle Edition. Amazon Digital Services.

Volumes 1 to 4. Individuation And The Collective Conscious (Kindle) Volumes 5 to 8. Marriage, Regeneration, And Aphorisms In Theistic

Psychology (Kindle)Volumes 10 to 12. Articles in Theistic Psychology (Kindle)***Volume 1. Individuation And The Collective Conscious: Discovering Our

Immortal Self In A Telepathic Universe. (Also in Print Edition)

Volume 2: Personality And Afterlife Lifestyles: Getting Ready For Eternity (Also in Print Edition)

Volume 3. Sacred Scripture, Dreams, And Archetypes: The Secret Connection. (Also in Print Edition)

Volume 4. Correspondences, Synchronicity, And The Spiritual Discipline Of Self-Witnessing. (Also in Print Edition)

Volume 5. Regeneration And The Vertical Community: How God Manages Our Psychological States. (Also in Print Edition)

Volume 6. Natural and Spiritual Marriage: Moving Into Eternity Together. (Also in Print Edition)

Volume 7. Sayings And Aphorisms In Theistic Psychology: Emanuel Swedenborg, Carl Jung, And Leon James. (Also in Print Edition.)

Volume 8. Topics And References in Theistic PsychologyVolume 9. Schematic Diagrams And Charts in Theistic Psychology Volume 10. Articles In Theistic Psychology (Part 1 of

3)Volume 11. Articles In Theistic Psychology (Part 2 of 3)Volume 12: Articles In Theistic Psychology: (Part 3 of 3)

** James, Leon (2018). *Principles of Theistic Psychology Series.* Kindle Edition. Amazon Digital Services.

Volume 1. Introduction To Theistic PsychologyVolume 2. Q&A On Theistic Psychology PrintVolume 3. Developmental Levels of Thinking About Theistic Psychology Volume 4. Extracting Theistic Psychology From Sacred Scripture Volume 5. Research Methods in Theistic PsychologyVolume 6. Personality And Spiritual GrowthVolume 7. Character Reformation And Levels Of Consciousness Volume 8. Learning, Cognition, And EducationVolume 9. Evolution And Stages Of Spiritual Development PrintVolume 10. The Daily Emotional Spin Cycle And Yoga Print

Volume 11. The Marriage Relationship: Wife-Centered Vs. Husband- Centered Print

Volume 12. The Heavenly and Hellish TraitsVolume 13. Religious Psychology And Rational Spirituality Volume 14. Scientific Meaning In Sacred Scripture Of Traditional Religions

About the Author

Beauty is to behold the order of God's creation. ~Leon James

Leon James has authored a series of books on what he calls theistic psychology. He describes his ideas as a new modern synthesis of the works of Carl Jung (1875-1961) and Emanuel Swedenborg (1688-1772). He has been Professor of Psychology at the University of Hawaii since 1971, and today he teaches all his psychology courses online.

His current research involves the attempt to synthesize the work of Jung and Swedenborg by constructing and presenting a narrative that fits into the point of view of contemporary thinking. Jung discovered the psychic world of archetypes as having an existence of its own and independently of the physical world. Swedenborg discovered the spiritual world of afterlife societies to be in eternity and not in physical time and space.

In the attempt to synthesize Jung and Swedenborg, Dr. James made the discovery that the "psychic world" of Jung and the "spiritual world" of Swedenborg refer to the same world. He then came to the conclusion that the psychic world and the spiritual world are the same world as the "mental world" in which we all live as human beings.

There is only one mental world and all human beings are born into it. Since there is no physical time or space in the mental world it is called the mental world of eternity. You are in it now!

A significant consequence of this identification between psychic world, spiritual world, and mental world, is to realize that we are born into the mental world of eternity with our immortal spiritual body, and therefore we are not really on earth, as it appears to be.

The existential illusion that we are on earth, and that our mind is in the physical body comes from the fact that our natural mind in eternity receives all its sensory input by correspondence from the physical body on earth. Our immortal spiritual body with which we are born into the mental world of eternity is connected by

correspondence to our temporary physical body on earth. This is the source of our belief

Moses, Paul, and Swedenborg

that we are on earth.

We are disconnected from the physical body through the two-day dying-resuscitation procedure. When this occurs we lose all contact with earth and we begin immortal life in the afterlife of mental eternity.

The purpose of being born temporarily connected to a physical body on earth is to provide the means by which human beings might acquire a natural mind that thinks with material ideas that are adapted to earth-time conditions and activities. Our natural mind becomes inactive in the afterlife of eternity but nevertheless serves as a basis for the use of our spiritual mind, which only then becomes fully active to eternity. We can then see and hear the environment of the afterlife world, and we can form normal relationships with those people who are already there.

Our immortal spiritual body is a lookalike of the temporary physical body and contains every part and organ that the physical body contains. The sensations and abilities of our spiritual body are far more exquisite and sharp than what we are experiencing now through our physical senses and body.

Swedenborg's observations confirm this explanation in that the afterlife world has a similar external appearance as what can be seen and heard on earth. We are all familiar with the experience of dreaming in which the setting resembles the physical world but the objects are not physical and therefore can appear or disappear according to our emotions and thinking. Without our natural mind and its connection to the physical world our dreams would have no content. Similarly in the afterlife, our natural mind is needed as a basis for providing us with material content in mental eternity, which is devoid of physical objects. And yet, the objects that appear in the mental world of eternity are far more beautiful and perfect than their material counterparts on earth.

Following the two-day dying-resuscitation procedure that Swedenborg describes from empirical observation and experience, we are no longer connected by correspondence to the physical body on earth. We seem to ourselves at that point to "awaken" in the afterlife world. We then seek, find, and settle in one of the numberless afterlife societies, some of which Swedenborg explored in his dual consciousness and described in his Writings. Which of the societies we settle in is determined by our personality inclinations. We are attracted to the afterlife society whose inhabitants have a personality structure that is compatible with ours.

Moses, Paul, and Swedenborg

Dr. James' current work involves showing the details of how God instructs us in Sacred Scripture regarding the psychology of regeneration, which is the systematic modification of our personality from the inherited inclinations that are based on self-love and self-interest, to a new acquired personality that is based

on altruism and mutual love. Our destiny and destination in eternity is determined by our personality.

Those in whom personality is based on self-love settle in one of the many "hellish" communities that are based on self-love, while those in whom the regenerated personality is based on mutual love settle in "heavenly" communities that are based on mutual love.

Knowledge of theistic psychology gives us the choice now of either remaining with our inherited inclinations or removing them by undergoing the psychological process of regeneration.

Dr. James shows that Jung's idea of "symbolism" is the same as Swedenborg's idea of "correspondences". As well, Jung's idea of "archetype" is the same as Swedenborg's idea of "ruling love" that characterizes the personality of the people in each afterlife society.

Further, the symbolism that we use in our dreams is the same symbolism that God uses in Sacred Scripture to instruct us about the psychology of regeneration. Without regeneration we cannot develop a personality that is able to live in a heavenly afterlife society.

How we can be successful in regeneration is of deep interest to everyone.

Dr. Leon James Professor of Psychology University of Hawaii Kailua, Hawaii 2018

Moses, Paul, and Swedenborg

Contents of Volume 1

Preface   3
17. Recapitulation and Study Questions and Exercises   5
17.2 True Science and Theistic Psychology   7
17.3 Why do scientists oppose scientific revelations in the Word of God?   8
17.4 Why do religious people oppose the idea that the Word of God is a scientific revelation?   9
17.5 What is the relation between the mind and the spiritual world?   10
17.6 What is heaven and hell?   12
17.7 Why do some people oppose the idea that hell is forever? 17.7 If God is omnipotent and pure love, why does he allow evil?   14
17.8 What are the three phases of consciousness?   22
17.9 What is the ennead matrix or the nine zones of spiritual development?   23
17.10a What are the laws of space and time in the spiritual world?
17.10b Are there devils and angels there?   28
17.11a What's the difference between sensuous and rational consciousness?
17.11b Is spirituality closer to mysticism or to rationality?   31
17.12 How does True Science view religious rituals and faith?   35
17.13 What is the Science of Correspondences?   39
17.14 Can it be shown that genuine spirituality is rational and scientific?   43
18. Discovering the Writings of Swedenborg   47
18.1 The Holy Spirit -- Rational Consciousness of God's Co-Presence   51
18.2 Dual Citizenship -- Horizontal and Vertical Community   53
18.3 As-of Self – First Fruits of Rational Consciousness   55
18.4 Self-Witnessing – The Psychology of Cooperation   58
18.5 What is God Talking About?   62
18.6 Christianity Demystified   67
18.7 Forming the New Church Mind in Ourselves   75
18.8 On Discrete Degrees and Correspondences   79
18.9 On Personality, Sacred Scripture, And the Afterlife   87
19. Further Exercises   104
19.1 Characterize the thinking and feeling levels of every day activities   105
19.2 Explain the level of thinking in each religious tradition sampled below   106
19.2.a Charity and Buddhism   106
19.2.b Charity and Christianity   107
19.2.c Charity and Judaism   107
19.2.d Charity and Islam   108
19.2.e Charity and Hinduism   109
19.2.f Charity and Secular Humanism   109
19.2.g Charity and New Church or New Christianity   110
Answer to 19.2.a Charity for Buddhism   111

Answer to 19.2.b Charity for Christianity 112
Answer to 19.2.c Charity for Judaism   114
Answer to 19.2.e Charity for Hinduism   116
Answer to 19.2.f Charity for Secular Humanism 117
Answer to 19.2.g Charity for New Christianity   118
Exercise 19.3 Use the ennead matrix to characterize Judaism, Christianity, New Church   121
Appendix: Diagnostic Test of Rational Spirituality 100 Items   183
ANSWER SHEET   184
ANSWER KEY   218
How to Interpret Your Score   220
Summary List of Characteristics for the Three Phases 221
Phase 1 Thinking   221
Phase 2 Thinking   222
Phase 3 Thinking   222
A Listing of the 100 Items Test Without the Alternatives   223
Other Recent Books by Leon James   228
About the Author   231
END   236

END

Made in the USA
Columbia, SC
04 November 2023